365 WAYS to **LIVE** GENEROUSLY

About the Author

Sharon Lipinski (Loveland, CO) is the founder of the nonprofit Change Gangs: Virtual Giving Circles, which helps people make small donations that make a big impact by pooling their small donations with the donations of other people who care about the same cause. She also maintains the largest repository of information documenting the tools, strategies, and accomplishments of some of America's eight hundred charitable giving circles.

365 WAYS to LIVE GENEROUSLY

Simple Habits for a Life
That's Good for You
and for Others

SHARON LIPINSKI

Llewellyn Publications
Woodbury, Minnesota

FIRST EDITION
First Printing, 2017

Cover design by Ellen Lawson

Forgiveness Meditation by Jack Kornfield © 2008 Bantam Dell, New York, New York.
All rights reserved. Used by permission.

Llewellyn Publications is a registered trademark of Llewellyn Worldwide Ltd.

Library of Congress Cataloging-in-Publication Data

Names: Lipinski, Sharon, author.
Title: 365 ways to live generously : simple habits for a life that's good for
you and for others / Sharon Lipinski.
Other titles: Three hundred sixty-five ways to live generously
Description: First Edition. | Woodbury : Llewellyn Worldwide, Ltd, 2017. |
Includes bibliographical references.
Identifiers: LCCN 2016039556 (print) | LCCN 2016044080 (ebook) | ISBN
9780738749600 | ISBN 9780738751313 (ebook)
Subjects: LCSH: Generosity.
Classification: LCC BJ1533.G4 L57 2017 (print) | LCC BJ1533.G4 (ebook) | DDC
179/.9—dc23
LC record available at https://lccn.loc.gov/2016039556

Llewellyn Worldwide Ltd. does not participate in, endorse, or have any authority or responsibility concerning private business transactions between our authors and the public.

All mail addressed to the author is forwarded but the publisher cannot, unless specifically
instructed by the author, give out an address or phone number.

Any Internet references contained in this work are current at publication time, but the
publisher cannot guarantee that a specific location will continue to be maintained. Please
refer to the publisher's website for links to authors' websites and other sources.

Llewellyn Publications
A Division of Llewellyn Worldwide Ltd.
2143 Wooddale Drive
Woodbury, MN 55125-2989
www.llewellyn.com

Printed in the United States of America

Dedication

To my mother, who taught me how to give

Contents

Introduction

We are cups, constantly and quietly being filled.
The trick is, knowing how to tip ourselves over
and let the beautiful stuff out.
—Ray Bradbury, *Zen in the Art of Writing*

You've read all the self-help books about being healthier and happier and more productive. So have I. You underline them. Fold the corners of the best pages. So do I. But not much changes. Sometimes self-help books become shelf-help books because that's where they stay. They don't provide actionable, easy-to-implement guidance, and you may not make the changes you know you should make. This book helps you do all the things you know you should do the only way it really happens—by doing it. Over and over. Until it becomes a habit.

But choose carefully the behaviors you make a habit in your life. No one intentionally creates a habit of hitting McDonald's every day, and yet plenty have that habit. The habits you'll practice in this book were carefully chosen to help you create a life in which you are healthy in body, mind, and spirit; in which you have deep relationships with family and friends; in which you experience less stress and more peacefulness; and in which you make the world a better place with powerful philanthropy. Often when people think about generosity, they think about other people. And yes, being generous is about tipping over your cup to give to others, but being generous to yourself means filling your cup so that you have even more to give.

The Seven Generosity Habits

1. Physical Health
2. Mindfulness
3. Relationships
4. Connecting with Yourself
5. Gratitude
6. Simplicity
7. Philanthropy

If you take care of your physical health, practice mindfulness, have strong relationships, connect with yourself, express gratitude, practice simplicity, and give time and money to causes you care about, your life will naturally unfold as a generous life that is good for you and good for others.

Many of these habits are about you taking care of you. That's because you are the foundation from which you give to others, so that foundation needs to be strong and solid. This is about filling up your cup so that you have the physical and emotional resources needed to give to others.

While taking care of yourself is critical, so is taking care of others. One of your deepest human needs is to make a contribution. At the end of your life, you're going to look back and ask, "Did my life matter?" And you can answer that question with a resounding "Yes!" when you make a positive impact on the world and improve the lives of others.

In this book, you'll discover why each habit is important; get tips based on the latest scientific research on habits; and gently, consistently practice these habits for the entire year.

Fundamentally, this book is about discovering through implementation the power of generosity to transform your physical, emotional, and spiritual health so you can create a life that is good for you *and* good for others.

Learning to Live Generously

I learned about giving from my mom. Her first instinct in any situation was to ask, "How can I help?" And for her, it wasn't just a rhetorical question. If you were carrying a big box, she'd drop everything to help you. If your car was stuck, she was out there helping you push it. If your kid needed to learn how to drive a stick shift, she was at your door the next weekend picking up your daughter to head over to a vacant parking lot. My mother loved giving, and people loved her for it.

Even though my mom was an incredibly generous person and time and again modeled for me everyday acts of kindness and generosity, I did not live up to her example. In fact, I'd say that I was a selfish person. If you want to be generous to me, you could say I was oblivious or lazy or too busy. But one day, a man I hardly knew helped me realize that I wasn't giving as much as I could and not nearly as much I wanted to.

Several years ago, I was a mortgage broker working sixty hours or more a week in a high-pressure job I hated. I had zero work-life balance because it was all work. I started waking up in the middle of the night with panic attacks, and I would sit up in bed with my heart pounding. I couldn't catch my breath, and I would sit there with my hand on the bedroom wall while I repeated to myself, "It's going to be okay." Eventually, it would pass. I'd get a couple hours of sleep and go back to work. One day at work, I said to a colleague, "If I have to do this for the rest of my life, I'd rather kill myself." Fortunately, I heard what I said, and I realized that I needed to make some changes. So I quit my job, and I spent the next year "discovering myself." I went on spiritual retreats and meditation retreats. I read, I listened, and I traveled. But I still hadn't discovered the answer.

I got this idea that spending a month alone contemplating and looking out over the stormy ocean would be just the ticket, so I rented a house in Newport, Oregon, for the entire month of November. While I was there, I would walk my dogs past the corner convenience store and chat with the older man who was living there as a caretaker. The store was closed because there weren't enough tourists in November to justify keeping it open, so he was always alone. We'd chat for a few minutes before I continued on my way, and I learned a little about him and his story. I learned that he was a recovering drug addict whose family no longer spoke to him. I learned that he spent most of his evening alone watching TV.

And I knew he would be alone for Thanksgiving. Nervously, I invited him to spend Thanksgiving dinner with me at a Chinese restaurant. Honestly, I hoped he'd say no, because I wanted to feel good for asking but didn't actually want to do it.

But he said yes. I picked him up, and we drove into town where we shared plates of sesame chicken and beef with broccoli while he talked about his kids. When I looked across the table, I didn't see a stranger. I saw a father who was proud of his kids. I saw a man who regretted his past. I saw a human being who rarely had an opportunity to talk with someone who cared about him or someone who listened to what was important to him. I realized that taking him out to dinner was such a little thing for me, but it was a big deal for him.

That was the moment I finally got it: it really is the small, everyday acts of generosity that make life worth living. This simple dinner with a stranger caused me to look back on my life. I had to admit that I wasn't giving very much *to* myself and I wasn't giving very much *of* myself—at least not in the ways that really mattered to me.

But I was a good person. I was honest, hardworking, and kind. Why wasn't I giving? I think for the same reasons many of us don't. I was so busy that sometimes I didn't have time to even notice an opportunity to give, let alone actually do something about it. I was afraid I'd do it wrong or be taken advantage of or look stupid. I told myself I'd do it later when I had plenty of time and money.

That was about to change. I was going to discover how to make giving easy and doable. It was going to be part of my daily life because I was ready to be the person I wanted to be and have the impact on the world I wanted to have. I was tired of being afraid. I was sick of waiting for a perfect someday that was never going to arrive.

I wanted to live generously—every single day.

What Is Generosity?

After reading and writing on generosity for the past several years, I believe that I have boiled it down to a simple but all-encompassing definition. Here is how I define it:

> *Generosity is intentionally, freely, and frequently giving to improve your life and the lives of others.*

Let's look at each component of this definition in more detail.

Intentionally

Give with the end in mind. Know what you want to accomplish and then give what is needed to reach that goal.

If you want to improve your own life, start with the question, "What will enhance my well-being?" Then give yourself what you need to improve your physical, mental, emotional, and spiritual health.

On the other hand, if you want to improve the lives of others, start with the question, "What will enhance *their* well-being?" When you're generous with others, you put yourself in their shoes, understand their lives, care what they care about, and then give them what they need. Generosity isn't giving what you have and hoping it's what someone needs—that's problem-solving. Throughout this book, I will help you keep your generous acts intentional and beneficial to both yourself and others.

Freely

Truly generous actions come from you freely and go to others freely.

From you freely: Sometimes there can be a lot of external pressure and expectations about what and when to give. I notice these situations because I feel trapped. I might say to myself, "I should give," "I need to pay it back," "It's my duty," or "I have to." I feel resentful and angry, and in my mind, I'm saying, "I can't believe you're making me …"

To others freely: Sometimes all kinds of subtle strings can be attached to a so-called generous act. If I do something nice for you, then you'll like me, do something nice for me, or act in a certain way. I notice I've placed conditions when I'm feeling hurt or resentful. I might say, "You didn't notice I did this" or "You didn't do something nice in return for me."

When you give because of outside pressure or with strings attached, generosity is transformed into an economic transaction where debts are tallied and balanced. Does the giving still count? As long as the strings attached aren't hurting anyone, then sure. But it doesn't feel good, and I don't think you should settle for giving without enjoying it!

As you explore being more generous, you will be invited to discover how you enjoy giving to others, how to transform obligatory giving into generosity, and how to say no when you're giving for the wrong reasons.

Frequently

Generosity is not a thought experiment. It does not exist until a generous act takes place. Therefore, to be generous, you must act generously, and the more often you act generously, the more generous you are!

Unfortunately, that is often easier said than done. In an experiment at Cornell University, 250 students were asked, "At the upcoming fundraiser for the American Cancer Society, how many daffodils would you buy?" More than 8 out of 10 students polled said they would buy flowers and that they would buy, on average, 2 flowers each.

The American Cancer Society Daffodil Fundraiser took place, and the researchers returned to the students to find out what actually happened. While 80 percent said they would buy a daffodil, only 43 percent actually did, and instead of buying 2 flowers, they only bought 1.2 flowers on average.[1]

We think we're generous. We would really like to buy two flowers to support cancer research. But when the rubber meets the road, we just don't give as much as we thought we would or think we should. Even though I've gotten a lot better, there are still times when the tongue in my mouth is not lining up with the tongue in my shoes.

This book helps you overcome that natural human tendency, and by the end of it you will have completed 365 intentional, generous acts. That's a lot of generosity!

Giving to Improve Your Life

When most people think about generosity, they think it means giving to other people. But what about being generous to yourself? If you were healthier, could you give more? If you understood yourself better, could you give better? If you had more time, could you give more often?

You must give to yourself intentionally, because only you can judge what improves your health and what doesn't. You must give to yourself freely because you are worth taking care of. And you must be generous with yourself frequently because you always need to be cared for.

To that end, this book will help you eat better, exercise, find time for meditation and/or prayer, and take other actions that are good for your physical, mental, emotional, and spiritual well-being.

Giving to Improve the Lives of Others

This is what people think of when they think about generosity. When it comes to being generous to others, there are two different areas in which you can help.

Giving to others: This addresses the immediate physical, emotional, and spiritual needs of others. You do this with friends and family all the time without even realizing what you're doing. When you do it for strangers, it's called charity. Giving to others makes an immediate and tangible difference in someone's life.

Giving to the world: This addresses the underlying issues that cause a problem so that other people won't experience the same problem. This is called justice. Giving to the world is a long-term investment in creating a world where fewer people suffer, where wrongs are righted, and where everyone can reach their potential regardless of where they were born.

For example, in your effort to give to others, you might teach literacy classes to adults who never learned how to read. In your effort to give to the world, you donate to a charity that helps keep kids in school so that they never become illiterate adults in the first place.

The daily lessons in this book will help you give in both areas so that you can be a well-rounded giver who is making the world a better place both right now and in the future.

Complete Generosity

So there you have it. When all those elements come together, you have true generosity. When you're giving yourself what you need to be physically, emotionally, and spiritually healthy; when you're giving to meet others' immediate physical, emotional, and spiritual needs; when you're working to solve problems at their roots so that fewer people will suffer in the future; and when you're doing it freely and frequently—that's complete generosity.

How to Use This Book

This is not a shelf-help book. The reality is that you know you need to exercise, eat right, and give time and money to causes you care about. If you're not doing it, it's not because of some moral failing. It's not because you're lazy. It's because it's not a habit. If you have to think about exercising (or some other desired behavior), there's only so long you can do that before something comes up and you forget. Suddenly, six months later, you're starting to exercise again.

This book is designed to help you create new healthy habits and break old bad habits and is based on the latest scientific research on how to do it. Each day focuses on one of the seven generosity habits and offers a suggested action you can take to practice that habit. Each habit appears once every week. The year begins with small actions that build in length and broaden in scope as the year progresses. If you want to focus on a specific habit, you can find an index at the back of the book with each day organized by habit.

In choosing how to make this book the most accessible and user friendly, I've grouped the habits together by week, some of which include a monthly check-in. Although this means some weeks have eight entries, it will make it easier for you to flip through the book to find a particular habit, since you know that every week contains all seven habits.

Journaling is a wonderful way to connect with yourself, and many of the daily practices begin with a journal entry to help you gain insight and clarity into your own desires and patterns. You can use your own journal, or you can download the Living Generously Resource Pack from www.LivingGenerouslyEveryDay.com /BookResources. It includes the daily practices plus a wide array of materials to help you with many of the habits.

Step by step. Action by action. Day by day. That's how change happens. That's how you create your best life.

The Giving Challenges

One day each month, a daily lesson will offer you the opportunity to consider a very specific giving scenario. Each of these giving scenarios reflects a different thread of this world's beautiful tapestry and allows you to explore the great variety of causes you may consider supporting.

Trust Yourself and Take What You Like

You are the expert on your own life, and no one knows better than you what is right for you. I encourage you to put on your detective hat and use this book to discover what works best for you. Discover how you need to exercise and eat to be healthy. Discover what kinds of charities you like to support. Discover how you like to connect with others. This is your life and your journey, and it's different from everyone else's. Trust yourself to live your generous life.

Many lessons in this book are approached from different angles, because one way of thinking about a problem may speak to you more than another. You may get more pleasure out of some daily lessons than others. Some daily lessons you may not need at all, so just ignore those days and move on to the next. Take what you like and leave the rest.

Enjoy the Journey

As I've learned to be more, to do more, and to give more, I've come to feel greater acceptance, peacefulness, love, and understanding no matter what is going on in my life. I know that this world is a better place because I am here, and that gives me a great sense of fulfillment.

But it's still a process and a journey. I'm still learning to love who I am unconditionally and not be so hard on myself. I still notice that sometimes I'm withholding when I could be giving—but, hey, at least I'm noticing it! That's progress!

Becoming the person you want to be and having the impact on the world you want to have is a journey without a final destination. You travel this path your entire life, getting better each step of the way. Maybe you even take a step back once in a while. That's okay, too, as long as you start moving forward again.

I hope this book helps you find the courage, strength, and motivation on your journey to give more of who you are and what you have to give to yourself, to your loved ones, and to the world.

Week 1

Day 1: Taking the First Step
Habit: Physical Health

*Take the first step in faith. You don't have to see
the whole staircase, just take the first step.*
—Martin Luther King Jr.

Becoming the person you want to be and having the impact you
want to have is a lifelong journey. Each step is really just the first
step from where you are right now toward where you want to be.

The most important part of any first step is that it's a first
step you *can* do. If you want to be healthy but walking around the
block is difficult, your first step isn't to start running. Instead, walk
around the block until you can walk it twice.

As you take each step in your journey, the next first step can
materialize.

Practice:

1. In your journal, identify any physical challenges or limitations
   you have. How have those physical challenges impacted your
   health? Given your physical challenges, list five physical activities you could do. Only list activities that can be done anywhere at any time—no special equipment or gym membership

required. Get ideas by searching online for "bodyweight exercises you can do anywhere."

2. Choose one of those physical activities to perform for one minute every day this week. (You should always consult a physician before beginning any exercise plan.)

3. Start now! Put down the book, perform that exercise for one minute, and for the next week, perform it for one minute sometime during the day. If you want to do more than one minute of physical activity, you are welcome to do so. Just do at least one minute.

. . . .
Day 2: Benefits of Mindfulness
Habit: Mindfulness

It's about living your life as if it really mattered,
moment by moment by moment by moment.
—Jon Kabat-Zinn

Scientific studies over the past two decades have shown that mindfulness improves nearly every aspect of your life. It boosts your immune system, increases positive emotions, decreases depression and anxiety, grows additional gray matter inside your brain, improves your ability to focus and complete tasks, fosters compassion and altruism (making people more likely to help others), and enhances relationships and feelings of intimacy.[2]

Be generous to yourself and enjoy the benefits that mindfulness will bring to your life.

Practice:

What is the next action you're going to take after putting down this book? As you are doing it, notice exactly what you are doing, how you are doing it, what's around you, how your body is moving, and what you're thinking and feeling while doing it. Notice as much as possible about this seemingly simply action.

. . . .
Day 3: Boundaries, Part 1
Habit: Relationships

People cannot go wrong, if you don't let them.
They cannot go right, unless you let them.
—Augustus William Hare and Julius Charles Hare,
Guesses at Truth, by Two Brothers

Sometimes you can be too generous or generous in the wrong ways. As a result, you can be taken advantage of or get involved in situations that are unhealthy. If you feel like you have to "save" people, if you get sucked into drama, if you swing between loving and hating your friends or lovers, then you might have boundary issues.

Poor boundaries result from misunderstanding who is responsible for what. Each person is responsible for their own actions, their own emotions, their own responses to their situation, and their own happiness or lack thereof. While you can provide guidance, inspiration, and some tools, you undermine their self-respect and self-agency when you disregard their personal responsibility to help them with things they should do and learn for themselves.

Practice:

1. Tomorrow, you'll explore your personal boundaries, but first, examine how you may be violating other people's boundaries. Take out your journal and write for five minutes. What are you taking responsibility for in other people's lives? When do you do things for people that they should do for themselves? Whose happiness do you feel responsible for?

2. Who needs you to generously respect their competency, autonomy, and choices? Send a greeting card or an e-mail, write a note, or choose some other method to communicate your love for that person.

. . . .
Day 4: Boundaries, Part 2
Habit: Connecting with Yourself

*The greatest thing in the world
is to know how to belong to oneself.*
—Michel de Montaigne, *Essays*

Boundaries work both ways. You are responsible for your actions, your emotions, your responses to your situation, and your happiness or lack thereof. When you expect other people to do certain things for you, to act toward you in certain ways, or to make you feel loved or happy, you place control of your life in someone else's hands. Unfortunately, they can't fix you any more than you can fix them. Fundamentally, healthy boundaries are a result of healthy self-esteem. When you respect yourself, you take care of your physical, emotional, and spiritual health.

Practice:

1. Take out your journal and write for five minutes. What are you not taking responsibility for in your own life? What do you expect from other people? If you were more generous to yourself, what would you do for yourself?

2. Treat yourself to a random act of kindness, like taking a walk in the park, enjoying a nutritious salad, or getting back in bed for ten minutes to enjoy some quiet time.

. . . .
Day 5: Function of Gratitude
Habit: Gratitude

Gratitude is the memory of the heart.
—Jean Massieu, *A Collection of the Most Remarkable Definitions and Answers*

We are about to embark on creating one of the most important habits of all: gratitude. After conducting and reviewing hundreds of studies, the University of California, Berkeley, concluded that gratitude is one of the most reliable methods for increasing happiness and life satisfaction. It boosts feelings of optimism, joy, pleasure, and enthusiasm. It reduces anxiety and depression, strengthens the immune system, lowers blood pressure, reduces symptoms of illness, and makes us less bothered by aches and pains. It encourages us to exercise more and take better care of our health. Grateful people get more hours of sleep each night, spend less time awake before falling asleep, and feel more refreshed upon awakening. Gratitude makes people more resilient and helps them recover from traumatic events.[3]

In short, gratitude is a keystone habit whose good effects cascade through your life, improving nearly every area: physical, emotional, spiritual, work, and personal relationships. You name it—gratitude helps.

Gratitude is a simple affirmation of goodness that acknowledges that the goodness comes from some place outside yourself, according to Robert A. Emmons, PhD, the world's leading scientific expert on gratitude.[4] Saying thank you is a grateful act, but you can also become a grateful person who looks at the world as a source of goodness. Every week you will have the opportunity to intentionally express gratitude so that feeling grateful becomes a habit.

Practice:

1. Take out your journal and list five people, places, things, or events you are grateful for.
2. Choose one and describe it in more detail. Why you are grateful for it? What does it bring to your life? What would it mean if it was suddenly gone?

· · · · · · · · · · · · · · · · · · · ·
Day 6: Value of Simplicity
Habit: Simplicity

*It seems that perfection is attained not when there is nothing
more to add, but when there is nothing more to remove.*
—Antoine de Saint-Exupéry, *Terre des Hommes*

Be generous to yourself by living simply so that you have the time
and attention to give to what is good for you and what is most important to you. When it comes to living simply, there are four areas
to focus on.

+ *Mind:* A calm, balanced mind provides clarity of thought that
  will help you be more productive and effective in every area of
  your life.

+ *Schedule:* At the end of your life, you'll wish you spent more
  time with friends, with family, and on hobbies, so create a
  schedule that focuses on the activities that are most important to you.

+ *Nature:* At first blush, you may think spending time in nature
  has nothing to do with living generously. But actually, it touches
  on a number of the generosity habits: physical health, mindfulness, connecting with yourself, gratitude (although in nature it's
  often better-called awe), and most importantly, simplicity.

+ *Home:* Having what you need where you need it creates space
  for family and frees up time and energy.

Practice:

1. On a scale from 1 to 10, 1 being not at all and 10 being utterly, how overwhelmed are you?

2. On a scale from 1 to 10, 1 being not at all and 10 being insanely, how busy are you?

3. On a scale from 1 to 10, 1 being not at all and 10 being like a souvenir shop, how cluttered is your home?

4. For the next week, place a twenty-four-hour waiting period before buying anything that isn't an essential food item. When you want to buy something, ask, "Where did the impulse to buy it come from?" If the desire to buy it is still there twenty-four hours later, ask, "What need will this purchase meet? Is it worth the money and space and emotional energy?" If yes, then buy it.

. . . .
Day 7: Role of Philanthropy
Habit: Philanthropy

What we think, or what we know, or what we believe is, in the end, of little consequence. The only consequence is what we do.
—John Ruskin, *The Crown of Wild Olive*

Philanthropy has nothing to do with *how much* you donate and everything to do with *how* you donate. A philanthropist is someone who...

+ has a picture of how the world should be

+ donates with the intention of bringing that picture to life

+ takes the necessary steps to evaluate if a particular donation of money or time will foster that vision

You can donate twenty-five dollars and be a philanthropist, but someone could donate a million dollars and not be a philanthropist.

Philanthropy is where the rubber meets the road. It's where the tongue in your mouth lines up with the tongue in your shoe. If you want to make the world a better place, then you have to *do something* about it. Philanthropy is you doing something about what you believe so that the world will be a better place.

Practice:

1. What reason primarily drives your giving? Rank the responses below. I donate because …

   ____ I have so much! I want others to have the same opportunities I had.

   ____ I've been there, and I don't want others to go through the same thing.

   ____ It's my duty and responsibility to give back.

   ____ I'm spiritually or religiously called to give.

   ____ Donating makes me feel good, like I'm making a difference.

   ____ Other: _____.

2. Take out your journal. What causes do you care about? What keeps you from doing more to support these causes? How would you feel if you died without supporting the causes you care about?

Week 2

Day 8: Thoughtless Habits
Habit: Physical Health

The diminutive chains of habit, as somebody says,
are scarcely ever heavy enough to be felt,
till they are too strong to be broken.
—Maria Edgeworth, *Moral Tales for Young People*

What time did you wake up this morning? Did you pop right out of bed when the alarm clock went off, or did you press snooze? What did you do next when you got out of bed—brush your teeth or make coffee? Likely, it was the same thing you did yesterday and the day before that, because for the vast majority of your day, your brain goes into autopilot and your habits take over.

This makes sense for the brain. Relying on habit frees up your brain for other activities, but it's a double-edged sword. It also means that new healthy habits are hard to start and bad habits are hard to break because you aren't actually thinking about your habits when you're doing them.

The first step is to understand your existing habits.

Practice:

1. What is your morning routine?

2. What is your lunchtime routine?

3. What is your afternoon or home-from-work routine?

4. What is your pre-bedtime routine?

5. At what point in your day does it make the most sense for you to get some physical activity? Morning, lunch, after work, other?

6. Double your daily physical activity to two minutes. The goal right now is not to get healthy. It's to create a habit of daily physical activity, which is what will get you healthy in the long run. Give yourself the best chance to create new healthy habits by making it easy to accomplish. You can do two minutes of physical activity every day. Anyone can! If you want to do more than two minutes of physical activity, you are welcome to do so. Just do at least two minutes.

· ·
Day 9: What Is Mindfulness?
Habit: Mindfulness

*This is the real secret of life—to be completely engaged with
what you are doing in the here and now.
And instead of calling it work, realize it is play.*
—Alan Watts, *The Essence of Alan Watts*

The word "mindfulness" is tossed around a lot, but what does it really mean? It's simple, really. Mindfulness is noticing each thought, feeling, body sensation, and surrounding environment in the moment as you're experiencing it without judging it as good or bad.

Practice:

Brush your teeth mindfully. While you're brushing your teeth, don't think about what else you need to do. Do nothing but brush your teeth. Pay attention as you place the toothpaste on the brush, feel the tube squeeze in your hands, notice the color and smell of the toothpaste. What sensations do you feel as you bring the toothbrush into your mouth? Feel each tooth that you're brushing. Experience the brush rubbing against your gums. If you notice you start thinking about something else, notice that. Then bring your attention back to your mouth and the sensations of the bubbles in your mouth.

· ·
Day 10: What's Your Impact?
Habit: Relationships

The purpose of life is not to be happy at all. It is to be useful, to be honorable. It is to be compassionate. It is to matter, to have it make some difference that you lived.
—Leo Rosten, "The Myths by Which We Live"

There's only one way to make the world a better place: you have to make an impact on others. The hermit isolated in a mountain retreat doesn't make the world a better place. But you're not a hermit, so you will have an impact. The question is, what will it be?

Practice:

1. Take out your journal and write for five minutes. What kind of impact are you making right now? How do you feel about the impact you are making? What kind of impact would you like to make?

2. Perform a random act of kindness today, like bringing a plant into the office; leaving random, positive sticky notes; or donating art supplies to a local school.

. . . .
Day 11: In Control
Habit: Connecting with Yourself

To love oneself is the beginning of a life-long romance.
—Oscar Wilde, "Phrases and Philosophies
for the Use of the Young"

Psychologists identify a strong internal locus of control as an important component to self-esteem. In other words, if you believe you have very little control or influence over what happens to you, it's difficult to feel good about yourself. But if you feel like a good part of your destiny is in your own hands, you'll take more action, take more responsibility for those actions, and, as a result, have higher self-esteem.

Finding a meaning for your life, meditating, exercising, and forgiving those who have harmed you are just a few actions that can create a sense of internal control. These also happen to be generous actions because they are gifts to yourself.

Practice:

1. On a scale from 1 to 10, 1 being feeling absolutely worthless and 10 being totally confident that you are awesome, how much self-esteem do you have?

2. In your journal, write about what in your life feels out of your control. What do you have control over in that situation? Take an action that exercises some control over your life, like enrolling in a class, seeking an expert opinion, or getting a good night's sleep.

. . . .
Day 12: Undeserved Gifts
Habit: Gratitude

My wealth has come from a combination of living in America,
some lucky genes, and compound interest. Both my children
and I won what I call the ovarian lottery.
—Warren Buffett

Throughout your life, you've received many gifts that had nothing to do with something you did or something special about you. You received them because of choices other people made or by virtue of where you live and who you were born to.

If you were lucky, your parents gave you food, shelter, and plenty of love. Maybe you also got music lessons, rides to soccer practice, birthday presents, and countless everyday acts of kindness, support, and life lessons.

If you were lucky, you got to go to school and get an education. If you were really lucky, you got a teacher who believed in you and inspired in you a love for science or books.

If you were lucky to be born in a developed nation, you received sanitation, running water, transportation infrastructure, health care, and a law enforcement system.

If you were lucky to be born after 1962 and in America, you could get a polio vaccine and grow up without the fear of being killed or disabled by this terrifying disease.

All around you is a large and often invisible network of people and institutions who give you tangible and intangible gifts that help you live and learn.

Practice:

In your journal, list five gifts you've received because of where you live, who you were born to, or choices other people have made. Then take a moment to appreciate the impact of these gifts on your life.

· ·
Day 13: Short Life in a Very Old World
Habit: Schedule Simplicity

We are like butterflies
who flutter for a day and think it's forever.
—Carl Sagan, *Cosmos*

The best science currently estimates that the universe is 13.8 billion years old. But that number is so big, it doesn't really mean anything. To put it in perspective, Carl Sagan introduced the Cosmic

Calendar and collapsed the entire history of the universe into just a single year. Neil deGrasse Tyson updated that timeline in the 2014 TV series *Cosmos*.

On January 1, all the matter in the universe was compressed into a dense and hot mass that for some, as of yet unknown, reason began to expand rapidly. Over the next eight months, the universe took shape. Elements like hydrogen and helium appeared, stars formed, galaxies coalesced. It wasn't until August 31 that our solar system formed around our sun. Then it took a month for the earliest known organisms, the single-celled bacteria and algae that led to all the diverse plant and animal life we have today, to appear on our planet. December is half over before life ventures out of the water and onto the land. For just a few days at the end of December, dinosaurs rule the land before their extinction gives room for mammals to thrive.

The first humans don't appear until the last day of the year at 9:45 p.m., and in a matter of hours, we learn how to use fire and tools. We discover agriculture and give up the nomadic life 60 seconds before the year ends. We invent writing 14 seconds before the year ends. In the final seconds, we discover how to work with bronze and iron; develop algebra, geometry, and physics; and invent cars, computers, and space travel.

On January 1 at 12:00 a.m., you arrive for 0.16 seconds.[5] That's how long your 80-year life registers in cosmic time.

Practice:

1. In your journal, identify four to five priorities. What are the most important things for you to focus on and accomplish

in your 0.16 seconds? List ten actions for each priority that would move that priority forward or that would strengthen that priority in your life.

2. Choose one of those actions and do it.

. . . .

Day 14: Month 1 Giving Challenge: Homelessness
Habit: Philanthropy

Charity literally translated from the original means love,
the love that understands, that does not merely share
the wealth of the giver, but in true sympathy and wisdom
helps men to help themselves.
—Franklin D. Roosevelt, 1936 speech at the
Democratic National Convention

The US Department of Housing and Urban Development estimates that each homeless person costs their community about forty thousand dollars a year due to incarceration, police intervention, emergency room visits, and temporary housing. But these expenses don't solve the underlying problems, and often people remain stuck in a cycle of homelessness, illness, and violence. On the other hand, permanent supportive housing programs provide housing plus health services, addiction recovery, and job training so that people can get off the streets for good. It turns out that in the long term, permanent supportive housing programs save more money than they cost.[6]

But the biggest cost to our communities is the unrealized potential of the men, women, and children who are suffering from homelessness. What talents and energies could they contribute to our community if they were mentally and physically healthy?

We can end homelessness in the United States by tackling its root causes: lack of affordable housing, poor access to the appropriate physical and mental health care, low wages, and not having the job skills and education needed by employers.

Practice:

Locate a homeless shelter in your community and call the staff. Ask them about the extent of homelessness in your community, what they are doing to solve it, how they know what they're doing is working, and how you can help.

Week 3
· · · · · · · · ·

Day 15: Triggers
Habit: Physical Health

It was the peculiar artifice of Habit
not to suffer her power to be felt at first.
—Samuel Johnson, "The Vision of Theodore,
the Hermit of Tenerife, Found in His Cell"

Last week, you discovered that you do your habits without even thinking about them. But wait…If you're not thinking about a habit when you're doing it, how do you know it's time to start it? Because you've been triggered.

Trigger: Alarm clock. Routine: Hop out of bed, put on a pot of coffee, jump in the shower, brush your teeth, get dressed, drink coffee, grab a snack out of the pantry, grab your briefcase and car keys, open the garage door, get in your car, turn the radio on, drive to work.

Trigger: Get home from work. Routine: Take off your shoes, grab a beer, turn on the TV, watch the evening news, order a pizza.

And you didn't have to think about any of that. You just did it. Use this to your advantage by using an existing trigger to build a new habit. For example, starting your pot of coffee can be the trigger for one minute of push-ups. Or taking your shoes off when you come home from work could be the trigger for putting on sneakers and going for a short run.

Practice:

1. Review your routines from day 8. As you look to strengthen your daily physical activity habit, choose an existing habit that will happen right before your new exercise habit. It will be your trigger, so you know when it's time to exercise.

2. Create a reminder to exercise and have what you need to exercise at the place where your trigger occurs.

3. This week, double the time of your minimum daily physical activity to four minutes. If you want to do more than four minutes of physical activity, you are welcome to do so. Just do at least four minutes.

. . . .
Day 16: Limits of Mindfulness
Habit: Mindfulness

Man is a mystery: if you spend your entire life trying to puzzle it out, then do not say that you have wasted your time.
I occupy myself with this mystery, because I want to be a man.
—Fyodor Dostoyevsky, 1839 personal correspondence

The human brain is still a vast, unexplored, unknown territory. Even as we understand more and more about how it functions, we still know very little about why it functions, where it breaks down, and how to change it. Mindfulness helps people cope with their changing mental and emotional states, but sometimes it needs to be partnered with expert guidance from a mental health professional trained at navigating the mysteries of the human mind. Be generous to yourself and give yourself the mental health care you need.

Practice:

1. Do you experience prolonged, extreme, or dramatic changes in your emotional states?

2. Do you abuse drugs or alcohol or have strange, confused, suicidal, or violent thoughts?

3. Would you benefit from the guidance of a mental health counselor? If so, collect three names from friends, family, your doctor, or your insurance company, and have a brief, introductory conversation with them about your needs and their services.

. . . .
Day 17: Loving Requires Giving
Habit: Relationships

One can give without loving,
but one cannot love without giving.
—Amy Carmichael, *A Chance to Die*

Can love exist without giving? I don't know. Does a tree falling in the forest make a sound if no one is around to hear it? I don't know that either. But I do know that love without giving is pointless. How will people know you love them if you don't give them anything?

I've given thoughtfully selected presents that were exactly what my husband wanted. I've given my best friend a pep talk when she needed it most. I've given my cousin a night off by babysitting her daughter. What do you give to those you love?

Practice:

1. Starting with your immediate family and then extending out in expanding circles, write the names of people you love.
2. Choose one person. Treat them to a random act of kindness like preparing their favorite meal, leaving them a loving note, or complimenting them on how they handled a situation.

. . . .
Day 18: A Feeling of Belonging
Habit: Connecting with Yourself

Your level of belonging, in fact, can never be greater
than your level of self-acceptance,
because believing that you're enough is what gives you
the courage to be authentic, vulnerable and imperfect.
—Brené Brown, "Brené Brown's Top 4 Life Lessons"

The more you are able to be who you really are and be accepted for it, the more self-esteem you'll have. The more self-esteem you have, the more you are able to express yourself, act authentically, and be fully present with others, and that means greater feelings of belonging. It's a virtuous feedback loop where more self-esteem creates more belonging and more belonging creates more self-esteem.

You can increase your sense of belonging and acceptance by expressing gratitude to others, practicing random acts of kindness, and volunteering. Be generous to yourself by being generous with others.

Practice:

1. Take out your journal. On a scale from 1 to 10, how lovable and valuable do you feel? List five aspects of your personality that you like, five past actions you're proud of, and five reasons you're a good friend.

2. Spend time with a friend in person or on the phone. Listen to what's going on in their life, admire their positive qualities, and practice accepting them for who they are.

. . . .
Day 19: Ask a Better Question
Habit: Gratitude

It is not in the still calm of life, or in the repose of a pacific station, that great characters are formed. The habits of a vigorous mind are formed in contending with difficulties.
—Abigail Adams, 1780 letter to John Quincy Adams

"Why me?" It's a question we all ask; unfortunately, it's a lousy question that prompts self-pity. People indulge in self-pity because even though they're feeling bad, they can feel better about feeling bad. And while it's true that there is plenty of suffering and misfortune in your life, there is also so much good fortune and maybe much, much more to be grateful for.

Asking a different, better question changes your focus from what's wrong in your life to what's right and provides more context and perspective for the situation. It gives you permission to take action, to try something new, and to feel good about who you are despite the current difficulty.

Isn't that better than feeling good about feeling bad?

Practice:

1. Recall a situation or an issue that made you feel sorry for yourself. In your journal, answer these questions. Why not you? What can you do with or learn from this situation? If this were serving a higher purpose, what would it be? How does this help you be better, faster, stronger? What do you need to believe about this situation to see the gift inside the difficulty?

2. Take an action to transform tragedy into triumph, such as connecting with others who've been through the same thing, sharing your experience with others, or expressing gratitude for what remains.

. . . .
Day 20: Importance of Nature
Habit: Nature Simplicity

There is something infinitely healing in the repeated refrains of nature—the assurance that dawn comes after night, and spring after the winter.
—Rachel Carson, *The Sense of Wonder*

Each month, you will be invited to connect with nature, because it is in nature that life gets the most simple. Ordinarily, your mind and body move at the busy pace of modern life. But nature moves at its own speed. It cares nothing for your schedule. Nature is concerned with its own intricate dance of life and death. It is indifferent to your survival. Being with nature is an opportunity to connect with the simplest truths of life.

Practice:

Find something in your natural world that is bigger than you: a creek, a river, a lake, a large tree, a mountain, a meadow, or the sky. Gaze at it. Sense the slow inevitability of its gradual changes. Become aware of the blind, immense, unconscious, impersonal, and neutral forces that created it and will endure beyond you and despite you. Feel the smallness of the human world's petty activities and desires. Accept that, underneath it all, there is a unique rightness and beauty to life.

· · · · · · · · · · · · · · · · · · ·
Day 21: Money vs. Time
Habit: Philanthropy

In Faith and Hope the world will disagree,
But all Mankind's concern is Charity.
—Alexander Pope, *An Essay on Man*

Is it better to give money or time? To get at this question, consider the following situation.

Your neighbor knocks on your door and asks you to help him move next weekend. Do you eagerly give him your time, groan but do it anyway, or decline?

Now imagine that same neighbor knocks on your door. This time, he asks to borrow fifty dollars to help make ends meet until the next payday. Does that feel different?

Is it better to give money or time? They are equally important but different, and they give you different benefits. If you happen to find yourself with more money than time, then give more money than time. If you have more time than money, then give more time. But always try to give a little of each.

Practice:

1. In your journal, write on the following questions. How do you feel when someone asks you for your time? How do you feel when someone asks you for your money? Do you have more money than time or more time than money?

2. Today, perform a charitable action like writing your church's newsletter, coaching a local children's sports team, or making a small donation.

Week 4

Day 22: Plan for Success by Planning for Failure
Habit: Physical Health

It does not do to leave a live dragon out of your calculations,
if you live near him.
—J. R. R. Tolkien, *The Hobbit*

Creating a new habit can be challenging, and the best-laid plans will falter as life unfolds on a daily basis. What are the dragons that will disrupt your best-laid plans for being physically active?

- *External dragons:* What challenges will work and life offer you? A hectic and inflexible work schedule? Your boss? A friend who means well, but...? Car accidents?
- *Family dragons:* What challenges will your kids, spouse, parents put in your way?
- *Internal dragons:* What obstacles will you put up in your own way? What are you afraid will happen if you accomplish your goal? What rationalizations will you give yourself about why it's okay not to meet your goal?

What will you do to meet your goal when life isn't working out exactly as planned?

Practice:

1. In your journal, consider the following question: What challenges will you face in being physically active every day? What will you do when you encounter an obstacle? What do you need, where do you need it, and how do you need to be reminded to complete your daily physical activity?

2. Set yourself up for success. Put what you need where you need it. Put your reminders in place. Know your backup plan.

3. Increase your minimum daily physical activity to six minutes. If you want to do more than six minutes of physical activity, you are welcome to do so. Just do at least six minutes.

· · · · · · · · · · · · · · · · · · · ·
Day 23: Raisin Meditation
Habit: Mindfulness

If the doors of perception were cleansed
everything would appear to Man as it is: infinite.
—William Blake, *The Marriage of Heaven and Hell*

Spending time being mindful is a gift to yourself that creates space for you to feel more, think more, be more. Fortunately, it's also simple. Take this exercise, for example, adapted from *The Mindful Way through Depression*, in which you explore the seemingly infinite details of a common object and experience.[7]

Practice:

1. Hold a raisin in your hand. Imagine where it all began—a flower on a far-off vine. Imagine the sun and water nurturing it to maturity, it being plucked from the vine, and it drying out in sun. Imagine the many hands it went through before ending up here in your hand.

2. Observe it closely. What does it look like? Describe it in detail, including size, shape, color, imperfections. What does it smell like? What does it feel like? If you squeeze it, does it make any noise?

3. Place it in your mouth. What do you notice? How is your body responding to food? How is your mind responding? Chew the raisin—slowly. What do you notice? How does it taste? What is the texture? What does it feel like to swallow the raisin?

4. How did your experience of eating this raisin differ from the other times you've eaten a raisin?

. . . .
Day 24: Introverts vs. Extroverts
Habit: Relationships

It is easy in the world to live after the world's opinion;
it is easy in solitude to live after our own;
but the great man is he who in the midst of the crowd keeps
with perfect sweetness the independence of solitude.
—Ralph Waldo Emerson, *Self-Reliance*

I'm an introvert. Sometimes I think that if I never left my house again, I'd be okay with that, because my house is the most beautiful and comfortable place in the world to me. I love reading. I love hanging out with a few people that I know really well. But I don't always enjoy sharing my emotions with others, and I tend to be more reserved around large groups of people. Even if you're an introvert like me, connecting with others is not only possible, it's necessary. You just have to discover *how* to connect in a way that fits your personality.

Practice:

1. Are you an introvert or an extrovert? Do you prefer one-on-one activities (introvert) or group activities (extrovert)? Does the idea of spending a weekend at home alone sound heavenly (introvert), or do you prefer to fill your weekend with social events (extrovert)? Do you like to work on one task at a time without interruptions (introvert), or do you like lots of projects and activity around you when you work (extrovert)? Do you weigh your words carefully after thinking about many facets of an issue (introvert), or can you offer an opinion quickly without even being asked (extrovert)?

2. Perform a random act of kindness sometime today that fits your personality. For example, if you're an extrovert, you could bring cookies for the entire office, or if you're an introvert, you could gift your favorite book to someone sitting across from you on the subway.

. . . .
Day 25: Self-Confidence
Habit: Connecting with Yourself

The confidence which we have in ourselves
gives birth to much of that which we have in others.
—François de La Rochefoucauld, *Premier Supplement*

Self-confidence is the feeling that you're good at something, getting better at something, or could do something. The more self-confidence you have, the more inclined you are to do things that lead to more successful experiences, leading to even more self-confidence. More than that, your self-confidence can give you the courage to be more generous more often and with more people.

Increase your sense of confidence by practicing an existing skill, learning a new skill, setting a goal and celebrating when you achieve it, remembering your past victories, or even doing something as simple as exercising.

Practice:

1. Take out your journal. On a scale from 1 to 10, how worthy and capable do you feel? List five things you're good at. List five things you've accomplished in the past.

2. Take an action to increase your self-confidence, like practicing something you already feel good at, learning something new, or celebrating a past achievement.

Day 26: Who Inspires You?
Habit: Gratitude

*The hero may be compared to one who kindles a great light in
the world, who sets up blazing torches in the dark streets of life
for men to see by. The saint is a man who walks through the
dark paths of the world—himself a light!*
—Felix Adler, *Ethical Addresses*

There are so many men and women throughout history who have
done great things. Famous people like Helen Keller, Martin Luther
King Jr., Marie Curie, and George Washington show the potential
of the human spirit for courage, love, and achievement. But sometimes our best inspirations live quiet, anonymous lives known only
to a few lucky people.

I am so grateful for those who illuminate the best qualities of
the human spirit, lead with their example, and reveal the potential
inside each one of us. They are human just like me. If they can do it,
then I can do it, too. My personal inspirations include Oprah Win-
frey, Mahatma Gandhi, Tony Robbins, and my parents.

Practice:

1. Who inspires you with their humanitarian actions?

2. Who inspires you by living the kind of life you want?

3. Who inspires you with their uniqueness and authenticity?

4. Who inspires you with their confidence?

5. Who inspires you with their message or their achievements?

6. Who else are you grateful to for their example of how to live?

7. Take a moment to appreciate these men and women. Choose one who is alive and you can contact. Write a brief note, greeting card, or e-mail expressing your appreciation.

. . . .
Day 27: The Necessity Drawer
Habit: Home Simplicity

If you look at your entire house as one unit of junk,
you'll never do anything because the job is too overwhelming.
Take it one drawer at a time.
—Janet Luhrs, *The Simple Living Guide*

Do you have an "I don't know where to put this, so I'll put it here" drawer? An "I don't have time to deal with this, so I'll put it here" drawer? A "Maybe I'll use this again someday" drawer?

Today, transform a junk drawer into a necessity drawer that has what you need where you need it.

Practice:

1. *Dump It:* Everything that is in the drawer must come out.

2. *First Pass Trash/Recycle:* The dried up pens, old receipts, chargers for cell phones you no longer have, and takeout menus should go into the trash or a recycle pile.

3. *Sort:* Group like things together.

4. *Rehome:* Relocate the items that belong somewhere else. Buttons go in your sewing kit, and paper clips go in your desk.

5. *Second Pass Trash/Recycle:* Be tough. If you haven't used it in years or if you forgot it was there, trash, recycle, or donate it.

6. *Organize:* Place all the items you decided were necessary back in the drawer. Use drawer organizers, ziplock baggies, or even old plastic storage containers to keep the items grouped together in their appropriate categories.

. . . .
Day 28: Giving Time
Habit: Philanthropy

Too often we underestimate the power of a touch,
a smile, a kind word, a listening ear, an honest compliment,
or the smallest act of caring, all of which have the potential
to turn a life around.
—Leo Buscaglia, *LOVE*

Volunteering is a unique way for you to be philanthropic. Volunteering opens you up to new experiences, builds skills, and reveals new interests. It gives you the opportunity to connect with people, and that can change your life in ways you can't anticipate. In the introduction, I shared my own personal experience with the transformative potential of connecting with people. I couldn't have imagined that a Thanksgiving dinner with a stranger would totally change my life.

Walking dogs at your local animal rescue or serving meals at a homeless shelter are magnificent contributions to your community. But formal volunteering is not the only way you can give your time. Mentoring a friend's child, writing your church's newsletter, or coaching your child's baseball team are also wonderful ways to give your time.

Practice:

1. In your journal, write about where you have given your time in the past. Where are you giving your time right now? Do you enjoy it? What would you enjoy? Are you giving more or less time than you'd like to give?

2. If you're giving too much time, put boundaries on how much time you give and take an action to reduce your time commitment. If you're giving too little, how much time would you like to give? Create a list of ways you would like to give. Choose one, and then take an action to make it happen.

Week 5
· · · · · · · ·

Day 29: Use Rewards
Habit: Physical Health

*Exercise and application produce order in our affairs,
health of body, cheerfulness of mind, and these make us
precious to our friends.*
—Thomas Jefferson, 1787 letter to daughter Martha

Habits are hard to change because you get a reward every time that habit is completed. The reward for your daily cup of morning coffee is a jolt of energy. The reward for your after-work cocktail is releasing stress.

Unfortunately, the rewards of a new healthy habit are often long term. Eventually, exercising will give you more energy to be more generous to those around you. Eventually, exercising will lead to better health, better sleep, better sex, more energy, and so on. *But* you won't feel those results for some time, and willpower is not sufficient to make you do something you don't like for very long.

Instead, unlock your brain's motivation by finding a reward that motivates you right now. A reward should be healthy, be cheap, and happen as close to end of the action as possible. Avoid big, end-of-the-line rewards like a new iPad for exercising for a month. This type of reward sets up an endpoint, which will derail habit creation. Instead, choose a reward that engages your body with physical activity (like a celebration dance), causes a physical reaction (like a cup of coffee), creates a sense of accomplish (like placing a check mark on a calendar to create a long string of successes), is an enjoyable activity (like listening to a great song), or provides social stimulation (like calling a friend).

Practice:

1. In your journal, brainstorm ten feelings, goals, accomplishments, foods, or other things that would feel good to you as a reward for completing your physical activity goal.

2. Choose three rewards you want to experiment with this week.

3. Keep your minimum daily physical activity at six minutes and do it consistently as part of your morning, lunch, or home-from-work routine (change the trigger if the trigger you chose isn't working). After your physical activity, reward yourself with one of your chosen rewards. How does it feel? Does thinking about the reward motivate you to exercise? Try other rewards throughout the week to discover which one will keep you exercising until the long-term rewards start kicking in.

. . . .
Day 30: Monthly Check-In

Genius is often only the power of making continuous efforts.
—Elbert Hubbard, *The Book of Business*

Time to check in on your progress. This is not a guilt-inducing exercise designed to shame you for all you haven't accomplished yet.

Instead, it's a gentle reminder about what's important to you and what you want to change.

Enjoy the journey. Be gentle with yourself. Keep growing.

Practice:

- What did I do last month that I'm proud of?
- Are my relationships with others improving or deteriorating?
- What do I need to do less of/quit/get rid of/delegate this month?
- What experiments did I try? What lessons did I learn? What is going well?
- What isn't working, and what do I want to change?
- Habit to focus on next month:
- Why do I want to establish that habit?
- What is a first step I can take toward making this a habit?
- What trigger will I use?
- How will I reward myself?
- What obstacles will I face in establishing this habit and how will I overcome them?
- Notes on successes, long-term goals, and personal changes I'm working toward:

Day 31: Wash a Bowl
Habit: Mindfulness

If I am incapable of washing dishes joyfully,
if I want to finish them quickly so I can go and have a cup
of tea, I will be equally incapable of drinking the tea joyfully.
—Thich Nhat Hanh, *The Sun My Heart*

Being present in the moment will allow you to express your full range of generosity. Thich Nhat Hanh, a Buddhist monk, suggests practicing on simple, everyday events—even something as simple as washing a bowl.

Practice:

After your morning cereal, take your bowl to the sink and focus all your attention on the action of washing the bowl. Pay attention as your hand turns the water on. If you bring your hand under the faucet to test the temperature, notice the feel of the water against your skin. Feel the texture of the sponge in your hand. Hear the water falling against the sponge. Hear the squish as the soap is squeezed in the sponge and begins to foam. Smell the scent of soap. Bring the sponge to the bowl and feel the pressure of the bowl pressing into one hand while you wipe with the other. Feel a moment of gratitude for the craftsmanship of the bowl and how it served you this morning. When you are done, place the bowl in the dish rack or dry it and put it away—experiencing each moment of that action as you take it.

· ·
Day 32: Tools for Introverts
Habit: Relationships

*You just stay here in this one corner of the Forest waiting for
others to come to you. Why don't you go to them sometimes?*
—Rabbit in *The House at Pooh Corner*, A. A. Milne

Here are a few strategies you can use to turn your introversion into
a powerful tool for social connection.

1. *Take alone time.* As an introvert, you will always need to re-
   charge, so take the alone time you need to calm, center, and
   energize yourself.
2. *Prepare.* As an introvert, you feel more confident when you
   are prepared, so have a few ice breakers ready, find out about
   the other attendees, learn about the history of the event, and
   write out what you want to say.
3. *Visualize success.* Before an event, stand in a confident posture and imagine feeling good about interacting with other
   people.
4. *Listen closely and ask questions.* This is what you do best, and
   this is wonderful—because you know what people *love* to do?
   Talk about themselves! Brilliant. Easy.
5. *Focus.* As introverts, we can get overwhelmed, so focus on
   just a few areas where you want to be social.

6. *Get comfortable with being uncomfortable.* It's okay to be scared and awkward. It's okay to try something new and not be very good at it. Show up anyway.

Practice:

1. In your journal, write about your comfort in social situations. What tools (from the list above or any other ideas) will you experiment with?

2. Is there a social interaction you've been avoiding? If so, choose your strategy and engage. If not, reach out to an old friend or acquaintance you haven't spoken to in a while.

· ·
Day 33: What Is Happiness?
Habit: Connecting with Yourself

*It is a characteristic of the American culture that, again and again, one is commanded and ordered to "be happy."
But happiness cannot be pursued; it must ensue.
One must have a reason to "be happy."*
—Viktor E. Frankl, *Man's Search for Meaning*

Positive psychologists point out that there are three components to happiness: pleasure, engagement, and meaning. But pleasure is the least important factor. Long-term, foundational happiness isn't pursued with pleasure. It ensues from a feeling of well-being and contentment with who you are and your contribution to the world.

Practice:

1. In your journal, consider the following questions: How happy are you with your contribution to the world? How happy are you with the person you are now and the person you are becoming? How engaged are you with your life, work, family, and friends? How clear are you on your purpose and the meaning of your life? Is it more important for you to focus on increasing your contribution, to become more with some aspect of your life, or get clear on your purpose? Brainstorm a list of actions that would get you closer to that goal.

2. Choose one to do today.

. . . .

Day 34: A Cure for Affluenza
Habit: Gratitude

Most human beings have an almost infinite capacity
for taking things for granted.
—Aldous Huxley, *Themes and Variations*

Affluenza is "a painful, contagious, socially transmitted condition of overload, debt, anxiety and waste resulting from the dogged pursuit of more."[8]

A tongue-in-cheek diagnosis, the symptoms include boredom; envy of other people's homes, cars, clothes, etc.; dissatisfaction with your material possessions; desire for more stuff; running out of room to store your stuff; a below-the-surface restive irritability; depression; lack of purpose; low energy; a vague sense that there must be something more to life; a need to stay distracted; workaholism; addiction to chaos; low self-esteem; inability to delay gratification; and feelings of frustration. In other words, almost all of us suffer from affluenza at some time!

Affluenza occurs when one has a high standard of living but a poor quality of life. Acquiring things creates a high standard of living; instead, give yourself the gift of curing affluenza by improving your quality of life and appreciating what you have.

Practice:

In your journal, list five objects in your life that make your life better and describe how they improve your life. Choose one of those items to focus on. What does this object mean to you? How much did you pay for it? Did you pay more or less than the value it brought to your life? Where was it made? Who made it? What materials is it made from? Where did those materials come from? How long will it last? What will happen to it in the future?

. . . .
Day 35: More Money
Habit: Mind Simplicity

Money is better than poverty, if only for financial reasons.
—Woody Allen, *Without Feathers*

When people say that money can't buy happiness, they're not exactly right. You need to have enough to meet your basic needs, but *more* money does not make you happier.

When people can afford more, they want more. The car they drive gets more expensive, their house gets larger, their clothes get more expensive. That means more expenses and more pressure to earn.

Practice:

1. In your journal, consider the following questions: Do you have enough income to meet your expenses? How stressful is your money situation to you? Are your wants exceeding your budget? Does maintaining your lifestyle increase your financial stress or busy schedule? What pressure do you feel to maintain appearances with other families? Can you downsize or eliminate some bills to lower your expenses?

2. When you spend money today, ask, "Is this purchase improving the quality of my life in the long run?"

. . . .

Day 36: Giving Money
Habit: Philanthropy

A wise man ought have money in his head,
but not in his heart.
—Jonathan Swift, 1729 letter to Lord Bolingbroke

How much money you make can comfort, motivate, or terrify you. Will there be enough today, this month, in retirement? Will it be lost, stolen? How much money you make can define you. Are you poor, middle class, rich?

Thoughts of money influence your life and choices in countless ways, and one of the best tools for lessening money's control over you is to give it away. Giving money reminds you that you are the temporary steward of money. You can't take it with you when you go, so your job is to care for it and use it while you have it. Giving money reminds you that money is a tool to provide for and support the things you love.

Money doesn't define who you are. Your actions define who you are, and how you use your money is an action that defines you.

Practice:

1. In your journal, consider the following questions: Where have you given your money in the past? Where are you giving your money right now? Are you giving more or less money than you'd like to give? How much would you like to give ideally?

2. Choose a dollar amount (no amount is too small) and give it away to a charity or to someone in need.

Week 6

Day 37: Variety Is the Spice of Life
Habit: Physical Health

*True enjoyment comes from activity of the mind and exercise
of the body; the two are ever united.*
—Wilhelm von Humboldt, featured in *A Dictionary of Thoughts*

The University of Florida's Department of Exercise and Sport Sciences discovered that variety and structure were critical to a successful exercise program. Their study divided 114 men and women into three groups: (1) those given specific exercises to do, but those exercises were different on different days; (2) those given specific exercises that were exactly same at each workout; and (3) those given no direction at all and able to do whatever exercises they desired whenever.

Researchers discovered that group 1, the group with structure *and* variety, enjoyed their workout sessions 20 percent more than the members of group 2 and 45 percent more than members of group 3. Most importantly, they were 15 percent more likely than group 2 and 63 percent more likely than group 3 to exercise on a regular basis.[9]

Create some structure and add some variety to your physical activity routines.

Practice:

1. Choose three different types of exercises you would enjoy and want to incorporate into your regular physical activity. If your chosen activities require that you leave your house or have specific equipment, how will you set yourself up for success?

2. Create a schedule. What activity will you do on Monday? Tuesday? Wednesday? Thursday? Friday? Saturday? Sunday? Be sure to schedule days of light physical activity like walking or dancing to give your body time to recover.

3. Increase your daily physical activity to eight minutes. Perform your chosen physical activities consistently as part of your morning, lunch, or home-from-work routine, and reward yourself with one of your chosen rewards. If you want to do more than eight minutes, you are welcome to do so. Just do at least eight minutes.

. . . .
Day 38: Loving Kindness Meditation
Habit: Mindfulness

If you want others to be happy, practice compassion. If you want to be happy, practice compassion.
—Tenzin Gyatso, 14th Dalai Lama

The loving kindness meditation can help you feel greater compassion for yourself and for others, and if you feel more compassionate, then eventually you'll treat yourself and others more compassionately.

Practice:

Close your eyes. Start this meditation by saying, "May I be happy. May I be healthy and strong. May I be filled with peace." Then repeat the phrases while directing them in your mind to someone you love while saying, "May you be happy. May you be healthy and strong. May you be filled with peace." Then think of someone you feel neutral about and say, "May you be happy. May you be healthy and strong. May you be filled with peace." Next, bring your thoughts to a person whom you are having some difficulty with and say, "May you be happy. May you be healthy and strong. May you be filled with peace." Finally, think of the seven billion people on this planet and say to the entire human race, "May you be happy. May you be healthy and strong. May you be filled with peace."

· · · · · · · · · · · · · ·
Day 39: Shyness
Habit: Relationships

Many a man is praised for his reserve and so-called shyness when he is simply too proud to risk making a fool of himself.
—J. B. Priestley, *I for One*

Shyness and introversion are often confused, but they are completely different. Introversion and extroversion are personality traits: introverts are more internally directed while extroverts are externally directed. Both introverts and extroverts can suffer from shyness because shyness is about fear. It's feeling tense or uncomfortable in social situations because it's not safe to be yourself or express your opinion.

Practice:

1. In your journal, explore the fears you have about interacting with others. What strengths do you have in social situations? For example, are you a good listener? Do you accept people for who they are? Do you understand people well? Do you handle one-on-one conversations well? Do people like themselves when they are around you? What strengths do you want to have?

2. Today, go out of your way to help someone feel safe to be himself or herself.

. . . .
Day 40: Your Eulogy
Habit: Connecting with Yourself

May you live all the days of your life.
—Jonathan Swift, *Polite Conversations*

Begin with the end in mind. If you know what a successful life looks like to you, you have a better chance of making it happen.

Practice:

1. In your journal, write a short eulogy. What do you want people to say about you at your funeral? What kind of person were you? How did you impact those around you? What did people admire about you? What will people miss about you?

2. Reflect on what you just wrote and ask, "Am I doing the things and spending my time in ways that help me achieve that?"

3. Choose one quality you want to express more often or an action you want to engage in more often. How can you incorporate this quality or action into your day?

. . . .
Day 41: Memory Stacking
Habit: Gratitude

God gave us memory that we might have roses in December.
—J. M. Barrie, *Courage*

Every moment of every day, you are creating memories. And while many moments are unremarkable, there are many that are worth remembering. There was your first kiss, that first time you saw the ocean, moved into a new apartment, fell in love. You can call on those memories when you need them most.

Practice:

1. In your journal, create a list of positive memories. When was a time you laughed uncontrollably? When was a time you cried tears of joy? When was a time you surprised someone you love? When was a time you were pleasantly surprised? When was a time you made someone laugh? When was a time you felt strong and healthy? When was a time you felt proud of an accomplishment? When was a time you felt carefree? When was a time you learned something exciting? When was a time you felt loved? When was a time you thought, "Wow! That's amazing!"

2. For each memory, close your eyes and relive it, feeling what you felt, seeing what you saw. Now take that memory and put it in some place on your body—like an earlobe or the tip of your nose. Now, anytime you want to relive that memory, touch that place. Some memories may have their own body part, or you can stack a bunch of positive memories on the same place so you can be flooded with positive emotions at the touch of a nose or the pinch of an earlobe.

3. Each day this week, touch your memory stack, feel all those positive emotions, and send a silent thank-you up and out in gratitude for all the moments in your past that felt so good.

. . . .
Day 42: Curate Your Time
Habit: Schedule Simplicity

You can't have it all at once. Over my lifespan,
I think I have had it all. But in different periods of time,
things were rough.
—Ruth Bader Ginsburg, 2014 interview with Katie Couric

You're a finite being, and time and money are limited resources. Instead of trying to have it all, curate your life. Choose to spend your time and money on what fits within your values, your budget, and your available time.

Practice:

1. What commitments do you have? Do you have a job, a side business, a family, kids' sports, hobbies, clubs you belong to,

recurring board meetings, school events, after-school events, classes, etc.? Who expects you to be where and do what inside the home and outside the home?

2. Which of these commitments do you hate doing?

3. Which of these commitments do you love doing?

4. Which of these commitments line up with the most important priorities you listed for day 13, "Short Life in a Very Old World"?

5. Which of these commitments do not line up with those priorities?

6. Choose one commitment that's not adding to your life or not helping you accomplish your long-term goals.

7. Remove yourself from this commitment.

. . . .

Day 43: Month 2 Giving Challenge: Seniors
Habit: Philanthropy

Age should not have its face lifted, but rather teach the world
to admire wrinkles as the etchings of experience
and the firm lines of character.
—Ralph Barton Perry, *Plea for an Age Movement*

Many seniors find themselves with lots of time on their hands that they might spend thinking about the loves they've lost over the years or wondering if they are still loved and needed by anyone. There are so many ways you could bring a little happiness to the heart of a senior, so get creative. Today, let a senior know that they are loved and needed.

Practice:

1. Is there a senior in your life you'd like to give a little extra special attention? If your grandparents are still alive, you could pull out the family photo album and ask for the story of how they met and fell in love. Give them an opportunity to relive a great memory. If you have an elderly neighbor, you could surprise them with a card, share a cup of tea together, or ask for their advice.

2. If no, reach out to a local senior center. They often host special dinners or dances, and they might need an extra hand to ensure a successful event.

Week 7

Day 44: The Four Steps to Creating a Habit
Habit: Physical Health

*This is the real power of habit: the insight that your habits
are what you choose them to be.*
—Charles Duhigg, *The Power of Habit*

Over the past several weeks, you have worked on creating your
physical activity habit. You can use these same steps to create any
new habit.

- *Start small.* What is a small first step that you can take every
  single day? See day 1.
- *Piggyback on an existing trigger.* What existing trigger can you
  use to start your new habit? See days 8 and 15.
- *Plan for success by planning for failure.* What do you need?
  Where do you need it? How will you remind yourself? What
  obstacles will you encounter, and how will you respond? See
  day 22.
- *Reward yourself.* What is your reward until the long-term benefits kick in? See day 29.

Practice:

Keep your daily physical activity at eight minutes. You are working on variety and consistency. Perform your chosen physical activities consistently as part of your morning, lunch, or home-from-work routine, and reward yourself with one of your chosen rewards.

. . . .
Day 45: Meditating with Kids
Habit: Mindfulness

If we are to reach real peace in this world and if we are to carry
on a real war against war, we shall have to begin with children.
—Mahatma Gandhi, *Young India*

Meditation is good for the whole family. At school, young people who practice mindfulness reduce their aggression and other behavioral problems while improving their ability to pay attention and increasing their level of happiness. At home, children of parents who practice mindfulness have better social skills and better relationships with their parents.[10]

If you want to introduce your children to mindfulness practices, keep in mind the age of your children, any learning challenges they have, and that mindfulness practices should never be used as punishment or discipline. Start slowly with them and only gradually increase the length of time if they are responding well. Talk about your experiences with mindfulness and ask them about their experiences.

Practice:

Either by yourself or with your kids, spend a couple minutes practicing the loving kindness meditation introduced on day 38.

. . . .
Day 46: The Definition of Connection
Habit: Relationships

I define connection as the energy that exists between people
when they feel seen, heard, and valued; when they can give and
receive without judgment; and when they derive sustenance
and strength from the relationship.
—Brené Brown, *The Gifts of Imperfection*

Connection is a two-way street. In order for you to feel connected, you must feel seen, heard, and valued. In order for someone to feel connected to you, they must feel that you see them, hear them, and value them. Clearly, this type of connection doesn't happen after one or two interactions. It takes time and repeated positive experiences, which is why this book will provide you with many opportunities to connect with others.

Practice:

1. In your journal, write about a person in your life you would like to strengthen your connection with. What is already good about your relationship with that person? What would you like to improve?

2. What action will you take to communicate to this person that you see, hear, and value them? Possible actions include a

supportive phone call, spending quality time together, gifting them with a present that supports one of their interests, or praising them in the presence of others.

. . . .

Day 47: Perseverance
Habit: Connecting with Yourself

Courage doesn't always roar. Sometimes courage is the quiet voice at the end of the day saying, "I will try again tomorrow."
—Mary Anne Radmacher, *Courage Doesn't Always Roar*

In September 2014, my mother was diagnosed with glioblastoma multiforme, a stage 4 brain cancer. As if the words "stage 4" and "brain cancer" aren't bad enough, they were followed by the words "aggressive" and "terminal."

My mom was only fifty-nine years old. She was a perfectly healthy adult, traveling the world and living her life, when suddenly she couldn't remember where she was, remember the day (or year or season), write down a telephone number, or even read. I had never realized before how quickly life could change, but suddenly here I was in this strange alternative universe where my mom had terminal brain cancer.

At first, I fell into confusion and despair as I tried to come to terms with the end of life as I knew it and with the painful knowledge that she would probably not have the opportunity to be an old woman. It turned out she wouldn't even live to welcome her first grandchild into the world.

As a family, we reached inside ourselves and discovered the courage to face the difficulty, to care for her, and to say, "I'll be here tomorrow, too." Each day through her illness, our biggest act of courage was to persevere. We kept showing up and doing the best we could.

Practice:

1. In your journal, reflect on a current or past difficult situation where you've been tempted to give up. What courage does it/ did it take to deal with it? Where do you find the courage to persevere?

2. Be generous to yourself and appreciate the courage and strength you have shown so far. What is the next step you need to take to meet this challenge or transform it into a meaningful experience?

. . . .
Day 48: Thank-You Spree
Habit: Gratitude

Silent gratitude isn't very much use to anyone who has done a lot for you.
—Gladys Bronwyn Stern, *Robert Louis Stevenson*

A thank-you is a simple way to express gratitude. Don't just throw your thank-you out there. Step your gratitude up a notch by following these steps for a truly generous and effectively delivered thank-you.

- Make eye contact.
- Smile.
- Speak in a clear, friendly voice.
- Be specific. What exactly are you thanking the person for? For example, "Thank you for holding the door for me" or "Thank you for thinking of me" or "Thank you for the heads up."
- Bonus points: Use their name in your thank-you.
- Bonus bonus points: If you know the person well, if it is appropriate, and if you're comfortable with it, you can add a light touch on the arm while you say thank you.

Practice:

Today, go on a thank-you spree. Take every opportunity to deliver a sincere and effective thank-you.

. . . .

Day 49: Where Do You Live?
Habit: Nature Simplicity

Come forth into the light of things,
Let Nature be your teacher.
—William Wordsworth, "The Tables Turned"

Your connection to the natural world is intimate and vital to your physical and mental health. Take the humble apple as an example. It took thousands of years of human and plant interaction to create large, juicy, sweet apples. From bloom, to blossom fertilization, to growth, to fruit harvest, to winter acclimatization, that apple arrived in your hand because of an intricate dance between weather, water, sunshine, and a vast array of animals, plants, fungi, and bacteria. It all seems to happen effortlessly, but it is neither simple nor guaranteed.

Practice:

1. In your journal, write about where you live and the natural world that begins at your front door. Where do you live? City, town, rural area? What was there before humans? How has the natural world around you changed as the human population has grown? What are the important geographical features around you: rivers, mountains, caves, lakes, ocean, plains? How do these geographical features impact how you live in this area? How do the seasons impact your life? How is life different in the summer, winter, spring, fall? Where does your food come from? What can be grown locally? How is it different from what you see in the grocery store?

2. Perform a generous action for your local environment, such as picking up trash, adding habitat for wildlife, or purchasing vegetables from your local farmer.

. . . .
Day 50: No Such Thing as a Small Donation
Habit: Philanthropy

Not he who has much is rich but he who gives much.
—Erich Fromm, *The Art of Loving*

In 2004, a tsunami hit Southeast Asia, causing $10 billion in damage and killing 230,000 people. In response to this unbelievable tragedy, everyday American citizens donated $2.78 billion for tsunami relief. And I mean everyday Americans. The average donation size was only $135, and the median donation was $50.[11]

In response to one tsunami, we created another—but this time it was a tsunami of money to help people. There is no such thing as a small donation, and it will save lives if it gets to the right charity.

Practice:

1. How much money can you donate every month no matter what? Remember, no donation is too small, and one dollar is a perfectly acceptable answer.

2. Start today. Give that amount to a charity or person in need.

Week 8
· · · · · · · · ·

Day 51: How Long Does It Take to Make a Habit?
Habit: Physical Health

Habit is a cable; we weave a thread of it each day,
and it becomes so strong we cannot break it.
—Horace Mann, featured in *Graded Selections*
for Memorizing by John B. Peaslee

How long does it take to create a new habit? Common wisdom suggests 21 days or 30 days. After tracking 96 participants in creating a habit of their choosing, University College London researchers observed that some habits were established in as little as 18 days, but many habits took even longer than the length of the study to establish—some even as long as 254 days.[12]

The plain truth is that how long it takes *you* to create a new habit depends on you, on the habit you're trying to form, on your motivation for starting it, how much pleasure you get from it, how much support you get from friends and family, and probably a host of other factors.

Sometimes you'll find it easy. But many people find exercise and meditation habits especially difficult to establish. Be patient. Keep weaving a new thread by taking your desired action every day. Eventually, you'll have the habit.

Practice:

1. Take a look back at the last week. How did you do with your physical activity? Did you make it the entire week? If so, congratulations! Why do you think you were successful? If not, what will you change—the first step, the trigger, the reminder, or the reward?

2. Perform ten minutes of physical activity *every* day. If you're still inconsistent, lower the time down to one or two minutes on days when you don't want to exercise. A simple walk around the block can qualify as physical activity.

. . . .
Day 52: Simple Breathing Meditation
Habit: Mindfulness

*Feelings come and go
like clouds in a windy sky.
Conscious breathing
is my anchor.*
—Thich Nhat Hanh, *Stepping into Freedom*

Your mind may be your most important asset. Moving your body, doing your job, loving your family, playing a game, preparing a meal—everything that you do requires your mind to engage, plan, direct. Meditation is a phenomenal tool for taking care of your mind so that you can do all the things you want to do and feel better doing them. Unlike exercising the body, which requires exertion, exercising the mind requires stillness.

Practice:

1. All you have to do is sit still and observe your breath as it goes in and out of your lungs without changing your breathing. Don't push or force your breathing or try to make it deeper. Simply observe your breath. If other thoughts creep into your mind (and they will), simply acknowledge them, and then resume your focus on your breathing.

2. Practice this simple breathing meditation for one to five minutes.

. . . .
Day 53: The Benefits of Relationship
Habit: Relationships

We do ourselves the most good doing something for others.
—Horace Mann, featured in *Thoughts*
by Jessie K. Freeman and Sara S. B. Yule

People who report feeling strong connections with others also report lower rates of anxiety and depression. They have higher self-esteem, are more empathetic to others, and are more trusting and cooperative. In a positive feedback loop, those behaviors strengthen their connections with others.[13]

It turns out that connecting with others isn't just good for your spirit. It's good for your body, too. Scientific studies reveal that strong social connections are associated with a 50 percent increased chance of longevity.[14]

Practice:

1. In your journal, write about the strength of your relationships compared to where you would like them to be. When is it easy for you to connect? When is it hard? What relationships would you like to strengthen? How can you do that?

2. Choose a relationship to strengthen. Reach out via phone, e-mail, or greeting card just to let them know you're thinking of them.

. . . .
Day 54: Fake It Until You Become It
Habit: Connecting with Yourself

A good stance and posture reflect a proper state of mind.
—Morihei Ueshiba, *The Art of Peace*

Being generous with others often requires courage and confidence, and surprisingly, you can use your body to increase your levels of confidence and thereby increase how often you are generous. In experiments, Amy Cuddy, professor and researcher at Harvard Business School, measured a 20 percent increase in testosterone and a 25 percent decrease in the stress hormone cortisol in participants after they adopted powerful body language. She observed more confident actions in these participants, and the opposite was true for people when they adopted submissive body language. She concluded that body language changed how people felt about themselves, which changed how they acted.[15]

Practice:

1. Bring your shoulders down, cross your arms around your body, get small, touch your neck. Notice how your breathing and your mood change.

2. Adopt a power pose for two minutes. Try opening up your chest and arms like a runner crossing the finish line or putting your hands on your hips like Wonder Woman. Notice how your breathing and your mood change. Adopt your power move in private for a few moments whenever you need to increase your confidence.

3. What would you do for yourself if you were feeling more confident? Do it!

. . . .
Day 55: Gratitude with Kids
Habit: Gratitude

The hardest arithmetic to master is that which enables us
to count our blessings.
—Eric Hoffer, *Reflections on the Human Condition*

If you want to raise children who are grateful for what they have, then you must teach them gratitude. The most important way they learn gratitude is by seeing you and hearing you practice gratitude.

But you may also encourage them to express their own gratitude by creating a gratitude jar for your home. A gratitude jar is simply a vessel you fill with short notes to remind yourself about what you were grateful for that day. You can have one gratitude jar for the family or every family member can have their own jar. You can choose a jar that's beautiful all on its own or you can decorate it with markers and colored paper. You can scribble your gratitude note on a scrap piece of paper or you can gracefully write it in colored marker on colored squares of paper that have been cut out using one of those fun patterned scissors that gives the paper a lovely edge. Are you getting the sense that there's no wrong way to do a gratitude jar? Exactly! Just get a jar and get going on the gratitude.

Each night, invite each family member to write down something they are grateful for that day and drop it in the jar. Every month or so, pull out some memories from the jar and read them aloud to remind everyone of all the good things that have happened so far.

Practice:

1. Gratitude jars aren't just for children. Everyone can benefit from the regular practice of writing and reflecting on their blessings. Find a jar that you can use for your gratitude jar.

2. Place a stack of papers and a pen next to the jar.

3. Schedule a time to review your gratitude jar with the family.

. . . .
Day 56: The Linen Closet
Habit: Home Simplicity

*The ability to simplify means to eliminate the unnecessary
so that the necessary may speak.*
—Hans Hofmann

Eliminating the unnecessary possessions so that the truly necessary can speak can begin in the simplest of places—like your linen closet. A cluttered, unorganized, precariously stacked linen closet is no way to treat possessions that bring so much value into your life. Knowing, appreciating, and caring for your possessions will allow you more time, money, and energy to give to yourself and to others in the ways that really matter.

Practice:

1. *Empty It:* Everything that is in the closet must come out.
2. *First Pass Trash:* Did you find old towels that are going to become rags, but you already have rags you don't use? A purple washcloth you keep because some day you might buy another set of purple towels? Expired medicines? Trash. Half-used bars of soap and bottles of lotion—finish 'em or trash 'em.
3. *Sort:* Group like things together.
4. *Rehome:* Are there items in your linen closet that belong in a different place?

5. *Choose:* Keep only what you need. I recommend no more than three sets of sheets and towels for each person: one in use, one in the hamper, and one clean and ready to use.

6. *Second Pass Trash or Donate:* Now that you've rehomed some items and chosen the important linens, what can you throw out? What can you donate?

7. *Organize:* Place your carefully curated items back into the closet neatly and nicely so that groups of related items remain together. Use containers for smaller items and leave space around your items so that your linen closet feels spacious and organized.

. . . .
Day 57: Be Like Batman
Habit: Philanthropy

Another definition of a hero is someone who is concerned about other people's well-being, and will go out of his or her way to help them—even if there is no chance of a reward.

—Stan Lee

Bruce Wayne is a man of action. At night, he roams the streets fighting crime and bad guys as Batman. But he knows that he can't just fight the bad guys. He has to stop the bad guys from becoming bad guys in the first place.

So he takes action of another kind: he donates money to fix the underlying problems in his community. He funds dozens of free medical clinics. He finances orphanages, soup kitchens, and schools.

Batman is different from other superheroes. He has no special powers or magic rings. He is a man. But he is a superhero because he acts to make the world a better place.

Practice:

1. Brainstorm three causes you feel passionate about. Choose causes that you care deeply about and that would make you feel like your life mattered if your actions helped fix these problems.

2. If only one of these could be fixed in your lifetime, which one would you pick? You've discovered your favorite cause. There are so many causes, and you can't support all of them. As we work through this book, focus on giving to your favorite causes.

Week 9

Day 58: The Family Doesn't Want to Change, Part 1
Habit: Physical Health

The great gift of family life is to be intimately acquainted
with people you might never even introduce yourself to,
had life not done it for you.
—Kendall Hailey, *The Day I Became an Autodidact*

Sometimes the people you love the most don't support you the way you want. They may even actively sabotage you or want no part of your changes. When that happens, follow these four steps:

+ *Step 1:* Accept them. Their path is their path to follow as is right for them.

+ *Step 2:* Understand their resistance. Could they feel insecure? "What if you get thin and decide to leave me?" Could they feel criticized and defensive? "What's wrong with the way we're living our lives? Aren't we happy?" Are they afraid to fail? "I've tried getting healthy before. I just can't do it."

+ *Step 3:* Thank them. Their resistance forces you to be more creative and resourceful and tests your resolve and commitment. It makes you stronger.

- *Step 4:* Appreciate your gift to them. Your family doesn't hear what you say; they see what you do. When they see you changing despite the odds and the obstacles, you show them what it means to persevere and overcome. When they see you accomplish a goal, you let them know they are part of a family of achievers. Your gift to them is being their role model.

Practice:

1. Additional tips will follow on day 66. In the meantime, reflect in your journal on how your family is responding to your changes. List three different emotions, fears, or concerns influencing their response. How will your improved health help your family?

2. Remember, taking care of your physical health is an act of generosity to yourself. Your ongoing goal is to complete ten minutes of physical activity *every* day.

. . . .
Day 59: The Meditation Habit
Habit: Mindfulness

*I have discovered that all the misfortunes of men
arise from one thing only, that they are unable
to stay quietly in their own chamber.*
—Blaise Pascal, *The Thoughts of Blaise Pascal*

This month, we'll start the meditation habit. Like all our habits, we're going to start off nice and slow. We're going to make it so easy that you'll have no reason not to do it.

Practice:

1. Find a place in your routine to add meditation (day 8), find a trigger that will launch your meditation habit (day 15), and give yourself a reminder.

2. Review day 22. What challenges will you face? How will you set yourself up for success?

3. How will you reward yourself (day 29)?

4. Practice the simple breathing meditation for one minute every day this week (day 52).

. . . .
Day 60: Monthly Check-In

*I think a hero is an ordinary individual who finds the strength
to persevere and endure in spite of overwhelming obstacles.*
—Christopher Reeve, *Still Me*

Time to check in on your progress. This is not a guilt-inducing exercise designed to shame you for all you haven't accomplished yet. Instead, it's a gentle reminder about what's important to you and what you want to change.

Enjoy the journey. Be gentle with yourself. Keep growing.

Practice:

+ What did I do last month that I'm proud of?
+ Are my relationships with others improving or deteriorating?
+ What do I need to do less of/quit/get rid of/delegate this month?

- What experiments did I try? What lessons did I learn? What is going well?
- What isn't working, and what do I want to change?
- Habit to focus on next month:
- Why do I want to establish that habit?
- What is a first step I can take toward making this a habit?
- What trigger will I use?
- How will I reward myself?
- What obstacles will I face in establishing this habit and how will I overcome them?
- Notes on successes, long-term goals, and personal changes I'm working toward:

. . . .

Day 61: The Risks of Not Connecting
Habit: Relationships

I tell ya a guy gets too lonely an' he gets sick.
—John Steinbeck, *Of Mice and Men*

People who lack a strong sense of connection to others are more vulnerable to anxiety, depression, antisocial behavior, and even suicidal behaviors. In a negative feedback loop, those behaviors tend to reinforce and increase their isolation from others.[16] This lack of social connection negatively impacts their health, and social isolation is a better indicator for mortality than being overweight, smoking, or having high blood pressure.[17]

This is why it's so important, even if you're an introvert who enjoys alone time, that you find ways to create and maintain meaningful relationships. Your generosity to others is truly generosity to yourself.

Practice:

1. In your journal, reflect on what keeps you from connecting with other people. How can you address those things? When do you feel lonely?

2. What interests do you have in common with other people? Find a group that meets in person or virtually on that topic and begin forming social connections with them.

. . . .
Day 62: Negative Self-Talk
Habit: Connecting with Yourself

You have been criticizing yourself for years, and it hasn't worked. Try approving of yourself and see what happens.
—Louise L. Hay, *You Can Heal Your Life*

Sometimes I say terrible things to myself about myself. "You're a loser, a failure, an embarrassment. You're getting fat, and your nose is too big. You're not very smart." Do you ever talk to yourself like that?

If you had a "friend" talk to you like that, you probably wouldn't hang out with them for very long. Would you even dream of saying something like that to someone you loved? Never! But we talk to ourselves like that all the time.

Practice:

1. In your journal, identify some of the hurtful things you say to yourself. Are they true? What else is true? Is it important? What is more important? What can you learn from this? What would you want to believe about this in five years? Reframe this negative thought by creating three alternative positive messages you could say to yourself instead.

2. Choose one positive reframe and program it into your phone to remind you once a day of this new belief you have about yourself.

. . . .
Day 63: Simple Pleasures
Habit: Gratitude

A morning-glory at my window satisfies me more
than the metaphysics of books.
—Walt Whitman, *Leaves of Grass*

I am not a morning person, but there is one thing that makes every morning better. When I wake up, I turn on my electric teakettle and pour hot water over my Lipton tea bag. Four minutes later, I scoop the tea bag out and add a teaspoon of sugar and enough milk to turn it a lovely tan. Sitting down at the kitchen table, I close my eyes and take a sip. Ahhh. Warm, sweet, and smooth. It's lovely. I look forward to my morning cup of tea every day. It's a simple thing that makes me grateful to be alive.

The secret to feeling satisfied from a simple pleasure is to notice it while it's happening and feel grateful for it. What are your simple pleasures? Taking a walk, sitting on the front porch, playing a board game, reading to your child, listening to a favorite song, enjoying a favorite meal, cooking, going on a picnic, watching a movie, hugging a loved one, looking through past photos, lying in the grass, walking your dog, drinking a cup of hot chocolate on a cold night, or the smell of apple pie?

Practice:

1. In your journal, reflect on these questions. When was the last time you enjoyed a simple pleasure? What was it? What are the simple pleasures that give you the most joy?

2. Choose a simple pleasure you will enjoy and feel grateful for today.

. . . .
Day 64: Money Can Buy Happiness
Habit: Mind Simplicity

If we command our wealth, we shall be rich and free; if our
wealth commands us, we are poor indeed.
—Edmund Burke, *Letters on a Regicide Peace*

Money can buy happiness when you use it in the right way. In experiments, researchers discover that people report higher levels of happiness when they buy something for someone or donate to charity instead of using their money for personal items like paying bills or buying something for themselves.[18] This is not surprising, because life is more enjoyable when shared or when helping others. Money is just another tool to create a great life.

Practice:

1. In your journal, explore your feelings about money. When does spending money feel good? When does it feel bad? How much money do you spend on others or give to charity? Do you feel differently about this money than money you spend on bills or on yourself?

2. Do something for someone, like inviting a friend to take a walk in the park, surprising a loved one with a small gift, or making a small donation to charity.

. . . .
Day 65: It's Working!
Habit: Philanthropy

And I avow my faith that we are marching towards better days. Humanity will not be cast down. We are going on swing- ing bravely forward along the grand high road and already behind the distant mountains is the promise of the sun.
—Winston Churchill, *Liberalism and the Social Problem*

It's a fact. The world is becoming a better place. In 2000, the United Nations created the Millennium Goals to identify the biggest problems facing the world and create a plan to address them. Fifteen years later they've recorded a drastic improvement. The number of people living on less than $1.25 a day has decreased by more than half. Today nearly 90 percent of children around the world have the opportunity to get a primary education. Child mortality rates have fallen by more than 50 percent. Globally, malaria infections have decreased by 37 percent, and malaria mortality rates are down 58 percent. Two billion more people have access to clean water.

But there is still much to be done. There are 860 million people who still live in extreme poverty, 57 million children who don't attend school, 2.4 billion people who lack access to improved sanitation facilities, and women all over the world who still to find it difficult to access education, secure employment, own economic assets, and participate in government.[19]

The improvements are due to the hard work, dedication, and financial resources of many people. Let's keep up the good work.

Practice:

1. Look back at the favorite causes you listed on day 57. For each of those causes, describe in your journal what this world would look like if it were solved. What difference will it make to you, your family, and the world?

2. Choose the cause you're most passionate about and identify three charities working to solve that problem.

Week 10

Day 66: The Family Doesn't Want to Change, Part 2
Habit: Physical Health

All happy families resemble one another;
every unhappy family is unhappy in its own way.
—Leo Tolstoy, *Anna Karenina*

On day 58, you discovered four steps for coping with your family's resistance. Here are a few more strategies that might help when your family doesn't want to change or even support your changes.

1. *Ask for specific but minimal support.* It might just be as simple as asking for space to do your own thing without criticism.
2. *Spend quality time with your family.* Make an extra effort to enjoy activities together.
3. *Find outside support.* Your family is not the only and often not the best place for support. Instead, enlist friends or look for people online or locally.
4. *Support their changes.* Support them in their hobbies and efforts the way you want to be supported in yours.
5. *Share your success.* When you notice the benefits you're getting, mention them.

6. *Invite them to participate.* Instead of nagging, scolding, or guilting, occasionally invite them to try out a change with you.

7. *Become a problem solver.* Ask, "How can I do this given my current circumstances and without their support?"

8. *Go slow.* Introduce changes slowly, and let your family adjust.

9. *Create family challenges.* Find common goals and create a challenge to reach that goal. Celebrate when you all reach it.

Practice:

1. In your journal, reflect on these questions. What support would you like to receive from your family, and how can you ask for it? How can you reach your goal even without their support? Which of these strategies will you employ with your family?

2. Keep caring for your health and being a great example for your family and friends. Perform ten minutes of physical activity *every* day.

. . . .
Day 67: A Successful Meditation
Habit: Mindfulness

Mindfulness isn't difficult; we just need to remember to do it.
—Sharon Salzberg, *Real Happiness*

Forget about reaching enlightenment. Stop hoping it will become easy. Don't worry that it wasn't like last time or isn't like someone else's experience. Mindfulness is a practice that will improve your mental, physical, and spiritual health. When do you stop practicing? Never. When do you stop being generous with yourself? Never.

Did you sit down for a few minutes to meditate? Then you've succeeded. It's that simple.

Practice:

1. Last week, you started meditating for one minute every day. Now take a look back at the last week. How did you do? Did you make it the entire week? If so, congratulations! Why do you think you were successful? If not, what will you change (the trigger, the reminder, or the reward) to make yourself successful this week?

2. Meditate for two minutes every day this week.

. . . .
Day 68: Be Selfish
Habit: Relationships

I am a greedy, selfish bastard.
I want the fact that I existed to mean something.
—Harry Chapin

The word "selfish" has a lot of negative connotations, but it's not an inherently negative word. Let's break it down:

Definition of "self": the entire person of an individual
Function of "-ish": of, relating to, or being
So we can define selfish as "of or relating to the individual."

That doesn't sound so bad, now does it? In fact, from this perspective, it's hard to imagine how anything that I do isn't selfish. Everything I say and do relates to me because I'm the one saying and doing it. The challenge is to choose selfish actions that are good for me and for others.

Practice:

Today, perform a random act of kindness like holding the door open, letting someone take a close parking spot, or making eye contact and nodding to the person you pass every day.

. . . .
Day 69: I Love You!
Habit: Connecting with Yourself

Do not judge but love and be loved,
if you want to be really happy.
—Sri Chinmoy, *Words of Wisdom*

There is so much to love about you. You have an amazing heart, and you care so much about people. You have interesting hobbies and unique insights. You love to laugh. The person you are inside is beautiful, and it's time you gave yourself as much love and acceptance as you give to those around you.

Look in the mirror and say, "I love you," and then say something you love about yourself. For example, "I love that you love children" and "I love that you hold the door open for others." I promise you that there are hundreds of things to love about yourself. Choose one and say it. Now choose another. And another. Practice loving yourself like you love your children, your spouse, your best friend.

Practice:

Practice the "I love you" exercise and say ten different things you love about yourself.

. . . .
Day 70: Everything Is a Miracle
Habit: Gratitude

We enjoy not only the privilege of existence
but also the singular ability to appreciate it and even,
in a multitude of ways, to make it better.
—Bill Bryson, *A Short History of Nearly Everything*

All of the matter in the universe was compressed 13.8 billion years ago into a space so small and hot our imaginations fail us for understanding how small and hot it was. For some reason, all the compressed matter began to expand rapidly in an event called the big bang. Once the big bang started, the universe grew to a million billion miles across, and 98 percent of the all the matter that exists today was created—in just a matter of minutes![20]

Somehow, our solar system has a star of the right age and size that a planet at just the right distance with the right composition of water, temperatures, and elements could, over millions of years, allow the simplest single-celled organisms to appear.[21] Over millions of years more, those single-celled organisms would evolve in response to a changing environment into fish, plants, butterflies, dinosaurs, primates, and eventually humans. Somehow every single one of your ancestors managed to avoid death for a long enough period of time that they could pass along their DNA. I can't even begin to cover the odds of your birth, but trust me, the odds of you arriving here from fertilization to birth are incalculable.

The fact that you exist here and now on this planet and in this universe is a freaking miracle.

Practice:

1. Pause to appreciate and marvel that you are a miracle living in a miracle. Feel awe and humility that somehow, in some way, you are connected to majestic and powerful forces.

2. What would a walking, breathing miracle do to improve the existence of others today?

. . . .
Day 71: Your Brain Is for Processing
Habit: Schedule Simplicity

Good order is the foundation of all good things.
—Edmund Burke, *Reflections on the Revolution in France*

Your brain is for processing, not for storage. As a storage device, the brain is unreliable at best. It forgets things it's supposed to remember or remembers things at the wrong time—usually when you're trying to fall asleep. Your brain knows this about itself, so if it knows you're relying on it, it's always worried. Help your brain out by collecting and organizing your life.

Practice:

1. Do a brain dump and write down everything that's in your head but can be stored on paper.

2. Collect to-do's and tasks and put it all in one "inbox."

3. Process your inbox. Add things to calendars that need to be added to calendars. Create lists like possible vacation destinations, home improvements, and gift ideas that you can refer back to whenever you need them. Create files like school projects and add an appointment on your calendar to review the file on a regular basis. Do, delegate, shred, delete, file, or schedule followups for all the information you've collected. You may not be able to organize your brain dump in one day; in that case, just spend an hour a day until you are caught up.

4. How will you capture things that come up in the future?

5. How often do you need to update your to-do list? How will you remind yourself to add new items to your to-do lists and cross off completed or no-longer-needed items?

. . . .
Day 72: Month 3 Giving Challenge: Pets
Habit: Philanthropy

*If a man aspires towards a righteous life,
his first act of abstinence is from injury to animals.*
—Leo Tolstoy, *The First Step*

Each year, 6 to 8 million cats and dogs enter shelters, but only 3 to 4 million of them will be adopted. That means 2.7 million adoptable cats and dogs will be euthanized. Here are five ways you can give for pets this month:

1. *Spay or neuter your own pet.* If you've been putting it off because you think you can't afford it, contact your local no-kill animal shelter and ask them if they know about any low-cost options in your area.

2. *Adopt.* Do you have space in your home for a homeless pet? Then adopt!

3. *Foster.* If your home is complete with the animals you have, can you foster a dog or cat until a forever home is found?

4. *Give money or goods.* A cash donation lets shelters buy exactly what they need when they need it, but they might also need specific items like food or blankets.

5. *Give time.* Dogs need to be walked and brushed. Litter boxes need to be cleaned. Websites maintained. Letters sent to past donors. Your local animal rescue may gladly welcome your time and expertise.

Practice:

Locate an animal shelter or rescue in your community. Call and ask about the extent of animal homelessness in your community, what they are doing to solve it, how they know what they're doing is working, and how you can help.

Week 11

Day 73: One Habit at a Time
Habit: Physical Health

*The drop, by continually falling, bores its passage through the
hardest rock. The hasty torrent rushes over it with hideous
uproar, and leaves no trace behind.*
—Thomas Carlyle, *The Life of Friedrich Schiller*

Only start one new habit at a time and only when you are feeling
comfortable and confident in the habit you've just created. Otherwise, you risk starting no new habits at all. Even if you only started
one new habit per month, you'd end the year with twelve new
healthy habits, and you will be miles closer to being the person you
want to be and having the impact you want to have.

Practice:
Continue being generous to yourself so that you have more energy
to give to others by performing ten minutes of physical activity *every* day.

. . . .
Day 74: Where Should You Meditate?
Habit: Mindfulness

Within you there is a stillness and a sanctuary to which you
can retreat at any time and be yourself, just as I can.
—Hermann Hesse, *Siddhartha*

You can meditate anywhere. At home. At work. In your car. In your bed. You can have a whole room dedicated to your meditation practice, but you can also meditate in the bathroom.

Meditation is the simple practice of stilling your mind, so wherever you are, you can meditate. Some places are more difficult to meditate in than others, so do your best to choose a place where you have some peace and quiet and give yourself the gift of visiting your sanctuary.

Practice:

1. Last week, you started meditating for two minutes every day. How did you do? What's working well? Where do you need to improve (the trigger, the reminder, or the reward) to make yourself successful this week?

2. Meditate for four minutes every day this week.

Day 75: Good for You and Good for Others
Habit: Relationships

When you look for things like love, meaning, motivation,
it implies they are sitting behind a tree or under a rock.
The most successful people recognize,
that in life they create their own love,
they manufacture their own meaning,
they generate their own motivation.

—Neil deGrasse Tyson, Reddit community interview

There are four types of actions. There are actions that are (1) good for you and good for others, (2) good for you but not for others, (3) good for others but not for you, and (4) bad for you and bad for others.

Fill your life with as many actions as possible that are good for both you and others, and when it's not possible, choose carefully an action that will be either good for you or for someone else *and* also meets your higher purpose. At all costs, avoid actions that are bad for both you and others.

Practice:

1. In your journal, reflect on an upcoming situation. Is it possible to choose an action that is good for you and others? If not, what is the higher purpose you want to accomplish? What action will help you achieve that?

2. Today, perform a random act of kindness that is good for you and good for others, like walking a shelter dog, donating your

old sports equipment, or welcoming a new neighbor to the neighborhood.

· ·
Day 76: Forgive Yourself, Step 1
Habit: Connecting with Yourself

There is no love without forgiveness,
and there is no forgiveness without love.
—Bryant McGill, *Chicken Soup for the Soul:*
The Magic of Mothers & Daughters

Do you feel bad for having hurt someone at some time? There are three steps to self-forgiveness; step 2 is covered on day 83, and step 3 is on day 91. But first, acknowledge that you've done something wrong. After you've admitted it to yourself, you may want to admit it to the person you've wronged or to a group of supportive people such as a church group (or other spiritual gathering) or a recovery meeting (Alcoholics Anonymous, Al-Anon) or even just a very supportive friend. In any case, apologize sincerely for the harm you've caused.

Practice:

1. In your journal write about someone you've harmed in the past. How did you harm them, and how bad do you feel about it? Write an apology.

2. Do you think acknowledging and apologizing for this harm directly to them would help you or them heal? Do you need to enlist a support group or good friend who can listen nonjudgmentally to your guilt?

. . . .
Day 77: Gratitude Letter
Habit: Gratitude

*It does me good to write a letter which is not a response
to a demand, a gratuitous letter, so to speak, which has
accumulated in me like the waters of a reservoir.*
—Henry Miller, *The Books in My Life*

At some point in your past, there was a moment when someone made your life better and helped you become the person you are today. Maybe a teacher encouraged you to write, a friend gave you a place to crash, a coach showed you that you were tougher than you thought, a coworker recommended you for a promotion, an employer took a chance on you, a relative believed in you, or a parent taught you to never give up. It's very possible this person has no idea what they did for you, that it mattered to you at all, and that it's made your life better.

The impact of their act of kindness on your life grows every day. Like the waters of a reservoir, the unexpressed words of gratitude need to be released.

Practice:

1. In your journal, remember a time when someone made a difference in your life. Who did this? What did it mean to you then? What does it mean to you today? How did it shape your life?

2. Tell them about it in a letter!

3. Mail or e-mail the letter.

Day 78: Discover Something Unusual
Habit: Nature Simplicity

All my life through,
the new sights of Nature made me rejoice like a child.
—Marie Curie, *Pierre Curie*

You won't believe the amazing creatures in the world. Even if you were gifted with a great imagination and excellent artistic skills, you wouldn't come up with something like the Chilean stag beetle, the pink fairy armadillo, the Dumbo octopus, the Patagonian mara, the naked mole rat, the Irrawaddy dolphin, the gerenuk, the dugong, the babirusa, the fossa, the star-nosed mole, the Sunda colugo, or the yeti crab.

Nature is remarkable in its diversity and creativity.

Practice:

1. Search online for "remarkable animals" and browse a few photos and descriptions. Imagine seeing them with the eyes of a child.

2. In your journal, consider the following questions: What is the purpose of this biodiversity? How is it good for you? the planet? the ecosystems they live in? How are they impacted by human behavior? How would you feel if this amazing creature disappeared from the planet?

3. Vote with your wallet by choosing sustainable products like Rainforest Alliance Certified coffee, Forest Stewardship

Council certified wood products, fair trade clothing, and Energy Star appliances.

....
Day 79: How Much Should I Donate?
Habit: Philanthropy

Don't look for big things, just do small things with great love.
—Mother Teresa, *Mother Teresa: Come Be My Light*

How much you should donate is a deeply personal question, and the answer depends on your situation. Ten percent may be too much for a family of four trying to make ends meet, but it might not be enough for a person making millions a year. Use this strategy to find how you much you will donate each month (and you can use it for saving money, too).

Practice:

1. Total your nonnegotiable expenses: Rent/mortgage, groceries, electricity, cell phone bills, etc. Clothing is not a nonnegotiable expense, because you can go a month or more without buying clothes. But if you don't pay your cell phone bill, you won't be able to use your cell phone. Some budget items fluctuate. In those cases, choose a dollar amount that's a little on the high side of what you pay on average.

2. Subtract it from your take-home pay. What's the dollar amount?

3. Based on this dollar amount, how much are you comfortable donating every month? If you are not donating on a regular basis yet, choose a dollar amount that you know you can

achieve. Remember, there's no such thing as a small donation. The trick here is to build the giving habit. So start small and give yourself the best chance of succeeding. Even if it's one dollar a month, just make sure you give that one dollar every month.

4. Include donating to charity on your nonnegotiable expense list. When you pay your monthly bills, also donate to charity.

Week 12

Day 80: What Are You Eating?
Habit: Physical Health

Food is an important part of a balanced diet.
—Fran Lebowitz, *The Fran Lebowitz Reader*

Changing your eating habits can be one of the most difficult endeavors, and it's best to begin by understanding them. In 2008, Kaiser Permanente's Center for Health Research released their findings from one of the largest and longest-running weight loss maintenance trials ever conducted. Nearly 1,700 participants were asked to keep food diaries, turn them in at weekly support group meetings, follow the DASH (Dietary Approaches to Stop Hypertension) diet, and exercise moderately for at least thirty minutes a day.

The researchers concluded that the food journal was critical to losing weight. "The more food records people kept, the more weight they lost. Those who kept daily food records lost twice as much weight as those who kept no records," said lead author Jack Hollis, PhD.[22]

Practice:

1. Find a notebook, phone app, sticky notes—whatever works for you—to keep track of your eating this week. You'll be reviewing this record over the next several weeks.

2. At a minimum, note the time, description of food, and degree of hunger every time you eat. Consider including where you ate (i.e., location) and how you felt before, during, and after eating.

3. Record each item as you're eating it. Something is better than nothing, so if you forget, go back and fill it in to the best of your ability. You are gathering important information that will help you discover your food issues and eat healthier.

4. Don't judge yourself. If you are eating a sundae, write it down. Don't feel bad or ashamed or try to hide it. Just write it down.

5. Perform ten minutes of physical activity *every* day.

. . . .
Day 81: Three Skills of Meditation
Habit: Mindfulness

If we spent half an hour every day in silent immobility,
I am convinced that we should conduct all our affairs,
personal, national, and international,
far more sanely than we do at present.
—Bertrand Russell, *Mortals and Others*

Meditation develops three important skills.

- *Allowing:* Whatever you're feeling and thinking is okay. You're not judging it, hiding it, or forcing it down. Whatever is, is.
- *Staying:* You are no longer blown about on the stormy winds of your emotions. Instead, you can stand in the eye of the storm and feel it.
- *Accepting Impermanence:* Your thoughts, your emotions, your aches and pains, your heartaches, your fears, and even your own body are temporary and in constant flux. By observing your emotional and physical state, you gain the wisdom to experience pain without suffering.

Meditation helps you feel whole, feel others, and show up even when life is tough, scary, or heartbreaking, and that will allow you to be more generous to others more often.

Practice:

1. Last week, you started meditating for four minutes every day. How did you do? What's working well? Where do you need to improve (the trigger, the reminder, or the reward) to make yourself successful this week?

2. Stick with four minutes every day this week.

Day 82: Giving at Work
Habit: Relationships

*It is a bit embarrassing to have been concerned with
the human problem all one's life and find at the end
that one has no more to offer by way of advice than
"Try to be a little kinder."*

—Aldous Huxley, featured in *The Little, Brown Book
of Anecdotes* by Clifton Fadiman

In *Give and Take: A Revolutionary Approach to Success*, Adam Grant delves into the dynamics of successful givers. He knows that people are wary of being too generous at work. At work, being too generous can get you in trouble. At work, nice guys finish last.

He discovers that yes, sometimes nice guys finish last, but sometimes they finish first. Grant's research reveals that across the board, the highest performers are givers. Grant writes, "Over the course of medical school, being a giver accounts for 11 percent higher grades …" In sales, "the top performers were givers, and they averaged 50 percent more annual revenue."[23] The trick, he shares, is being strategic so that you give the right amount to the right people at the right time.

Practice:

1. In your journal, reflect on your behavior at work. How generous are you at work? Do you share your expertise? Give credit to others? Create a positive work environment? What

are your fears about being generous at work? How can you balance being generous with others and taking care of your own career?

2. Choose a way to be generous at work today, such as mentoring the newcomer, sharing an article on industry trends, or bringing cookies in for the team.

. . . .
Day 83: Forgive Yourself, Step 2
Habit: Connecting with Yourself

Surely it is much more generous to forgive and remember,
than to forgive and forget.
—Maria Edgeworth, *Tales and Novels*

On day 76, you acknowledged a harm you did. Now, don't forget it. Because the second step to self-forgiveness is to change yourself or your life so that you won't commit that same sort of transgression again. On day 91, you'll discover the third step to self-forgiveness.

Practice:

In your journal, revisit this harm. What were the circumstances that led to this transgression? Will those same circumstances happen again? If so, how do you need to change your life (such as leaving an abusive relationship) or yourself (quitting drinking, learning to handle stress, or expressing emotion more appropriately) so that you won't cause this kind of harm again?

Day 84: Whose Shoulders Are You Standing On?
Habit: Gratitude

If I have seen further it is by standing on ye sholders of Giants.
—Isaac Newton, 1676 letter to Robert Hooke

The history of human civilization includes one advancement after another. From humble beginnings, we decorated our caves with finger paints and illuminated them with fire. Step by step, we moved out of the caves into cities. We learned how to elect political leaders, to mine and create metal tools, to use electricity, and to fly. Each discovery made possible by the one before it. Looking back, we can see our inexorable march toward a better world.

Isaac Newton, Marie Curie, and Albert Einstein were leaders in science, while Pablo Picasso, Jane Austen, and Michaelango led in the arts. Religious leaders like Buddha, Confucius, Jesus, and Mohammad and thought leaders like Leonardo da Vinci, Socrates, and Avicenna lit the way. Invention, business, politics, social justice—in every field, there are men and women who have accomplished much. They've become giants, and they've helped shape thousands or millions of people who have followed behind them.

Practice:

1. In your journal, consider the following questions: Who in history has made what you do possible, what you think possible,

and what you believe possible? What cultures and values in your society make it a better place to live? Who can you thank for that?

2. Take a moment to appreciate these people. Choose one and share the story of this person's accomplishments with someone else.

. . . .

Day 85: Your Clothes Closet
Habit: Home Simplicity

And, after all, what is a fashion? From the artistic point of view, it is usually a form of ugliness so intolerable that we have to alter it every six months.
—Oscar Wilde, "The Philosophy of Dress"

There may be no area of my home that has given me more heartache than my closet. Here is my best advice for simplifying your clothes closet.

Practice:

1. *Empty It:* Everything must come out. If your closet is a disaster and tackling the whole thing overwhelms you, focus on just one part of the closet.

2. *First Pass Trash/Donate/Store:* Create three piles. Trash for clothes that are worn out or damaged. Donate or sell clothes you know you'll never wear again. Store seasonal clothes or other clothes you're not ready to get rid of.

3. *Simplify:* Identify your duplicates. Do you wear the duplicates? If not, store, donate, or sell them.

4. *Choose the Best:* Hang up the clothes you wear all the time, the clothes you love, and the clothes that you look great in. As you're hanging each garment, consider if it has a color or shape that flatters you. If not, store it, donate it, or sell it.

5. *Second Pass Trash/Donate/Store:* Take another look at what's left. Is there anything that can now be trashed, donated, or stored?

6. *Hang Backward:* Hang the remaining clothes so that the hanger hook faces you. The next time you want to organize your closet, the clothes that are still on backward hangers have not been worn. It's a safe bet that it's time to donate it.

7. *Acquire Consciously:* Make thoughtful additions to your closet. Ask, "Does this fit me? flatter me? Is the color compatible with my other clothes? Does it fill a niche not already being served by something I already own?"

· ·
Day 86: Your Donation Rules
Habit: Philanthropy

Charity is a virtue of the heart, and not of the hands.
—Joseph Addison, *The Guardian*

To be a good philanthropist, you will need to say no, and I'll help you with that on day 94. But first, you must know when to say yes. This exercise helps you create your donation rules.

1. *How much will you give?* What is your monthly donation budget? How much time each month will you give for volunteering or mentoring?

2. *What causes do you support?* You can't support all the worthy causes out there, so focus on the ones that are most important to you. Personally, I support charities that help people become self-sufficient and ones that support pets, veterans, women, or the environment.

3. *What don't you support?* If there are any causes you know you don't support, list them.

4. *Any other rules?* I always research a charity before I donate, and I only give to charities that respect the dignity of the people they help. Other rules could include discussing a donation with a spouse or donating anonymously.

Practice:

In your journal, create your donation rules:

1. How much money will you donate every month? How much time?

2. What are your top three causes that you want to support?

3. What causes do you not support?

4. Any other donation rules?

Week 13

Day 87: My Favorite Food Advice
Habit: Physical Health

Tell me what you eat, and I will tell you what you are.
—Jean Anthelme Brillat-Savarin, *Physiologie du Goût*

Michael Pollan opens *In Defense of Food* with my favorite food advice: "Eat food. Not too much. Mostly plants."[24] It's that simple.

+ *Eat food*—fruit, vegetables, grains, nuts, meat, and fish. When you're eating food, the ingredient list is small, like in a tomato and mozzarella salad with fresh basil leaves, drizzled with balsamic vinegar. When you're eating food, the state in which you consume it is very similar to that in which it was harvested—like sautéed carrots. Processed products like high-sugar breakfast cereals have a long ingredient list, don't resemble the grains harvested to make them, and don't spoil like natural, unprocessed foods do.

+ *Not too much.* Eat until full but not stuffed.

+ *Mostly plants.* Plants are packed with nutrients to power your body and fiber that fills you up for longer.

Practice:

1. Last week, you started keeping a food journal. Now browse through that journal. What do you notice? Are there patterns about what you eat, when, and why? How do you feel about what and how you ate last week?

2. Continue your food journal this week and try to notice these patterns as they're happening. You'll be revisiting this food journal again next week.

. . . .
Day 88: Meditation Eases Physical Pain
Habit: Mindfulness

The more you try to avoid suffering, the more you suffer,
because smaller and more insignificant things begin to torture
you, in proportion to your fear of being hurt.
—Thomas Merton, *The Seven Storey Mountain*

Pain is a fact of life, and it turns out that meditation actually decreases how painful pain feels. Fadel Zeidan, Katherine Martucci, and their team published a study called "Brain Mechanisms Supporting the Modulation of Pain by Mindfulness Meditation." In this study, fifteen volunteers reported a 40 percent drop in pain intensity and a 57 percent drop in the unpleasantness of the pain when using a simple breathing meditation.[25]

Practice:

Meditate for six minutes every day this week.

. . . .
Day 89: Pay Attention
Habit: Relationships

Attention is the rarest and purest form of generosity.
—Simone Weil, 1942 letter to Joë Bousquet

Giving someone your full attention makes them the center of your universe for a moment in time, and doing so is no easy feat. That's why it is so rare. It is the most generous thing you can give, because it speaks to people's deepest human need: to be worthy of love.

When who they are, what they want, what they need, what they're going through, or what makes them light up becomes the sole occupation of your mind and heart, they will feel loved. When you don't interrupt, offer advice, or compare problems, they will feel loved.

Practice:

1. Who needs your full attention today? Why?

2. How will you offer this person your undivided attention?

. . . .
Day 90: Monthly Check-In

Think of three Things, whence you came, where you are going, and to whom you must account.
—Benjamin Franklin, *Poor Richard's Almanack 1755*

Time to check in on your progress. This is not a guilt-inducing exercise designed to shame you for all you haven't accomplished yet.

Instead, it's a gentle reminder about what's important to you and what you want to change.

Enjoy the journey. Be gentle with yourself. Keep growing.

Practice:

- What did I do last month that I'm proud of?
- Are my relationships with others improving or deteriorating?
- What do I need to do less of/quit/get rid of/delegate this month?
- What experiments did I try? What lessons did I learn? What is going well?
- What isn't working, and what do I want to change?
- Habit to focus on next month:
- Why do I want to establish that habit?
- What is a first step I can take toward making this a habit?
- What trigger will I use?
- How will I reward myself?
- What obstacles will I face in establishing this habit and how will I overcome them?
- Notes on successes, long-term goals, and personal changes I'm working toward:

. . . .
Day 91: Forgive Yourself, Step 3
Habit: Connecting with Yourself

*A stiff apology is a second insult. … The injured party does
not want to be compensated because he has been wronged; he
wants to be healed because he has been hurt.*
—G. K. Chesterton, *The Common Man*

Step 1 to forgiving yourself is to acknowledge (day 76), step 2 is to change (day 83), and step 3 is to give. Give unconditionally—without expectation of return—to the person you've hurt. "Without expectation of return" is critical because they won't be sure you really mean it. They may not trust you. They may be waiting for you to go back to your old ways. That's okay. You can't control how they will react. But you can give. If you repeatedly give with love and respect for them and their needs, you are doing what you can to rectify the situation.

If it's not possible to give to the person you've hurt, give to others to create new experiences that remind you that even though you may have done some bad things, you are still a good person.

Practice:

1. Look back through your journal at the harm you've caused. Is it possible to give to the person you've harmed? If so, how will you do so respectfully, humbly, and unconditionally? If not, what can you give to others?

2. Perform a random act of kindness, such as buying the person in line behind you their coffee or planting a container of flowers for others to enjoy.

. . . .
Day 92: Good Morning
Habit: Gratitude

It was a morning like other mornings
and yet perfect among mornings.
—John Steinbeck, *The Pearl*

The sun makes its way over the horizon, slowly at first and then all in a rush. The world comes back to life. As the first rays of light touch each living creature, they sing, chirp, and twitter to welcome this new day and announce that they are showing up for this thing called life.

As you begin your day, you have another opportunity to live, laugh, and love. Another day to do your best, to inspire others, and to be kind. Another day to sing your song.

Practice:

1. In your journal, write about what makes your morning better. A comfortable bed, a hot shower, a great cup of coffee? Who makes your morning better? Whose face do you like to see? What can you do this morning that you do every morning but some people never get the chance to do? For example, if your eyes work, you can check your reflection in the mirror.

What opportunities will you have today that some people never have the opportunity to do?

2. If you did just one thing to feel like your day was a success, what would it be?

. . . .
Day 93: The Advertising Affliction
Habit: Mind Simplicity

Many a small thing has been made large
by the right kind of advertising.
—Mark Twain, *A Connecticut Yankee in King Arthur's Court*

Globally, companies were expected to spend $540 billion on advertising in 2015.[26] That's a lot of messages telling you to buy, buy, buy! And not just you, but your kids, too. American children watch an estimated sixteen thousand television commercials every year.[27] Companies advertise because it works.

Reducing your exposure to advertisements is one way you can protect yourself from being triggered to buy things that you don't want, don't need, can't afford, or won't appreciate for very long or that won't actually make you feel better, smarter, or more beautiful. Avoid that, and you'll have more time, energy, and money to give to others.

Practice:

1. In your journal, consider the following questions: Where are you exposed to advertising? How can you reduce your exposure to ads? You might try ad blockers for your computer or

watching prerecorded TV so you can fast-forward through the commercials.

2. Implement one strategy to reduce the number of ads you see.

. . . .
Day 94: How to Say No
Habit: Philanthropy

We're told every day,"You can't change the world."
But the world is changing every day.
Only question is … who's doing it? You or somebody else?
—J. Michael Straczynski, 1996 forum post

Saying no is a vital skill for a good philanthropist. When a request for your time or money violates your donation rules, follow these three steps.

1. *Listen and evaluate.* First, truly listen to their request and understand what and why they're asking. Then evaluate it. When a request violates one of your rules, move to step 2.

2. *Appreciate then decline.* That's the formula: appreciate and then decline. For example:

   ### Requests for Money

   I love that you are so passionate about this cause. I focus my giving on supporting causes that support veterans, pets, and help people get out of poverty. That's what I'm passionate about, so I can't donate, but I wish you a lot of luck in raising money for this cause.

Requests for Time

I love that you are so passionate about this cause, but I'm not the right person for this. I don't have the attention for detail needed to do a good job.

or

I love that you are so passionate about this cause, but I've got too much other stuff going on right now, and I just don't have the time.

3. *Stand your ground.* If someone isn't taking no for an answer, simply reply, "Yeah, thanks for asking. I'm flattered you thought of me, but I just can't. Good luck with your project."

Practice:

1. Write out your appreciate and decline response to a donation request you don't want to do.

2. Are you currently giving your time or money to a place you don't want to? If so, prepare an appreciate-and-decline response and then quit.

Week 14

Day 95: Health vs. Weight
Habit: Physical Health

Healthy emotions come in all sizes.
Healthy minds come in all sizes.
And healthy bodies come in all sizes.
—Cheri K. Erdman. *Live Large!*

Common wisdom says, "A pound of fat equals 3,500 calories, so to lose a pound, all you need to do is cut out 3,500 calories." Unfortunately, it isn't true. In the article "Myths, Presumptions, and Facts about Obesity," researchers reviewed numerous weight loss studies and concluded that individual weight loss or gain varied significantly and did not follow the predicted amount of weight loss.[28]

As a general rule, to lose weight you must burn more calories than you take in, but as a practical matter, some people will find it easier than others. Simple lifestyle changes that improve your eating habits and increase your exercise may be all you need to do to lose weight. Or it may be more difficult for you and require diligently recording in your food and exercise journal, counting calories, and occasionally using meal replacements and low-calorie diets.

How much you weigh is only one component of your physical health, and it isn't always the most important. Focus on your healthy habits and talk to a doctor about any underlying health issues that could be affecting your weight.

Practice:

1. In your journal, describe your history with weight. Do you struggle with your weight? When did your struggle begin? Describe your ideal relationship with food and exercise. What does it mean to you to be healthy?

2. Review your food journal for the past few weeks. Are there patterns about what you eat, when, and why? What pattern will you work on changing? What will you do today to change that pattern? If you're finding it helpful, continue your food journal.

. . . .
Day 96: Excuses
Habit: Mindfulness

For like a poisonous breath over the fields,
like a mass of locusts over Egypt, so the swarm of excuses
is a general plague, a ruinous infection among men,
that eats off the sprouts of the Eternal.
—Søren Kierkegaard, *Purity of Heart Is to Will One Thing*

Sometimes change is hard and doesn't stick right away. Exercise and meditation may be two of the most difficult habits to establish, but don't give up. Whenever you notice you haven't followed through for any reason, pause. Be generous to yourself. You're a work in progress. Now, get back to it!

Practice:

1. In your journal, reflect on a habit you're struggling to create. Why is it important to you? What benefits will you get? What is the smallest step you can take? What trigger or reward will you use?

2. On days you are feeling substantial resistance to exercising or meditating, just do one or two minutes to keep the habit alive.

3. Meditate for eight minutes every day this week.

. . . .
Day 97: Enlist Support
Habit: Relationships

If you want to walk fast, walk alone.
If you want to go far, walk together.
—Proverb

You can go it alone, and you might go very fast. But how long until you run out of energy? How long until you get bored? How long until you get distracted?

Other people can cheer you on, so you find the energy to keep going. They can make it more fun, so you don't even realize how far you've gone or how far you have left to go. They can keep you focused, remind you of your purpose, and inspire you to recommit to your journey.

In return, you do the same for them. You give them hope, inspiration, encouragement, support, and insight. Together, you can go farther.

Practice:

Who do you know who is trying to accomplish the same thing you are? Enlist their support in a mutually beneficial effort to reach this goal.

. . . .
Day 98: Feeling Important
Habit: Connecting with Yourself

Half of the harm that is done in this world
Is due to people who want to feel important.
—T. S. Eliot, *The Cocktail Party*

Some people feel important because of how much money they make, while others feel important because they dismiss economic achievements as important. Some people feel important because they are beautiful or skinny, while others feel important because they reject traditional beauty standards. Some people feel important because they're smart, while others take pride in their ignorance. Some people feel important through their hobbies and accomplishments, while others take in pride in things they don't do.

No matter how they do it, everyone finds a way to feel important.

Practice:

1. In your journal, reflect on what makes you feel important. Are these good for you? good for others? What would be a better way to feel important?

2. Perform a random act of kindness that makes you feel important, like letting the person in line behind you go ahead or dropping off a meal for a new mom.

. . . .
Day 99: Good Night
Habit: Gratitude

Finish every day and be done with it. . . . You have done what you could: some blunders and absurdities no doubt crept in; forget them as soon as you can.

—Ralph Waldo Emerson, *Selections from Emerson's Poems and Essays*

Like Ralph Waldo Emerson advised, you should finish every day and be done with it. But before you are done with it, there are some moments worth remembering. In addition to your blunders and absurdities, you did something kind, funny, or important. Because of your blunders and absurdities, you learned a few things. Despite your blunders and absurdities, there were magical moments.

Practice:

1. In your journal, consider these questions: What happened that was great today? What made you laugh? What did you

learn? What are you proud of? What surprised you? What were you grateful for today? What do you want to remember? What opportunities did you have today that some people never have the opportunity to do?

2. Take a moment to appreciate your day.

. . . .
Day 100: No Dinging
Habit: Schedule Simplicity

*Technology ... is a queer thing. It brings you great gifts with
one hand, and it stabs you in the back with the other.*
—C. P. Snow, quoted in the *New York Times* in 1971

While monitoring e-mail behavior, Dr. Thomas Jackson of Loughborough University discovered that people responded to 70 percent of arriving e-mails within 6 seconds and 85 percent within 2 minutes. He also confirmed that it's a huge waste of time. It took, on average, 64 seconds for people to resume their original project after checking e-mail, which could add up to 8.5 hours of lost productivity a week.[29] What would you do with an extra 8.5 hours?

Practice:

1. E-mail is mail. You fetch it when you're ready for it. Turn off the new mail notifications on your computer and smart phones.

2. If you have e-mails that you must absolutely respond to immediately and you know they always come from the same

person, set up an alert to let you know that you've received an e-mail from this very important person.

. . . .

Day 101: Month 4 Giving Challenge: Environment
Habit: Philanthropy

When we try to pick out anything by itself,
we find it hitched to everything else in the universe.
—John Muir, *My First Summer in the Sierra*

Our lives are made possible because of this amazing planet. Her air fills our lungs. Her water quenches our thirst. Her plants and animals provide our shelter and food. If we love ourselves, we must love and care for that which makes our lives possible.

Here are three areas where you can make this planet and us just a little healthier.

1. *Lower your home's energy impact.* Can you install weather stripping, caulk around windows, replace your lightbulbs or toilet with higher efficiency models, or increase the temperature on your thermostat so your air conditioning runs less often?

2. *Reduce your consumption impact.* Can you bring reusable bags to the grocery store, avoid single-serve items, compost kitchen and yard waste, shop at secondhand stores, use a travel mug, or make your own chemical-free cleaners? Look for opportunities to reduce, reuse, and recycle.

3. *Increase your environmental activism.* Can you call your congressperson and tell them that clean air and water are important to you, sign a petition asking a multinational corporation to use fair trade policies, buy from companies pursuing local and sustainable practices, visit a national park, or pick up garbage?

Practice:

1. What one thing can you do today to lower your home's energy impact or reduce your consumption impact?

2. Increase your environmental activism by calling your congressional leader. The website www.contactingthecongress.org will provide you the name and phone number of your representatives.

Week 15

Day 102: Food Doesn't Fix That
Habit: Physical Health

We all eat, and it would be a sad waste
of opportunity to eat badly.
—Anna Thomas, *The Vegetarian Epicure Book Two*

Do you eat more when you're feeling tired or stressed or bad about something? Does eating make you feel better, safe, certain, or loved? Do you reward yourself with food? Do you feel like you have no control over when you eat, how much you eat, or what you eat? Do you feel guilty or ashamed after you eat? If so, you may be an emotional eater. Although everyone eats emotionally from time to time, is your emotional eating causing problems in your life?

Your primary tool to curb emotional eating is to feel your feelings. Don't suppress them or avoid them. You might be stressed, angry, unhappy, scared, hurt, uncertain about the future, bored, lonely, or ashamed. Name it. I am feeling _____.

Now breathe. It's just a feeling. It's not permanent. It's not who you are. It's not going to kill you. Sit with it. Get curious about it. What does it feel like to feel _____? How often do you feel like this? When do you tend to feel like this? Can you use this feeling to fuel your commitment to change?

Practice:

1. In your journal, explore when you eat emotionally. Do certain situations or feelings make you want to eat? Looking through your food journal will help you identify these times. In the future, when you encounter this feeling and the urge to feed it, what will you do instead? You've paused to feel your feelings. Then what? Some ideas are calling a friend, having a cup of tea, putting on a favorite song, meditating, or going for a walk.

2. Choose one specific food behavior to change. What is it, why do you need it change it, and how will you change it? Remember, being generous to yourself means giving yourself space to feel and allow your emotions in a way that takes care of your physical health.

. . . .
Day 103: Meditation Improves Focus
Habit: Mindfulness

We live, in fact, in a world starved for solitude, silence, and privacy: and therefore starved for meditation and true friendship.
—C. S. Lewis, *The Weight of Glory*

In a study, cognitive scientists monitored the brain activity of eight long-term Buddhist practitioners and ten student volunteers. They found that gamma activity associated with focus was thirty times greater in the meditating monks than in the students. Even when the monks weren't meditating, their brain's resting state exhibited substantial differences from that of the students.[30] What could you do in your life if you had even more focus than you have now?

Practice:

Congratulations! You've reached your goal of ten minutes of meditation *every* day. Keep up the great work. Your increasing ability to be in the moment with your own thoughts and emotions will make you a better friend, lover, and parent.

. . . .
Day 104: Celebrate Their Success
Habit: Relationships

Celebration is an active state, an act of expressing reverence or appreciation. ... Celebration is a confrontation, giving attention to the transcendent meaning of one's actions.
—Abraham Joshua Heschel, *Who Is Man?*

Of course you want to be there for people when times are tough, but what about when times are good? According to research by Shelly Gable of the University of California, Santa Barbara, couples who don't celebrate their partner's successes are less likely to be happily married than those who are enthusiastic, interested, and demonstrative about good news.[31]

If you really want to make someone feel special, show that you understand why their accomplishment is important and make a big deal out of it.

Practice:

Who do you know who has had something positive happen in their life? Help them celebrate it.

. . . .
Day 105: The Desired Things
Habit: Connecting with Yourself

Go placidly amid the noise and the haste, and remember
what peace there may be in silence. As far as possible, without
surrender, be on good terms with all persons.
—Max Ehrmann, "Desiderata"

As a teenager, my mom purchased a scroll inscribed with the prose poem "Desiderata" (Latin for "The Desired Things"). Every time she moved, she carefully rolled it up only to pin it back up on the wall at her next home. Almost forty years later, that scroll finally got framed, and I love looking at all the pin marks in the corners.

This poem influenced my mother deeply, and I think of it as her North Star. It reminded her of what was important, told her how to live a good life, and comforted her that she was doing her best.

Practice:

1. In your journal, write about your desired things. What's important to you? What advice would you give to others about how to live a good life?

2. What is one thing you could do today to live up to your own advice?

· · · · · · · · · · · · · · · · · · · ·
Day 106: Gratitude Stroll
Habit: Gratitude

An early morning walk is a blessing for the whole day.
—Henry David Thoreau, 1840 journal entry

The world is an amazing place. You just have to step outside to see it, hear it, smell it, and touch it.

+ *See it:* Use your eyes to notice plants and animals that are perfectly adapted to their environments. Observe the remarkable achievements of human engineering. Look at the cloudless sky that kisses your skin with warmth, a starry sky on a moonless night, or a magnificent full moon resting on the horizon.
+ *Hear it:* Use your ears to absorb the sounds of birds. Hear children laughing. Enjoy an outdoor concert.
+ *Smell it:* Use your nose to appreciate the smell of freshly baked bread. Enjoy the fragrance of blooming lilacs. Revel in the fresh air after a rain.
+ *Touch it:* Use your hands to discover the roughness of bark. Feel the silky smooth petals of a flower. Caress the wiry fur of a dog.

Practice:
Go for a walk. Concentrate on your breathing for a few moments to shake off the cares and worries of the day and to get focused on the moment. As you walk, look at everything you pass and feel grateful for it. Say thank you to the tree, the flowers, the spiders. Do you

notice any pleasant smells? Say thank you for great smells or for the ability to smell. Do you hear any pleasant sounds? Say thank you for beautiful sounds or the ability to hear. Do you pass a beautiful yard? Say thank you for people who care about their homes. As you walk, express as much gratitude as possible for everything you see, hear, smell, and feel.

- -
Day 107: Don't Just Do Something, Sit There
Habit: Nature Simplicity

You must have been warned against letting the
golden hours slip by. Yes, but some of them are
golden only because we let them slip.
—J. M. Barrie, *Courage*

Spring in Georgia is truly spectacular with its comfortable temperatures, blooming flowers, and singing birds. As I sit outside, a slight breeze ruffles my hair. My toes soak up the afternoon sun. A sense of calm and peace settles around my heart and mind, and I smile warmly to my husband while I give his hand a firm squeeze. My heart feels full, and I give thanks that I have the physical, mental, and emotional capacity to appreciate this beautiful world. This feeling of gratitude nurtures a desire to be generous to the planet and encourages me to take actions that will care for and protect it.

Practice:

1. Sit down outside. What do you feel on your skin? Pay even closer attention. What else do you feel on your skin? What

sounds do you hear? Listen harder and further. What else do you hear? How far away is it? Where is it coming from? What do you smell? Even if it smells unpleasant, what else do you smell? What do you see? Look closer. What else do you see? Look even closer. What else do you see?

2. Close your eyes. Feel that you are part of this world. The air that moves through your hair also moves into your lungs, giving you life. Plants nourish your body and soul. Just sit there appreciating that your life is possible because of nature's gifts: her air, food, water, shelter. If you feel moved to do so, thank her for her gifts.

3. Perform a generous action for the environment today, such as using mass transportation, wearing out your clothes before replacing them, or avoiding poisons for weed and pest control.

. . . .
Day 108: Giving with Kids: Guiding Principles
Habit: Philanthropy

What is the use of living, if it be not to strive for noble causes and to make this muddled world a better place for those who will live in it after we are gone?
—Winston Churchill, 1908 speech at Kinnaird Hall, Scotland

Use these four guiding principles to help your children grow into generous adults.

1. *Model generous behavior.* Take time to point out things you're grateful for. Talk about causes you donate to and why. Plan activities for your own special days (your anniversary, your birthday) that involve giving to others.

2. *Keep it small.* Avoid overwhelming them with big problems with big solutions or too many choices. Focus on one part of a problem they can help with and only consider a couple charities.

3. *Be patient.* Young children are unpredictable and older children can be rebellious. If your child doesn't want to give, it doesn't mean your child is selfish. They may need more time and distance from that toy. They may need more perspective or empathy about the person they could be helping. There will be more opportunities to learn and practice generosity.

4. *Repeat often.* Experiment with different ways to express gratitude and different opportunities to give. The family can volunteer together, host an open house for a local charity, or hand out flyers to raise awareness. There are countless ways to give.

Practice:

1. In your journal, ask yourself, "How am I currently modeling generous behavior? How does that differ from the generous behavior I would like my children (family, friends, community) to see me doing—in other words, how can I do better?

2. Either by yourself or with or in front of your kids, perform a philanthropic action like donating lightly worn clothes or making a small donation.

Week 16
· · · · · · · · · ·

Day 109: To Cook or Not to Cook?
Habit: Physical Health

You could probably get through life without knowing how to roast a chicken, but the question is, would you want to?
—Nigella Lawson, *How to Eat*

If you were stranded on a deserted island, the first thing you would think about when you woke up in the morning is "What am I going to eat today?" Eating is the most important thing you do every day. And because you must eat, you must cook. There's no way around it. Unless money is no object and you can hire a personal chef, you must cook, because no one else will care about your health as much as you should care about your health.

Healthy cooking is a new habit to create that we'll take one step at a time, building on the skills you have and adding new skills. Over time, you'll create an arsenal of tools to help you cook cheaply, quickly, and often.

Practice:

1. In your journal, note: How often do you cook? How often do you eat out? What drives your decision to eat out? What are your fears and concerns about cooking more?

2. Create a first, small step you could take to cook at home more often. How many meals will you prepare at home this week?

. . . .

Day 110: Greeting Yourself with Friendliness
Habit: Mindfulness

*Meditation practice isn't about trying
to throw ourselves away and become something better.
It's about befriending who we are already.*
—Pema Chödrön, *Comfortable with Uncertainty*

While you're meditating, you may experience strong physical or emotional sensations.

Whether you think the feeling is positive or negative, greet it as an old friend who is popping in for a short visit. Notice the feeling. Define it. Is it anger, joy, disappointment, betrayal? Observe yourself feeling this emotion. What is happening to your body and in your mind in response to this emotion? How long does the emotion last? If the emotion becomes overwhelming, try bringing your hand to your heart and repeating a reassuring phrase or switching to a meditation technique like body scanning. Seek outside advice if these emotions are impacting the quality of your life.

Practice:
Keep up the ten minutes of meditation *every* day!

Day 111: Takers
Habit: Relationships

How people treat you is their karma; how you react is yours.
—Wayne W. Dyer, quoted in
Don't Die with Your Music Still in You

Takers put their own interests ahead of other people's interests. As a giver, it's important to avoid overgiving to takers, because not only will they not reciprocate, making them a black hole of positive energy, but they may actively harm you when it serves their needs.

Practice:

1. In your journal, reflect on a time when you gave to a taker. How could you have known? What were you hoping to gain by giving to them? Is this something they could have given you? Were you violating their boundaries or your own (days 3 and 4)? What are some ways to spot takers? Next time, how will you handle a taker?

2. Who in your life is a giver? Do something nice for them like treating them to coffee or washing their car.

Day 112: Let Your Light Shine
Habit: Connecting with Yourself

And as we let our own light shine, we unconsciously give other
people permission to do the same. As we are liberated from our
own fear, our presence automatically liberates others.
—Marianne Williamson, *A Return to Love*

Your commitment to creating a better world gives me hope. Your
life gives me an example to live by. Your presence gives me courage.
Your laughter, wisdom, and passion inspire me. Thank you for being you.

Practice:

1. In your journal, write about the times or places where you min-
   imize yourself or your accomplishments. What parts of you
   are you trying to hide or hoping other people don't discover?
2. Commit to letting your light shine more brightly more often. Start with sharing with a trusted friend something about
   yourself that you are proud of but most people don't know
   about you.

Day 113: What Do You Have?
Habit: Gratitude

He who knows that enough is enough will always have enough.
—Lao Tzu, *Tao Te Ching*

Do you feel like you don't have enough? Do you wish you had more? A bigger house, a faster car, that cute pair of shoes? Do you wish you could afford a boat, a better vacation, a bigger birthday party for your kids? Me too. We all do. It's human nature. It doesn't matter how much we have, we still want more. Even the richest people in the world want more.

If you are not satisfied, perhaps it's because you've forgotten how much you already have.

Practice:

1. In your journal, consider the following questions: What financial resources do you have? What is good about your financial situation? What possessions do you have in your home that make your life better? What intellectual resources do you have? What do you know about? What could you teach someone? What passions do you have? What emotional resources do you have? What are your good character traits? What relationships do you have? Who do you love, and who loves you? What is good about your health? What positive experiences have you had? What has made you the

person you are today? What truths do you know about the human condition?

2. Pause to appreciate how much you have.

. . . .
Day 114: Purse or Wallet
Habit: Home Simplicity

Simplicity is the keynote of all true elegance.
—Coco Chanel, quoted in *Harper's Bazaar* in 1923

The American Chiropractic Association warns that any purse that weighs over three pounds can lead to spine and back pain. Today, simplify your purse.

Practice:

1. *Empty It:* Everything must come out.

2. *First Pass Trash.*

3. *Sort:* Group like things together.

4. *Rehome:* Relocate the items that belong somewhere else.

5. *Choose:* What do you need in your purse or wallet?

6. *Organize:* Use bags to keep similar stuff together. Your cheapest and most practical option is a simple, clear ziplock bag, but use any small bag that can be sealed. An office bag is for a pen, a highlighter, a pad of paper, and other similar items. The health bag is for aspirin, tissues, hand sanitizer, bandages, and so on. The cosmetics bag is for a small bottle of hand lotion, a

small nail file, a mirror, and lip balm. The electronics bag is for items like charging cables.

7. *Weigh:* If your bag weighs more than three pounds, go back through it and remove large or heavy items, downsize to travel sizes, and get rid of more items.

. . . .
Day 115: Giving with Kids: In Practice
Habit: Philanthropy

If you wish to be like a little child,
study what a little child could understand—nature;
and do what a little child could do—love.
—Charles Kingsley, *Charles Kingsley:*
His Letters and Memories of His Life

When giving with your children, consider these three strategies.

1. *Use group activities.* Group activities can get kids excited about doing something for others without becoming too emotionally attached to those things they'll be giving. For example, plan a day for kids to fill backpacks with school supplies for low-income children.

2. *Give how your child likes to give.* Structure opportunities that allow your children to participate in ways that they enjoy. Do they like to build things, work with animals or seniors, give money, or use their technical skills? For young children,

money may not mean much. Instead, let them give tangible objects like books for a school or cookies to a senior center.

3. *Grow with them.* When they start getting an allowance, start the "Spend some, save some, give some" lesson and help them direct their money in equal parts toward fun purchases, savings, and philanthropy. When they get older, they can research charities or suggest areas of interest for the family's philanthropy. Don't underestimate your kids. Challenge them, educate them, and grow with them as their skills and interest in giving grow.

Practice:

1. In your journal, identify the stage of giving your children are at. How can you engage them at that level? Is your child drawn toward one style of giving over another? What giving event will you undertake with your children?

2. Either by yourself or with or in front of your kids, perform a philanthropic action like donating old books to your library or making a small donation.

Week 17

. . . .

Day 116: The Essential Pantry
Habit: Physical Health

There's nothing like a home-cooked meal—nothing!
When people ask me what the best restaurant in L.A. is,
I say, "Uh, my house."

—Giada De Laurentiis, 2011 interview with *Redbook*

It's been a long day. You haven't been to the grocery store in a week. What are you going to make for dinner?

Stop. Before you pick up the phone to order pizza, take a look at your pantry. As you've discovered in building your other new healthy habits, planning for failure is critical to success. What are you going to make for dinner in this situation?

If you have a well-stocked pantry, there are countless dishes you can make in less time than it takes for the pizza guy to arrive. If you have a package of frozen spinach, parmesan cheese, two eggs, and chicken broth, you have stracciatella, a comforting yet light Italian soup. If you have some garlic, a few olives, capers, and anchovies, plus a can of diced tomatoes and a box of spaghetti, you've got pasta puttanesca in the time it takes to boil pasta.

A well-stocked pantry is your secret to quick, tasty, healthy meals. My well-stocked pantry always has these items:

- onions, garlic, potatoes, carrots, and ginger
- cans of diced tomatoes, chickpeas, black beans, kidney beans, coconut milk, olives, capers, pickles, and anchovies
- chicken broth, salsa, peanut butter, and tahini
- rice (or other grain), pasta, and corn meal
- in the refrigerator: eggs, milk, sour cream, bacon, parmesan, and cheddar cheese
- in the freezer: spinach, tortillas, and pitas

Practice:

1. What does your pantry look like? What do you need to add? Go grocery shopping to add needed pantry supplies.

2. Create five simple, go-to recipes you can make with ingredients you have in your pantry. If you need ideas, search online for "pantry meals" or "last-minute meals," so you're prepared to cook when you don't feel like you have the time.

3. How many meals will you prepare at home this week?

. . . .
Day 117: Prayer vs. Meditation
Habit: Mindfulness

The greatest wisdom is listening to the guidance of the heart.
—Kabir Helminski, *The Knowing Heart*

Prayer can be a beautiful expression of faith, hope, and healing. Prayer can be a wordless outpouring of grief and request for help. Traditionally, prayer comes from you and goes out.

On the other hand, meditation is about listening, waiting, and watching. Something may or may not arrive from the outside. Something may or may not well up from inside you. Whatever happens, happens. You are there. Waiting. Watching. Listening. There is no greater act of generosity to yourself than to truly listen to yourself.

Practice:

1. Keep up the ten minutes of meditation *every* day!

2. Remember to allow and acknowledge your feelings. Attach no expectations or goals to your meditation practice. Seek outside guidance for advanced instruction and training in meditation and mindfulness practices.

. . . .
Day 118: Matching Giving and Taking
Habit: Relationships

Just as the wave cannot exist for itself, but is ever a part of the heaving surface of the ocean, so must I never live my life for itself, but always in the experience which is going on around me.
—Albert Schweitzer, *Philosophy of Civilisation*

Givers can end up as burnt-out doormats who gave too much too often and to the wrong people. As a giver, it's important to know your limits and to avoid giving to takers who put their own interests ahead of everything else and don't reciprocate your generous acts.

When it comes to giving, we can learn by watching the matchers, reveals Adam Grant, author of *Give and Take*. Matchers balance giving with getting, make sure the takers get what's coming to them, and ensure the givers get rewarded.

Practice:

1. In your journal, consider your giving and receiving behavior. When is it okay for you receive? Are you a balanced giver and receiver? Where do you need to be more strategic with your giving?

2. Think of someone who has helped you out and find a way to repay them, such as with a gift certificate or a home-baked goodie.

. . . .
Day 119: Shit Happens
Habit: Connecting with Yourself

If we had no winter, the spring would not be so pleasant:
if we did not sometimes taste of adversity,
prosperity would not be so welcome.
—Anne Bradstreet, *Meditations Divine and Moral*

People get sick, get hurt, and lose jobs. Cars need repairs, plumbing leaks, and air conditioners break. Tornados, earthquakes, and hurricanes wreak havoc. Sometimes shit happens, and it's no one's fault.

Practice:

In your journal, identify a difficult situation you are dealing with now or have experienced in the past that felt out of your control.

What can you learn from it? Given the circumstances, what's the best possible outcome? What action can you take to bring yourself closer to your desired outcome?

. . . .

Day 120: Monthly Check-In

We should face it [the future] seriously,
neither hiding from ourselves the gravity of the problems before
us nor fearing to approach these problems with the unbending,
unflinching purpose to solve them aright.
—Theodore Roosevelt, 1905 inaugural address

Time to check in on your progress. This is not a guilt-inducing exercise designed to shame you for all you haven't accomplished yet. Instead, it's a gentle reminder about what's important to you and what you want to change.

The outcomes are less important than your continued growth into your full potential as an individual, family member, friend, and philanthropist. In fact, sometimes your desired outcomes change.

Enjoy the journey. Be gentle with yourself. Keep growing.

Practice:

- ✦ What did I do last month that I'm proud of?
- ✦ Are my relationships with others improving or deteriorating?
- ✦ What do I need to do less of/quit/get rid of/delegate this month?

- What experiments did I try? What lessons did I learn? What is going well?
- What isn't working, and what do I want to change?
- Habit to focus on next month:
- Why do I want to establish that habit?
- What is a first step I can take toward making this a habit?
- What trigger will I use?
- How will I reward myself?
- What obstacles will I face in establishing this habit and how will I overcome them?
- Notes on successes, long-term goals, and personal changes I'm working toward:

. . . .
Day 121: Unhistoric Acts
Habit: Gratitude

The growing good of the world is partly dependent on unhistoric acts; and that things are not so ill with you and me as they might have been, is half owing to the number who lived faithfully a hidden life.
—George Elliot, *Middlemarch*

That things are not so ill with me as they might have been is owing to my parents, who faithfully lived a hidden life but set an example of hard work, integrity, and generosity for me to follow. My parents would be the first to say that there is nothing special about them. But what they take for granted about themselves is what's so remarkable. For example, my mom was my biggest cheerleader. She didn't think she was special for cheerleading. She thought I was special enough to deserve cheerleading. But what would have happened to me without that vote of confidence? Would I have had the self-esteem to travel the world, marry a wonderful man, write a book? Yes, her cheerleading was unhistoric, but it made my life better. Now, I do my best to pay that forward and help the world become better, too.

Practice:

1. Look around at your friends, family, neighbors, coworkers. What do they do that is helping the world be a better place and they don't even know it? Take a moment to appreciate the people who are doing their best to make the world a little better for their friends, family, and communities.

2. Send a card, e-mail, or text thanking this person for their actions.

. . . .
Day 122: Your Brain on Scarcity
Habit: Mind Simplicity

A man is rich in proportion to the number
of things which he can afford to let alone.
—Henry David Thoreau, *Walden*

Eldar Shafir, Princeton psychologist and author of *Scarcity: Why Having Too Little Means So Much*, discovered that people experiencing financial difficulty spend so much time on questions like

"Where will get I enough money? What has to be paid? Where can I spend less?" that they don't have enough time to plan for the future and anticipate unforeseen expenses. As a result, things get paid late, money is spent on the wrong things, and in a perverse cycle, they continue to struggle financially.[32]

And it doesn't happen just with money. A busy person makes decisions that leave them with even less time. A lonely person has difficulty making friends.

Practice:

1. In your journal, ask yourself where in your life you feel the most scarcity. Time, money, relationships? Something else? How does that concern impact your life? What would you do differently if it wasn't a concern? How would you feel if you had plenty of it? What would solve your problem (a savings account, fewer commitments, a stronger sense of self-esteem, etc.)?

2. What is one thing you will do today to get closer to that solution?

· ·
Day 123: Charity Research, Level 1: Orientation
Habit: Philanthropy

To decide to whom to give it, and how large a sum,
and when, and for what purpose, and how,
is neither in every man's power, nor an easy matter.
—Aristotle, *The Neomachian Ethics of Aristotle*

A donation starts with your heart, but a good donation happens when you use your head. Here are the first four questions you should ask before you give:

1. *What problem is the charity trying to solve?* Use simple and clear language.
2. *How are they solving it?* There are lots of ways to solve any problem. How is this charity doing it?
3. *How do they know they are making a difference?* Do they know if they're making a difference? Or are they assuming their work makes a difference? Are they tracking the results of their work? Are they tracking the right results?
4. *Is that something I want to support?* Why? Do you like what they do and how they do it? Do you believe they are making an impact on the problem? If you support this charity, it might mean you can't support another, so is this the cause and charity you want to support with your scarce financial resources?

Practice:

1. On day 65, you identified three charities working on your favorite cause. For each one, answer, "What problem are they trying to solve? How are they solving it? How do they know it's working? Is that something I want to support?"
2. Do any of these charities warrant further research?

Week 18
· · · · · · · · · ·

Day 124: Picky Eaters
Habit: Physical Health

I'm President of the United States,
and I'm not going to eat any more broccoli.
—George H. W. Bush, 1990 news conference

Making healthy food changes can be especially difficult with children. Below you'll find a few tips for helping those picky eaters in your house, but for more advice, I encourage you to visit parenting forums to hear what works for other parents.

1. *Go slow.* Don't swap out all their favorite junk foods or highly processed dinners (e.g., chicken nuggets) right away. Bring in healthier items one at a time.

2. *Give them choices.* As you bring in the healthier items, let your child choose which healthier item and how much of it to add to their plate in addition to their typical chicken nugget dinner.

3. *Give them lots of opportunities.* Kids may not like something right away, and they need to be exposed to it over and over before they'll like or tolerate it. If they don't want to eat it now,

that's okay. Don't force it. Give them another chance another day.

4. *Make sure they're hungry.* If they come to the dinner table hungry, they may be more likely to try that new food.

5. *Be their example.* Let them see you try new stuff and enjoying it. In time, your example will rub off on them.

6. *Get them to help.* Kids who help you prepare dinner may be more interested in eating it.

7. *Avoid temptation.* Don't bring junk food into the house.

8. *Don't underestimate your kids.* Share with them the importance of good food and your experience with food.

Practice:

1. What challenges do you face in providing healthy meals for the whole family?

2. What strategies will you use to gradually help the whole family eat better?

3. How many meals will you prepare at home this week?

. . . .
Day 125: Different Types of Meditation
Habit: Mindfulness

Inner stillness is the key to outer strength.
—Jared Brock, *A Year of Living Prayerfully*

Although you could do the simple breathing meditation for the rest of your life, you may want to explore different kinds of meditation to discover if you like some methods better than others. Some meditation styles have formal schools and practices. You can take classes on meditation methods like Transcendental Meditation, Vipassana meditation, zazen, kundalini, and qigong. Aside from these formal practices, you might enjoy guided meditations in which someone speaks to you in a calm, soothing voice for a period of time. You might be drawn to meditating while listening to slow, peaceful music or gongs. You may find that small, intentional movements enhance your experience of meditating.

In the end, you are the expert on your own life, so choose what works best for you.

Practice:

1. Are there any meditation styles you already know you want to explore? If so, what are they? Where can you learn more about this meditation style?

2. Continue meditating for ten minutes *every* day.

. . . .
Day 126: Checking In
Habit: Relationships

Imagine an invisible sign around each person's neck that says, "Make me feel important!"
—Mary Kay Ash, *Mary Kay, You Can Have It All*

A text, an e-mail, or a surprise phone call to check in or to say you're thinking of the person lets them know they are important.

Let someone know they are important enough to you that you took time out of your busy day to show you care.

Practice:

Who do you want to make feel important today? Check in with them via text, e-mail, or phone to see how they're doing.

. . . .
Day 127: Repetition
Habit: Connecting with Yourself

Every man feels instinctively that all the beautiful sentiments
in the world weigh less than a single lovely action.
—James Russell Lowell

In the beginning, you don't have to believe that you can. You just have to take action toward your goal *as if* you believed it. Every little action you take adds to the action before it, and soon there is momentum. Eventually, your mind catches up and realizes it's been wrong this whole time. You can do it because you've already done it!

Practice:

1. You are now in the process of building three foundational habits that care for your health: physical activity, healthy eating, and meditation. Are you taking the daily actions suggested in this book? If not, what is stopping you?

2. What habit do you want to recommit to? Revisit day 44 to create your plan.

Day 128: Things You Don't Have to Worry About
Habit: Gratitude

We can only be said to be alive in those moments
when our hearts are conscious of our treasure.
—Thornton Wilder, *The Woman of Andros*

Each morning, our early human ancestors awoke and asked, "What am I going to eat today? Where will I collect water today?" They didn't understand what made them sick. They couldn't count on getting better. A big portion of their time and energy was taken up with the daily business of staying alive.

Today, if you're lucky, you have grocery stores, running water, electricity, sewage systems, and modern medicine.

All of these modern conveniences aren't just nice to have. They free up mental and emotional energy allowing you to focus on living, working, and playing better.

Practice:

1. In your journal, list the modern conveniences that make your life better. How do these help you spend more time on the things you love? Who doesn't have these things? How is their daily life different than yours because they don't benefit from these modern conveniences?

2. Take a moment to appreciate that so much is in place to help you live a better life.

. . . .
Day 129: Daily Routine
Habit: Schedule Simplicity

Simplicity is about subtracting the obvious,
and adding the meaningful.
—John Maeda, *The Laws of Simplicity*

Every decision you make depletes your brain's mental energy, and when you've made too many decisions, you get "decision fatigue." For this reason, many successful people reduce the number of unimportant decisions they have to make, so they have more energy for accomplishing the important tasks.

Routines are beautiful mechanisms for reducing the number of decisions you need to make. If you already know what you're going to do when you wake up in the morning, what you're going to eat, what you're going to wear, how you're going to get to work, then you can be more productive all day long.

Practice:

1. What in your life do you have to think about but could be automated or simplified, such as what you wear or what you eat?

2. What is your ideal morning routine at home? at work? Are you overcomplicating your morning routine with too many or unimportant activities?

3. What is your ideal end-of-day routine at work? at home? Are you overcomplicating your end-of-day routine with too many or unimportant activities?

4. Choose one action to eliminate from each of your routines.

Day 130: Month 5 Giving Challenge: Education
Habit: Philanthropy

Education is the most powerful weapon
we can use to change the world.
—Nelson Mandela, 2003 speech
"Lighting Your Way to a Better Future"

Across the developing world, girls are denied an education for no other reason than the fact they are girls. In poor and rural areas around the world, schools (if they exist) aren't equipped with the books and tools needed to prepare young people for today's world. Teachers don't always show up for work, don't always treat all students equally, aren't always trained to provide the best quality of education, and aren't always supported by their communities. Students everywhere look at the skyrocketing cost of a college education and wonder how they're going to afford it.

Yet study after study shows a direct benefit between education and personal gains like better health and higher income. Plus, it strengthens our communities and leads to stronger civic engagement in terms of voting, volunteering, political interest, and interpersonal trust.[33]

Practice:
Choose a way to support education. Monetary options could include a donation to a scholarship fund or a charity that builds schools in developing nations. Or you could donate supplies of pencils, crayons, and notebooks to a local school. Or you could give your time and mentor a young person.

Week 19

Day 131: Willpower Will Fail
Habit: Physical Health

Your task is not to foresee the future, but to enable it.
—Antoine de Saint-Exupéry, *The Wisdom of the Sands*

Stop beating yourself up about not having enough willpower to stick to your new healthy-eating resolutions. Recent psychology experiments reveal that you get a daily willpower account, and each time you draw on it, you have less willpower to call on for the next situation. Plus, being tired or hungry drains your willpower account so that it may not be available when you need it most.[34]

Following your healthy eating goals is not about willpower. It's about planning. Don't force yourself to rely on this unpredictable resource called willpower. Give yourself the best chance for success by planning ahead.

Practice:

Plan out your menu for the entire week. What do you need to buy at the grocery store to make it happen? What nights will you have time to cook at home? What nights will you need to have something already ready? What will you eat for lunch? Make it the night before, so all you have to do is grab it and go.

Day 132: Pain Journal
Habit: Mindfulness

Self-observation is the first step of inner unfolding.
—Amit Ray, *Meditation*

If you have chronic pain issues, a pain journal is a vital part of your mindfulness practice that will help you gain insight about your pain, how it changes over time, and what influences it. Living with chronic pain impacts the quality not only of your life but of those around you, so over the next few weeks, give yourself and them the gift of reducing the impact of pain on your life.

Practice:

Using a notebook, sticky notes, or a phone app (the phone apps for pain journals are kind of awesome, and you should definitely check them out), note the date and time of your pain episode, what you've been doing since the last time you had pain, where in your body you felt pain and if it moves around, the intensity of the pain (on a scale from 1, no pain, to 10, worst possible pain), how often you felt the pain, the duration of each pain episode, whether the pain interrupted a daily activity like sleeping or working, what medications you took or alternative treatments (like yoga or aromatherapy) you tried during the period and whether they gave you any relief, other actions (such as taking a warm shower, standing up, or walking around) that you took, and what emotions you felt that were connected to the pain. Do your best to record your entries at least every day.

Day 133: Appreciate
Habit: Relationships

To a large degree, our success and happiness in life depends
on how much people like themselves when they're with us.
—Joe Caruso

A simple thank-you can go a long way in letting someone know
you appreciate them. But don't stop there. Look for opportunities
to compliment and admire something they did or said, a way they
handled a situation, their family, or even one of their possessions. A
genuine, well-timed compliment lets someone know that not only
have you noticed them, but you like them, too.

Practice:

Who do you want to make feel liked today? What can you admire
about who they are or what they've done? Deliver your compliment
in person or via phone, text, greeting card, e-mail, or social media.

Day 134: Pamper Yourself
Habit: Connecting with Yourself

To sit in the shade on a fine day, and look upon verdure,
is the most perfect refreshment.
—Fanny in *Mansfield Park*, Jane Austen

Pampering yourself may seem silly or trite, but it's actually a powerful way to connect with yourself. A good dose of pampering puts

you in touch with your body and your spirit at the same time. Pampering reminds you that you are special, important, and worthy of being cared for. You would do it for those you love, so do it for yourself.

Practice:

1. In your journal, list activities that you love doing, that make your body feel nurtured, and that restore your spirit.

2. Choose one to indulge in.

. . . .
Day 135: Anonymous Kindness
Habit: Gratitude

Many of the bravest never are known, and get no praise. That does not lessen their beauty.
—Louisa May Alcott, *Eight Cousins*

An estimated one hundred billion humans have walked this earth.[35] Many of their actions have impacted the life you live today, and yet you'll never know who they are and you might not even know what exactly they did. There are men and women who stood up for what was right, giving you more freedom today. There are those who disbursed goods or ideas that you use today. And there are people who do something as simple as put change in your parking meter so you don't get a ticket. All around you are anonymous men and women making your world a better place.

Practice:

1. Take a moment to appreciate the generosity, kindness, and bravery of people you've never met, whose names you'll never know, and yet who have made your life better.

2. Perform a random act of *anonymous* kindness today, like putting coins in someone's parking meter or leaving notes of positivity for others to find.

. . . .
Day 136: Take a Walk
Habit: Nature Simplicity

A pedestrian is a man in danger of his life;
a walker is a man in possession of his soul.
—David McCord, *About Boston*

Every religion has called upon the power of the pilgrimage because wandering creates space in your heart for delighting in nature. Walking quiets your mind so that it can hear the voice of inspiration and spirit. Walking makes apparent the rhythms of and relationships between your body, your spirit, and the natural world.

Practice:

1. Find a place near you where you can walk. Ideally, it's a place nearby with a lot of nature that you can visit on a regular basis, but a small section of a riverfront, a tiny park, or a simple city street will do.

2. Observe carefully using all your senses. No electronics, no music. Walk slowly. Breathe slowly. Notice the nature around you. Are there insects hanging out on flowers? Do you hear birds? See birds? What kind are they? What kind of trees are around you? If you can't name them, describe them. What kind of bark does the tree have? What is the shape of the leaf? Does it have flowers? fruit? What season are you in? How is nature responding to that season? In the city, notice the corners, alleys, and decorations that you've driven past a hundred times and never noticed.

3. Savor your physical connection to nature. Remove your shoes and touch the earth with your feet. Caress the trees with your palms. Inhale the fragrance of a flower.

4. Revisit this place often, getting to know it intimately, so you know when and how it changes over time.

5. Look for opportunities to drive less, use mass transportation, or carpool.

. . . .

Day 137: Charity Research, Level 2: Reputation Research
Habit: Philanthropy

When faith and hope fail, as they do sometimes,
we must try charity, which is love in action.
We must speculate no more on our duty, but simply do it.
—Dinah Craik, *Christian's Mistake*

The next step in choosing a great charity is to research the charity's reputation.

1. *Check online sources.* The Internet is an invaluable resource for finding out more about a charity. Here are a few websites I always check: Give Well, Charity Navigator, Better Business Bureau, and Guidestar.

2. *Google the charity's name.* Google the charity's name with the word "problem," "concern," "controversy," or "criticism."

3. *Google the charity's work.* Google the charity's type of work with the words "criticism," "problem," and "controversy." Does this type of work make a difference? What are the pitfalls in this line of work? Could it do more harm than good?

Practice:

1. Choose a charity from day 123 to research further.

2. Check a few of the websites listed in step 1. Do you like what you find?

3. Do step 2. Are there any news articles or blog posts that give you pause?

4. Do step 3. What should this charity be doing if they're going to do this work right? Are they following the best practices?

5. Does this information change your desire to donate to this charity? Do you need to do more research? Do you want to call the charity and talk with them about it?

Week 20

Day 138: What's Stopping You?
Habit: Physical Health

How shallow to presume war exists only within the physical world. Battles are waged for mind and soul, where things far from comprehension are confronted.
—Christopher Hawke, *Unnatural Truth*

Sometimes when you're struggling to create a habit, it's a simple logistical problem. Maybe you haven't set yourself up for success by choosing a first step you can do, a trigger that works for your schedule, or a reward that keeps you motivated.

It's also possible that you have an inner conflict. For example, some people have been abused in their past, and they developed a subconscious belief that if they were heavy, no one would find them attractive enough to abuse again. This belief sabotages their efforts to lose weight.

We all have beliefs that guide our behavior, that influence what we expect from the world, how well we treat ourselves, and how we interact with our friends, family, and coworkers. If you're struggling to accomplish something you know in your head is good for you, it's likely that you are harboring a secret belief that is undermining your efforts to change.

Practice:

1. What goal or habit are you struggling with? In your journal, write about what you'd have to believe to do that, to act that way, to not take the action you know you should take. Write new, empowering beliefs that you will live by now.

2. Adopt your power pose from day 54. Repeat your new, empowering beliefs. You don't have to believe it yet. Just say it like you do.

. . . .
Day 139: Physical Pain Meditation
Habit: Mindfulness

Do you not see how necessary a World of Pains and troubles
is to school an Intelligence and make it a soul?
—John Keats, 1819 letter to his brother and sister-in-law

With practice, your small pains can cause you less suffering. With even more practice, your bigger pains may become less intense and less frequent. Chronic pain, a headache, or a cold is a great opportunity to practice this pain meditation.

Practice:

1. First and foremost, you should never put your health at risk by ignoring important pain signals that need to be addressed, so get medical help if needed. If your pain does not require medical attention, feel free to readjust yourself—although do so intentionally and mindfully. Try changing your posture,

moving your hands to a different position, or loosening your clothing. After each adjustment, pay attention to your body. Ask yourself, "How does that feel now?" and then carefully listen to your body.

2. Begin with your simple breathing meditation, and when you're feeling relaxed and centered, begin to observe your pain. Where is it? What does it feel like? Is it pulsating or vibrating? Is it solid? Does it move? Pay attention to how the pain changes. Then notice how you're responding to the pain. Are your muscles tense around the area where the pain is occurring? Are you tensing in other places in anticipation of the pain? How are you responding emotionally to the pain? Are you thinking, "I hate this pain" or "I'm sick and tired of feeling like this" or "I wish it would go away"?

3. Now relax. Relax the muscles around the pain. With each breath, let go of tension in your muscles. Next, let your emotions relax. Let go of your thoughts and emotions about the pain. Stop resisting. Breathe and observe the sensations of pain and how they're changing. When you're ready, experience the pain as the pain. Imagine you are the pain. Go right into the center of it, and feel the pain as *the pain*—not as *you feeling* the pain. It's hard to describe, but just give it a go.

4. Continue with your pain journal. You may jump ahead to day 154 if you want to review it now.

. . . .
Day 140: Powerful Body Language
Habit: Relationships

The human body is the best picture of the human soul.
—Ludwig Wittgenstein, *Philosophical Investigations*

On day 54, you learned that your body language changes how you feel about yourself. Not surprisingly, it also changes how others feel about you. Amy Cuddy, a professor and researcher at Harvard, discovered that participants who adopted a high-power pose (chest out, arms open) before giving a speech were rated as more confident, captivating, and enthusiastic than those who practiced a low-power pose (arms crossed, chest and shoulders pulled in) before giving the speech.[36]

Practice:

1. How do you usually stand and carry yourself? How does that posture affect how you feel about yourself? How does it affect how others view you? Continue practicing your power pose especially, in private, before an important event or conversation.

2. Perform a random act of kindness today like leaving an extra large tip for your barista or a token of appreciation for the office cleaning staff.

Day 141: Feedback Loops
Habit: Connecting with Yourself

The great moral teachers of humanity were, in a way,
artistic geniuses in the art of living.
—Albert Einstein, "Religion and Science: Irreconcilable?"

Good things feed off of good things, creating more good things.
It's a positive feedback loop. A morning that begins with exercise
and meditation can mean you arrive at work in a calm state and
interact with your coworkers in positive and productive ways. As
a result of your ability to handle stress and facilitate positive relationships between coworkers, you're asked to take the lead on an
exciting project. Exercising your creativity and autonomy at work
makes the hours fly by, and you arrive home with a smile on your
face and greet your spouse with a loving kiss, creating a more loving and rewarding relationship. Feeling a deep sense of security and
love at home, your children start to perform better in school, giving
you more time to just enjoy your kids.

Practice:

1. In your journal, identify an area where you can bring more
   love, attention, energy to create more positive experiences in
   your own life and those around you. Bad things feed off of
   bad things, creating more bad things. Where are you stuck in
   a negative feedback loop? How can you break the cycle?

2. Treat yourself to a random act of kindness, like watching your favorite TV show, going to a game, or hopping on the swings at a local park.

. . . .

Day 142: Mothers
Habit: Gratitude

To describe my mother would be to write about a hurricane in its perfect power. Or the climbing, falling colors of a rainbow.
—Maya Angelou, *I Know Why the Caged Bird Sings*

For much of my life, I did not fully appreciate my mom and her gifts. She was a big personality and a strong woman. Sometimes I felt bowled over; at other times, I felt I lived in her shadow. It wasn't until my mom got sick that I could get out from behind my story, look at her with clear eyes, and fully appreciate her.

The best gift my mother gave me was a gift that she didn't even have herself. She gave me and my sister a sense of self-worth. Who we were was who we were. What we wanted was important. What we cared about was interesting. She supported us no matter what and never made us feel like we were inferior or less than perfect. We were always enough and always worthy of her love. As a result, we knew we deserved to be treated well and so the people we invited into our lives were good people. We were confident to try new things and take risks.

It speaks volumes about who my mother was as a person that she could give us this gift. She could reach so deep within herself that she gave us something she never experienced. She transcended her limitations, and for that, I am eternally grateful. Thank you, Mom.

Practice:

1. In your journal, write about your mother. What was her childhood like? What was her greatest struggle? How did your mother shape you? What are you grateful to your mother for?

2. If your mother is still alive, tell her. Ask her questions about her life.

. . . .
Day 143: Papers
Habit: Home Simplicity

I have so much paperwork. I'm afraid my paperwork has paperwork.

—Aldous Ghent in *Elsewhere,* Gabrielle Zevin

Breathe. You are not the only one drowning in paperwork. We all are, and some portion of your scarce mental resources is being spent worrying about it. If your paperwork is out of control at home or at the office, this is the day to tackle it so that you can have more energy for what's really important to you. I encourage you to search online for "how to organize my paperwork" because there are a lot of people out there who love to organize and share their systems.

Practice:

1. Collect your paperwork. Bring all your loose paperwork together into your inbox.

2. Organize into trash, shred, scan, file, and action required piles.

3. Process your inbox. After trashing and shredding, file papers into their appropriate hanging folders. Scan and electronically file documents. Scanning is my favorite paperwork organization tool. I scan paid bills, receipts, articles. You name it. I scan it. I only keep the original documents for the really important stuff: marriage and birth certificates, titles, social security cards, and such.

5. Take action. What remains should be paperwork that needs to be addressed: bills that need to be paid, phone calls that need to be made, etc. Put important dates on your calendar now, and pay bills that need to be paid.

6. Ongoing: Choose a schedule that allows you to keep up with your paperwork. I review mine on the twelfth and the twenty-eighth of each month, so no bills fall through the cracks.

7. If you have piles of old paperwork, sit down once a week to review just one old folder or drawer. Can it be trashed, shredded, scanned? Return your necessary paperwork to the drawer.

Day 144: Charity Research, Level 3: Impact Evaluation
Habit: Philanthropy

*It's more rewarding to watch money change the world
than to watch it accumulate.*
—Gloria Steinem, 1986 letter to the editor of *People*

Do you want your donation to actually make a difference? Then ask these five questions designed by Sean Standard-Stockton of Tactical Philanthropy.[37]

1. *On what research or evidence did the charity design its programs?* Do they know what other people in their field are doing and what their results are? What does the research in their field show? Are they trying something new? Why?

2. *What information does the charity collect about the results of its programs?* Do they know how many people they've helped or how the situation has improved after their help?

3. *How does the charity systematically analyze the information it collects?* How and when do they review the data they're collecting above? Don't expect smaller charities to do the same in-depth tracking and analysis as large charities.

4. *How has the charity adjusted its activities in response to new information?* Discover what a charity has learned over the years and what they do differently now.

5. *Does the charity have an absolute focus on producing results?* Do they focus as much on the program results as fundraising and marketing?

Practice:

1. Choose a charity from day 137 or choose a new one to research further.

2. On what research or evidence did the charity design its programs?

3. What information does the charity collect about the results of its programs?

4. How does the charity systematically analyze the information it collects?

5. Does the charity have an absolute focus on producing results?

6. Does this information change your desire to donate to this charity? Do you need to do more research?

Week 21

Day 145: Bulk It Up
Habit: Physical Health

Cooking is at once child's play and adult joy.
And cooking done with care is an act of love.
—Craig Claiborne, *Craig Claiborne's Kitchen Primer*

If cooking and cleaning up after cooking every night is overwhelming, don't cook every night! Whenever possible, I make an extra large batch of dinner. We eat the leftovers for lunches or dinners for the next couple days.

The freezer is also an amazing tool for helping you provide healthy, home-cooked meals. You can always make a double or triple batch of dinner and then pop the extra into the freezer. This way you can accumulate a few extra meals that can be pulled out in case of emergencies.

Or you can have a "Freezer Day" where you spend several hours one day cooking a month's worth of meals that are frozen in dinner-sized portions. It's a lot of cooking and a lot of cleanup, but then you're done for the rest of the month. Enlist two or three friends in a Freezer Day swap where you trade some of your frozen meals, and then you'll get even more variety in your monthly freezer meals.

Practice:

1. Have you been successful in cooking more often? If not, what's stopping you? What reward can you give yourself to motivate you to cook more until cooking becomes part of your normal routine?

2. Review the strategies in day 116, "The Essential Pantry," and today's post and develop a plan for cooking more meals from home this week.

. . . .
Day 146: Emotional Pain Meditation
Habit: Mindfulness

Our feelings are our most genuine paths to knowledge.
—Audre Lorde, *Conversations with Audre Lorde*

Negative emotions are part of the human experience, but they can become a problem when they cause suffering long past the event that triggered them.

Practice:

1. Sit quietly as you recall a past experience that causes you pain. Don't judge it or push it away. Observe yourself responding to the memory. Describe the emotion you are feeling. What sensations do you notice in your body? Touch the part of your body that is hurting with this memory, acknowledge what you are feeling, and then breathe. Imagine saying to the

pain, "May you feel peace. May you be happy." Feel it release with each exhale. Love yourself for being brave enough to face your pain.

2. Continue with your pain journal. You may jump ahead to day 154 if you want to review it now.

. . . .
Day 147: Five-Minute Favor
Habit: Relationships

Good actions give strength to ourselves,
and inspire good actions in others.
—Samuel Smiles, *Duty*

If you find yourself spending so much time helping others that you don't have enough time and energy for yourself, Adam Rifkin's five-minute favor can be just the tool you need to balance giving to others and taking care of yourself.[38]

He suggests that if helping someone will take less than five minutes, go for it. A lot can be done in five minutes, but if it's going to take longer than five minutes, it's okay to say that you'd love to help if you had the time.

Practice:

Say yes or volunteer for an opportunity to help that will take less than five minutes.

Day 148: Role Models
Habit: Connecting with Yourself

Lives of great men all remind us
We can make our lives sublime,
And, departing, leave behind us
Footprints on the sands of time.
—Henry Wadsworth Longfellow, "A Psalm of Life"

Role models not only let you know what is possible, but they provide clues that you can follow to find your own success. Remember these people are still human and flawed, so don't expect them to be perfect. But the success they've achieved in one area can help you create that same success in your life.

Practice:

1. In your journal, create a list of people who live the kind of life you want to have, who express the kind of confidence you want to feel, who have accomplished things you want to achieve, who are the kind of person you want to be, and who have overcome a problem you are struggling with. Choose one of these people. In what ways is this person your role model? What do they have, do, and express that you want?

2. If you can, interview this person. If not, read about them and imagine what they have struggled with to get, do, or be who they are. Are their struggles similar to your struggles? What steps did they follow or actions did they take to achieve this? What would your life be like if you were more like this person?

3. Print a photo of this person and place it in a prominent place to remind you that what you want is possible, that someone else has done it, and that you can do it, too.

· ·
Day 149: Gratitude Rampage
Habit: Gratitude

Gratitude unlocks the fullness of life. It turns what we have into enough, and more. It turns denial into acceptance, chaos to order, confusion to clarity. It can turn a meal into a feast, a house into a home, a stranger into a friend.
—Melody Beattie, *The Language of Letting Go*

There is so much to say thank you for and so little time. Today, go on a gratitude rampage and thank as many people, objects, technologies as possible. Nothing is off limits. If it makes your life better, thank it. If it has positive qualities, thank it.

On your mark. Get set. Go!

Practice:

Starting in your home, thank all the people who make your life better. Feel grateful to your spouse, your children, your parents. Thank all the technologies that make your life better on a daily basis. Then moving out in an expanding circle, identify who and what you're grateful for in your neighborhood. Expand the circle to include your city. Who and what can you feel grateful for in your city? Expand again to include your entire state. Who and what can you feel grateful for in your state? What about your country, the world, the universe? Feel your connection to everyone and everything and thank it.

. . . .
Day 150: Monthly Check-In

To be what we are, and to become
what we are capable of becoming, is the only end of life.
—Robert Louis Stevenson, *Familiar Studies of Men and Books*

Time to check in on your progress. This is not a guilt-inducing exercise designed to shame you for all you haven't accomplished yet. Instead, it's a gentle reminder about what's important to you and what you want to change.

Enjoy the journey. Be gentle with yourself. Keep growing.

Practice:

- What did I do last month that I'm proud of?
- Are my relationships with others improving or deteriorating?
- What do I need to do less of/quit/get rid of/delegate this month?
- What experiments did I try? What lessons did I learn? What is going well?
- What isn't working, and what do I want to change?
- Habit to focus on next month:
- Why do I want to establish that habit?
- What is a first step I can take toward making this a habit?
- What trigger will I use?

- How will I reward myself?
- What obstacles will I face in establishing this habit and how will I overcome them?
- Notes on successes, long-term goals, and personal changes I'm working toward:

· · · · · · · · · · · · · · · ·
Day 151: Humility
Habit: Mind Simplicity

On the highest throne in the world,
we still sit only on our own bottom.
—Michel de Montaigne, *Essays*

Humility allows you to focus on what's most important because you know you are no better and no worse than anyone else. Humility helps you learn because you can admit you don't know. Humility helps you take action because you know you need to start somewhere. Humility keeps you moving forward despite setbacks because you don't expect yourself to be perfect.

Practice:

1. In your journal, write about who has helped you. Look at your family, your friends, and your community. Where do you get support, information, and resources? Look at the world around you. What part do you play in the world? What do you need? What limitations are there on your abilities and knowledge? Where have you refused to help because

you felt you're better than that? What have you strived for because you're trying to be better than someone else?

2. Go out of your way to help someone today. If you receive praise for your actions, accept it graciously, acknowledge those who contributed to the outcome, and refuse to entertain the belief that you are better than anyone else or above doing what needs to be done.

. . . .

Day 152: Charity Research, Level 4: Financial Research
Habit: Philanthropy

Love is an activity, not a passive affect; it is a "standing in,"
not a "falling for." In the most general way, the active character
of love can be described by stating that love is primarily giving,
not receiving.
—Erich Fromm, *The Art of Loving*

There is a range of documents that charities may file to account for their annual financial information. The steps below will help you evaluate any charity's financial situation.

Practice:

1. Use the charity from day 144 or choose a new one to research further.

2. Visit www.guidestar.org, search for the charity, and click the "Financials" menu option. (You may need to create a free account.) Does the charity file 990s?

a. If no, call and ask the charity, "Where does your income come from? Approximately how much income do you have? How do you spend it? Approximately how much are your expenses? How has your financial situation changed over the past few years? How do you feel about the financial future of your charity?"

b. If yes, review the last three years. What patterns do you notice? Is revenue going up or down (line 12)? Do they typically run a deficit (line 19)? Do they have assets to withstand tough times (line 22)? Are they heavy on a primary funding source that could leave them vulnerable if those sources dried up (Section VIII, and for large donors/private foundations check Schedule B, Part 1). In other words, you're trying to understand how stable they are. Are there at least five board members, most of whom are not paid (Section VII)? A large board that is not financially invested in the success of the charity is a good indication of strength and stability.

3. Does this information change your desire to donate to this charity? Do you need to do more research?

Week 22
· · · · · · · · · ·

Day 153: The Right Diet
Habit: Physical Health

Life is too short for self-hatred and celery sticks.
—Marilyn Wann, *Fat! So?*

Atkins, South Beach, Paleo, vegetarian, vegan, DASH, blood type, GAPS, macrobiotic, Mediterranean, Zone, gluten free—there's always a new diet fad promising to be the one that finally gets it right.

Will any of these work for you? I don't know. Some are complete bunk. Some contain kernels of truth. Some work for some people and not for others.

As a general rule, a diet that makes you feel restricted or deprived will not last. Instead, adopt a food lifestyle that allows you to eat healthy meals that you enjoy on a regular basis. Since your body changes over time, you may initially feel great eating one way, but at some point you can reach a weight plateau or suddenly have less energy.

Put your detective hat on to see if changing your regular food choices changes how you feel. Finding the right way for you to eat is part of your life's journey, and you may need to revisit your food choices periodically as you age.

Practice:

1. In your journal, write about how your food choices have changed over the past several months. Are you noticing any changes in your body or energy levels? Are they improving your ability to be there for others? What healthy practices are easier for you to do on a regular basis? What changes do you still want to make?

2. What one will you work on next? How will you do it (trigger, routine, reward)?

. . . .
Day 154: Practice with Physical Pain
Habit: Mindfulness

Mental pain is less dramatic than physical pain, but it is more common and also more hard to bear. The frequent attempt to conceal mental pain increases the burden: it is easier to say "My tooth is aching" than to say "My heart is broken."
—C. S. Lewis, *The Problem of Pain*

Physical pain is an opportunity to practice staying present even when it's not easy, so when emotional difficulty comes your way, you'll be better able to help yourself and others.

Practice:

1. Review your pain journal. What patterns are you noticing? Do you experience pain at specific times or after specific activities like eating a meal or exercising? Is your pain triggered

by stressful events in your life? Does your emotional state add to your pain? Does your pain help you avoid dealing with a situation you don't really want to deal with? What alleviates the pain? When is your pain the worst? When is it the least? What have you learned about your pain? What adjustments or new techniques do you want to make or try to see if they diminish the amount of pain you are feeling? If you are dealing with chronic pain, continue with your pain journal for as long as is necessary. Understanding your pain (what triggers it, how long it lasts, what it responds to, etc.) will drastically improve the quality of your life.

2. Practice the physical pain meditation from day 139.

. . . .
Day 155: Get Curious
Habit: Relationships

You can make more friends in two months by becoming interested in other people than you can in two years by trying to get other people interested in you.
—Dale Carnegie, *How to Win Friends and Influence People*

You know what everyone's favorite subject is? Themselves! Every person has hobbies, interests, experiences, beliefs, and possessions that are important to them, and when you take an interest in what's important to them, they feel that they as an individual must be important to you, too.

Practice:

Who do you want to learn more about? Find time to talk. Get to know them better by asking questions like these: How do you spend most of your time? What makes you laugh? If you had an extra hour per day, how would you spend it? If you could go anywhere on vacation, where would it be?

. . . .
Day 156: Something New
Habit: Connecting with Yourself

Change is not merely necessary to life—it is life.
—Alvin Toffler, *Future Shock*

In order for your life to change, something new must come into it or something new must come out of you. Don't wait around for something or someone new. Instead, focus on something new you can bring to your life that comes from inside *you*. Bring more enthusiasm. Bring a different perspective or a positive attitude. Bring a desire to serve people in whatever way they need your help. Bring curiosity, laughter, and a sense of humor.

When all this goodness comes *out* of you, you may be surprised at what new people and opportunities come into your life.

Practice:

1. In your journal, ask yourself, "What character trait do I want to bring more of to my daily life? Is there a particular situation that would improve if I brought more love and understanding?"

2. Perform a random act of kindness, like complimenting a stranger or gifting an iTunes song.

. . . .
Day 157: Fathers
Habit: Gratitude

I believe that what we become depends on what our fathers
teach us at odd moments, when they aren't trying to teach us.
We are formed by little scraps of wisdom.
—Umberto Eco, *Foucault's Pendulum*

You know what I love most about my dad? His playfulness. When we were kids, we were always doing stuff. He'd take us hiking, ice-skating, Christmas tree hunting. I remember he bought this huge role of butcher paper, and he would roll out these big sheets for us to drawn on. But we couldn't *just* draw on them. We'd have to try drawing with our left hands or drawing while blindfolded.

My dad taught me to love animals. We were the only kids on the block to have pet ducks follow us around. I remember one time when he found a litter of baby mice after clearing up a brush pile, and he brought the mice inside. We nursed those mice until they could be released back into the wild.

He was always asking "What if?" and "Why?" and pointing out little things we might never notice. Our little imaginations would light up with these questions, and he gifted me with an insatiable curiosity and appreciation for nature.

Practice:

1. In your journal, write about your father. What was his childhood like? What was his greatest struggle? How did your father shape you? What are you grateful to your father for?

2. If your father is still alive, tell him. Ask him about his life.

. . . .
Day 158: Get Things Done
Habit: Schedule Simplicity

Clutter is postponed decisions.
—Barbara Hemphill, *Taming the Paper Tiger at Work*

Keeping your word to yourself by finishing what you start and taking care of your business is critical to your ability to feel good about yourself and to move forward with confidence. If you have things piling up, this process may help.

1. *Collect:* Write down and collect all the undone things you need to catch up on.

2. *Eliminate:* Do you really need to do this? If you don't need it, then delete it, trash it, or cross it off the list. Make this your first choice.

3. *Delegate:* Are you the person who should be doing this? Can someone else handle it?

4. *Do:* If the task will take two minutes or less, just do it.

5. *Defer:* If it will take more than two minutes, add it to your to-do list.

6. *File:* If it's just something you need for reference, file it, scan it, or archive it.

7. *Do:* Go back to your deferred tasks. What is the most important task? What can you do right now on that project that will move it forward?

Repeat this process whenever you're feeling overwhelmed and need to catch up. Your brain will rest better knowing that you know what needs to be done and when it will get done.

Practice:

Is there an undone item on your to-do list that you'll feel better getting done? What is one action you can take to move that project toward completion?

. . . .
Day 159: Month 6 Giving Challenge: Food Bank
Habit: Philanthropy

The war against hunger is mankind's war of liberation.
—John F. Kennedy, 1963 speech to World Food Congress

There are 15.8 million American children who suffer from the life-long consequences of food insecurity. Their growing bodies and minds are damaged by insufficient nutrients, stunting their physical and intellectual growth. They also suffer emotionally. Hungry children find it difficult to focus and excel in school. As our nation's economic growth depends on the well-being of our children, the existence of childhood hunger in the United States threatens future American prosperity while robbing them of the opportunity to reach their full potential.

Your food bank is an incredibly important organization, and a donation to your local food bank goes right back into your community. What amazes me most about food banks is how incredibly efficient they are! A ten-dollar donation to your food bank can purchase forty pounds of food. That's equivalent to thirty meals! Here, a small donation really can make a big impact.

Practice:

Visit your local food bank's website and make an online donation of any amount or volunteer to stock their shelves.

Week 23

Day 160: Try a New Veggie
Habit: Physical Health

The greatest delight which the fields and woods minister is the
suggestion of an occult relation between man and the vegetable.
—Ralph Waldo Emerson, *Nature*

When I moved to Georgia, I had never eaten okra. When I joined my local community-supported agriculture program, they sent me a bag of okra—for several weeks in a row. Here's what I learned about okra: It's slimy. The more you chop it, the slimier it gets. Two things reduce the sliminess: oil and vinegar. That's why Southerners love it fried and pickled. I tried it fried, in gumbo and in pasta sauce. Nope, not liking the okra. I went a different direction and tried bhindi masala, an Indian curry, and it wasn't bad. Then I discovered whole okra, fresh tomatoes, corn, olive oil, and salt roasted it in a 400-degree oven and served with a filet of roasted catfish. Mind blown. Okra is so good this way that I don't know why anyone would eat it any other way!

Adding more vegetables to your diet is a sure way to add all those things your body thrives on: fiber, vitamins, minerals, and antioxidants. In addition to favorites like potatoes, carrots, and corn, there's a plethora of leafy greens to enjoy: collards, kale, mustard, watercress, arugula, chard, and spinach. The *Brassica* genus is powerfully nutritious and delicious with its cabbage, Brussels sprouts, broccoli, cauliflower, rutabaga, turnips, and kohlrabi. Explore the wild world of vegetables!

Practice:

1. How much plant-based food do you eat (fruit, vegetable, grain, or bean)? What is one vegetable you've never tried but will try this week?

2. Search online and choose three different recipes, like stir fries or soups, that use a lot of vegetables. Choose one to prepare tonight.

. . . .
Day 161: Dig a Well
Habit: Mindfulness

I wish that life should not be cheap, but sacred.
I wish the days to be as centuries, loaded, fragrant.
—Ralph Waldo Emerson, *The Conduct of Life*

As you experiment with different meditation styles, it's like digging a hole for a fence post. You try this technique for a little while, and you dig a few feet deep. Then you stop and try another technique. Then you've got another hole that's a few feet deep. Then you try another and another, and now you've got a straight line of shallow holes perfect for building a fence.

Instead, think of your meditation practice like digging a well. The more effort you expend in one place, the deeper you'll go and the more benefits you'll experience. Experiment, but eventually, you'll want to choose a meditation style and stick with it, digging deeper and deeper. You'll move away the rocks and the dirt until you have a deep well that provides life-sustaining water.

Practice:

1. In your journal, write about what you've enjoyed about your meditation. What have you struggled with? What changes have you noticed in yourself or how you interact with others?

2. Continue meditating for ten minutes *every* day.

. . . .
Day 162: The Wrong People
Habit: Relationships

We cannot tell the precise moment when friendship is formed.
As in filling a vessel drop by drop, there is at last a drop which
makes it run over; so in a series of kindnesses there is at last
one which makes the heart run over.
—James Boswell, *The Life of Samuel Johnson, LL.D.*

Being vulnerable and connecting with others does not mean doing so without discretion, because some people can't be trusted. Not everyone needs or wants to know all of your business. To avoid oversharing, ask first, "Is this mine to share? Why am I sharing this with this specific person? What am I looking for here?" Be cautious if you're sharing because you're seeking approval or looking to reduce your anxiety.

Always be you, but share yourself in stages. You can let people know that you're dealing with difficult situations without revealing all the gory details. As confidants prove themselves worthy, share more. When they show themselves to be unworthy, stand up for yourself and communicate your hurt. Never reward negative behavior.

Practice:

1. In your journal, consider these questions: Who in your life is treating you badly? How have you tolerated or rewarded this behavior?

2. Invite someone out for coffee, lunch, or drinks to get to know them better.

. . . .
Day 163: Prepared for Anything
Habit: Connecting with Yourself

Life is not lost by dying! Life is lost
Minute by minute, day by dragging day,
In all the thousand, small, uncaring ways.
—Stephen Vincent Benét, *A Child Is Born*

Not knowing how long we will live is a double-edged sword. On the one hand, it's kind of nice not to know; on the other, we can be lulled by the thought that we will have all the time we need. The trick is to balance the knowledge that no future moment is promised with the knowledge that we could live a long life. Balance actions that make every moment count with actions that provide for a long, happy life.

Practice:

1. In your journal, write about what you would do if you only had a month to live. What needs to be said, done, shared, resolved? What if you had a year left to live? Five years left to live? Twenty years left to live?

2. Choose something from this list and do it.

. . . .

Day 164: Thank Your Body
Habit: Gratitude

There is more reason in your body
than in your deepest wisdom.
—Friedrich Nietzsche, *Thus Spoke Zarathustra*

BODIES… The Exhibition is a traveling exhibit of preserved human bodies that have been dissected to display different bodily systems and health conditions. I walked this exhibit in awe of the complicated and amazing human body.

Some exhibits were a single organ or a related group of tissues, and some were the entire body. In one, a man was posed as if he was playing tennis—the tendons stretched and the muscles contracted in anticipation of striking the ball. In another, portions of the torso were pulled out as if they were dresser drawers revealing remarkable tightly packed organs, blood vessels, and fat.

Practice:

1. Whatever your health challenges, your body is still amazing and still doing a lot for you. Your lungs move in and out without you thinking about it, and your beating heart moves blood through your lungs, delivering oxygen to every cell in your body. Your legs take you where you want to go. Your feet help you balance. Your hands, your ears, your eyes, your nose, and your brain all serve vital functions. In your mind, touch each part of your body, and appreciate it for its amazing design and the work it does for you.

2. Treat your body to a random act of kindness, like a massage or a tall glass of cold water.

· ·

Day 165: Discover Something New about
Something You Already Know
Habit: Nature Simplicity

A lifetime can be spent in a Magellanic voyage
around the trunk of a single tree.
—Edward O. Wilson, *Naturalist*

There is probably no creature on earth more common than the ant. Not only do they appear on every single continent in the world (except Antarctica), but there are an estimated 1.5 million ants for every single person on this planet. Do you know that ants farm colonies of aphids and fungi? Or that they enslave and war with ants of other colonies or species? [39]

Ants serve important roles in the environment. Their tunnels aerate soil and bring nutrients back up to the surface. They disperse seeds, helping plants thrive in new environments. And maybe best of all, they dine on all kinds of bugs we don't like having around, including fly larvae, fleas, bedbugs, and cockroaches. They've even been known to keep termites at bay.

Practice:

1. Search the Internet for a creature that is ordinary to you. What don't you know about it? How does it live? What does it eat? How does it procreate? What purpose does it serve in the environment?

2. Perform a generous action for your local environment, such as stopping the delivery of paper statements, using less fertilizer on your lawn, or only running the dishwasher when full.

. . . .
Day 166: Calling the Charity
Habit: Philanthropy

Instead of exhorting you to Augment your Charity, I will rather utter an Exhortation, or at least a Supplication, that you may not abuse your Charity by misapplying it.
—Cotton Mather, *Magnalia Christi Americana*

A charity's website is a carefully crafted message, and a conversation can reveal more about who they really are. Are they organized enough to return phone calls? Are they professional and passionate? How well do they talk about their charity, their work, and their accomplishments?

When I call a charity, I ask questions like these:

+ How do you know what you're doing works?
+ What are you planning to accomplish this year?
+ How has your organization changed over the years?

Before I call, I've reviewed their website, their financials, and searched online for any criticisms of their charity. Sometimes, this review will create its own questions.

+ Last year, your expenses were significantly higher than the year before. What was that due to?
+ I noticed your website hasn't been updated for eight months. What activities and accomplishments are happening now?

Practice:

Choose a charity you are currently supporting or considering supporting. Call them. What do you discover about them that you didn't already know?

Week 24

Day 167: Just Say No Once
Habit: Physical Health

There is a certain degree of temptation
which will overcome any virtue.

—Samuel Johnson, quoted in *The Life of Samuel Johnson, LL.D.*

In many homes, one person makes most of the food decisions. According to Brian Wansink, PhD, of the Applied Economics and Management Department at Cornell University and director of the Cornell Food and Brand Lab, this "nutritional gatekeeper" accounts for 72 percent of all of the family's food decisions—and not just for food consumed in the home. The nutritional gatekeeper also influences school lunches, snacks, and eating out.[40]

The nutritional gatekeeper can wield this power for good and close the gate to unhealthy food choices. One of the easiest places to do that is at the grocery store where you only have to say no once: "No, I'm not buying that bag of chips." Once the chips are home, you have to say no over and over again. And I don't know about you, but I just don't have that much willpower.

Make it easier to make good food choices on a regular basis by keeping the unhealthy foods out of your home as much as possible.

Practice:

1. Who is the nutritional gatekeeper for your home?

2. Empower your nutritional gatekeeper to make healthy choices for the home.

3. List three items the nutritional gatekeeper should keep out of the home.

· ·
Day 168: Walking Meditation
Habit: Mindfulness

I only went out for a walk, and finally concluded to stay out till sundown, for going out, I found, was really going in.
—John Muir, *John of the Mountains*

It can be easy to maintain a sense of calmness and serenity while sitting in silence with your eyes closed, but most of your life is spent in action with your eyes open.

A walking meditation is a meditation in action whose practice can help you walk through the world with more grace, dignity, and peacefulness no matter what is going on around you.

Practice:

1. Find a place near you where you can walk. You can walk around a room in a circle, up and down a flight of stairs, around your block, or through a park. In fact, you can practice a walking meditation anytime you are walking.

2. Bring your attention to the act of walking and not to the destination.

3. Walk slowly, being aware of each movement of your legs and arms and torso.

4. Imagine a lotus flower blooming as you place each foot upon the ground and in order to care for that flower, you must place your foot with lightness, peacefulness, and love.

5. Feel your connection with the earth as you place your foot, seeing the spherical earth appear underneath you with each step.

. . . .
Day 169: Send a Card
Habit: Relationships

Shall we make a new rule of life from tonight:
always to try to be a little kinder than is necessary?
—J. M. Barrie, *The Little White Bird*

When my aunt was diagnosed with lung cancer, I was heartbroken. Since I lived two thousand miles away, there wasn't much I could do for her. But I wanted to do something, so I went to the store and bought dozens of greeting cards—mostly humorous. The cancer moved quickly and the treatment was difficult, but each week she was alive, I faithfully dropped another card in the mail. I know it wasn't much, but at least I could let her know I was thinking of her and maybe bring a smile to her day.

Practice:
Send a greeting card to someone you love.

Day 170: Three Words
Habit: Connecting with Yourself

Far away in the sunshine are my highest aspirations.
I may not reach them, but I can look up and see their beauty,
believe in them, and try to follow where they lead.
—Louisa May Alcott, quoted in *Elbert Hubbard's Scrap Book*

Your highest self knows who it is and what to do in any situation, but it isn't always easy to hear it and act on its advice. There is no greater gift to yourself than to behave in a way that is consistent with your deepest values. This exercise inspired by Brendon Burchard may help you clarify and remind you of what you value and how to act.[41]

Practice:

1. What three words reflect the best qualities you want to bring to your life every day?

2. What three words capture how you want to engage with others?

3. Post these three words where you can see them on a regular basis or program an alarm on your phone to remind you of your three words.

Day 171: Even Cancer Has Gifts
Habit: Gratitude

The deeper that sorrow carves into your being,
the more joy you can contain.
—Kahlil Gibran, *The Prophet*

At first, I wasn't grateful for the cancer that was killing my mom, but I've had to admit that in addition to the pain, it gave me four important gifts.

1. Even though the remaining days were tinged with pain, she wasn't taken from us without warning. We could create new memories, reminisce, laugh, share, and love in the time we had left.

2. It opened my heart to accept my mom for all her strengths and flaws and gave us an opportunity to heal any lingering misunderstanding, alienation, or regret.

3. It completely transformed my relationship with my dad. I used to go months without calling him, and now we speak every couple of days.

4. It freed me from my fear of rejection. I could go at any moment, so I didn't have time to waste on being afraid of what people thought about me. I still feel that fear, but it doesn't stop me anymore. I just ask myself, "What would mom have done if she knew she was only going to live to 59?"

Practice:

1. In your journal, reflect on a difficult time you've gone through in the past. What did you learn from it? How did it make you a better person?

2. Perform a random act of courageous kindness today, like introducing yourself to a person you haven't met yet at work or coming to the rescue of someone in need.

. . . .
Day 172: Simplicity with Kids
Habit: Home Simplicity

And I learned what is obvious to a child. That life is simply a collection of little lives, each lived one day at a time.
—Nicholas Sparks, *The Notebook*

Life with kids is going to be far more complicated than life alone. Here are four principles to simplifying life with kids:

1. *Be the example.* The most powerful lessons your children learn are those you teach through your everyday actions, and your example is a silent invitation to your children to simplify.

2. *Discuss simplicity together.* Discovering how to simplify is a process and a conversation the whole family should participate in.

3. *Foster self-sufficiency.* Teach your children to take care of themselves and contribute to maintaining the home—even if it

takes more time to teach them than doing it yourself or if it means accepting a completed task that isn't as good as what you would have done.

4. *Enjoy simple pleasures.* Find simple ways to enjoy each other's company such as cooking, reading, or playing outside.

Practice:

1. In your journal, ask yourself these questions: How much of your busy life with your kids is because of you? How much of the clutter in your home is from things your children don't really need and don't use? Do you feel the need to impress other parents? Do you pack your children's schedule because you're afraid they'll miss out on something? Do you say yes when you should say no? Do you choose to do something yourself because it's easier than taking the time to teach your children?

2. If you have children, start a conversation about simplicity; otherwise, ask yourself questions like these: What's necessary here? Why do we own things? Why do we do things? How would we want to experience this? How can we enjoy this more with less? What's important in this situation?

3. For the next week, place a twenty-four-hour waiting period before buying anything that isn't essential. When you want to buy something, ask, "Where did the impulse to buy it come from?" Twenty-four hours later, ask, "What need will this purchase meet? Is it worth the money, space, and emotional energy?"

Day 173: The Overhead Ratio Myth
Habit: Philanthropy

*The most useful and influential people in [a country] are those
who take the deepest interest in institutions that exist for the
purpose of making the world better.*
—Booker T. Washington, *Up from Slavery*

Before donating, many people ask, "How much of my donation
goes to help people in need?" Theoretically, if less money is spent on
administrative costs like salaries, office space, and fundraising costs
(often referred to as the overhead ratio), then there's more being
spent directly on programs. And that means your donation would
make a bigger difference.

Unfortunately, it's not true. A donation can go 100 percent to
programs and still be 100 percent wasted. What if they're helping
people who don't need help at all, have already been helped, or do
need help but the program doesn't actually help? Charities need to
invest in tools, training, and research to do good work.

Ignore overhead ratio. Instead, use the charity research tools in
this book to find good charities doing good work. Focus on their impact, not on their expenses.

Practice:

1. Have you discovered a charity you are excited about supporting yet? If not, find three new candidates.

2. Make copies of the four-level Charity Evaluation Worksheet located in the appendix and use it to research any charity before you donate.

Week 25

$\bullet$ $\bullet$ $\bullet$ $\bullet$ $\bullet$ $\bullet$ $\bullet$ $\bullet$ $\bullet$ $\bullet$

Day 174: Energy for Life
Habit: Physical Health

*Physical fitness is not only one of the most important keys
to a healthy body; it is the basis of dynamic
and creative intellectual activity.*
—John F. Kennedy, "The Soft American"

Having enough energy improves your mood and helps you make better decisions.

Let's get technical for a moment. Inside your cells are little things known as mitochondria. Your mitochondria create adenosine triphosphate, or ATP, and ATP is the main source of energy for your body. It's what every cell in your body uses to do its job. Need to digest your lunch? Your intestines need ATP. Need to strategize about your company's upcoming merger? Your brain needs ATP. The more ATP you have, the better your body can do its job, the more energy you will have, and the better you will feel.

If your mitochondria are the source of your energy, then it makes sense to take care of them. Do you know what's good for mitochondria? Exercise! Scientists have shown that mitochondria need oxygen and nutrients to do their work, and physical activity pumps oxygen-rich blood to the mitochondria, creating more ATP and more energy.

You're not just being physically active for you. You're being physically active for your mitochondria.

Practice:

1. Your goal is ten minutes of physical activity *every* day. If you're not there yet, what is stopping you? Recommit to being physically active every single day. On days you don't want to, do something—anything—to move your body, like walking, stretching, or dancing.

2. How do you feel about your current level of physical activity? Are you ready to increase the difficulty of your exercise? What will you change or add to your physical activity?

. . . .
Day 175: Mindful Eating
Habit: Mindfulness

There is no love sincerer than the love of food.
—George Bernard Shaw, *Man and Superman*

Nourishing your body is an act love. Mindful eating helps you become more aware of your physical and emotional relationship with food.

Practice:

1. When it's time to eat, turn off the TV, walk away from the computer, put down your phone. Just eat.

2. Observe. What does the food look like on your plate? What colors and textures do you notice? How hungry are you right now? How do you feel about the food you're about to eat? What do you want this food to do for you?

3. Focus on each bite. After taking a bite, put your fork down. What is the sensation of food in your mouth? Hot, cold, heavy, smooth? What is the flavor? Sweet, salty, spicy, tangy, sour, savory? Can you identify any of the individual ingredients? Does it make any noise when you chew it? Do you like what you're eating or not? Don't judge if liking or not liking it is good or bad. Just notice that you do. Has your level of hunger changed at all? Has your emotional state changed? Do you want to eat another bite?

· · · · · · · · · · · · · · · · · · · ·
Day 176: Cluster Giving
Habit: Relationships

I do not believe one can settle how much we ought to give. I am afraid the only safe rule is to give more than we can spare.
—C. S. Lewis, *Mere Christianity*

Sonja Lyubomirsky, psychology professor at the University of California, wanted to know if how you give matters. In a study, one group of students was directed to perform five random acts of kindness in a day. Another group was asked to perform five random acts of kindness spread out throughout the week. The control group was not asked to perform any special acts. She discovered that random acts of kindness increased happiness levels only for the group of students who performed five acts in a single day.[42]

Practice:

1. Today perform five random acts of kindness. If you need ideas, search online, but don't limit yourself. You can create nearly any opportunity to bring a little joyous surprise to someone's day.

2. Then, in your journal, consider if doing five random acts of kindness felt better or worse than a single random act of kindness. Which acts of kindness did you enjoy? Which did you not enjoy?

. . . .
Day 177: Be Proud
Habit: Connecting with Yourself

I am not where I need to be,
but thank God I am not where I used to be.
—Joyce Meyer, *Approval Addiction*

There is no word in the English language for giving yourself credit in a powerful, respectful, and appropriate way. Instead, when we talk about our own achievements, we are bragging and boasting, and nice people just don't do that.

But a little bragging is good for you. It reminds you what you've accomplished and inspires you to keep doing great things. Plus, it feels good to celebrate. Doing great things should feel great, too.

Practice:

1. In your journal, write at least five responses for these three sentence-starters:

    I am proud that I have created …

    I am proud that I have achieved …

    I am proud that I am …

2. Share your answers with a trusted friend.

. . . .
Day 178: Stormy Waters
Habit: Gratitude

I am not afraid of storms, for I'm learning how to sail my ship.
—Amy in *Good Wives*, Louisa May Alcott

A lot of stuff happens in your life that you have no control over, and sometimes it can feel like a boat being carelessly tossed about by a storm. Sailors can't control Mother Nature, so they developed a wide range of tools to handle the waves.

- *Heaving-to:* By counterbalancing the foresail and the mainsail, they can slow their forward progress.
- *Lying a-hull:* Downing all sails, battening the hatches, and locking the tiller downwind, they can drift at the mercy of the storm.
- *Using an anchor:* They could throw an anchor over the bow to keep the boat stationary and their bow facing into the waves.

+ *Throwing a drogue:* Deploying a drogue from their stern, they can slow their speed and keep their hull perpendicular to the waves.

When you hit stormy waters, what are your resources?

Practice:

1. In your journal, consider the following questions: What beliefs do you have that can empower you to rise to the occasion? What have you learned from past experiences about weathering tough times? Who do you have in your life who helps you batten down the hatches? What financial, emotional, and spiritual resources can you call on?

2. Take a moment to appreciate that you have so many tools at your disposal.

3. Treat yourself to a random act of kindness today, like enjoying a piece of chocolate or a bubble bath.

. . . .
Day 179: Memories
Habit: Mind Simplicity

We do not know the true value of our moments
until they have undergone the test of memory.
—Georges Duhamel, *The Heart's Domain*

When my grandparents moved into a nursing home, we had to give or throw away most of their stuff. There was no room in their new home or in ours for it. But the memories of my grandparents only take up space in my heart. I remember that my grandma's special treat was to take us to Red Lobster. I remember my grandpa kept the refrigerator stocked with Yoohoo, and I loved running in after playing outside to pull out an ice-cold, chocolaty drink. At my grandparents' sixtieth wedding anniversary, I remember giving them a mixed CD I made of songs that they might have played at their wedding. My grandpa pulled out the CD, looked at it, turned it over, and asked, "What is this?" So then I had to go to the store and also buy them a CD player. I cherish these memories of my grandparents.

Practice:

1. In your journal, write about some of your favorite family memories. Share one with someone who will appreciate it.

2. What stuff of yours do you hope your loved ones will cherish? Is there a memory attached to this item? Write it down so your loved ones will understand what it meant to you.

3. What new memories do you want your loved ones to have with you? What can you do to create a memorable experience?

. . . .
Day 180: Monthly Check-In

Human improvement is from within outwards.
—James Anthony Froude, *Short Studies on Great Subjects*

Time to check in on your progress. This is not a guilt-inducing exercise designed to shame you for all you haven't accomplished yet. Instead, it's a gentle reminder about what's important to you and what you want to change.

Enjoy the journey. Be gentle with yourself. Keep growing.

Practice:

+ What did I do last month that I'm proud of?
+ Are my relationships with others improving or deteriorating?
+ What do I need to do less of/quit/get rid of/delegate this month?
+ What experiments did I try? What lessons did I learn? What is going well?
+ What isn't working, and what do I want to change?
+ Habit to focus on next month:
+ Why do I want to establish that habit?
+ What is a first step I can take toward making this a habit?
+ What trigger will I use?
+ How will I reward myself?
+ What obstacles will I face in establishing this habit and how will I overcome them?
+ Notes on successes, long-term goals, and personal changes I'm working toward:

. . . .
Day 181: How Do You Feel about Money?
Habit: Philanthropy

Riches are a good handmaid but the worst mistress.
—Francis Bacon, *De Augmentis Scientiarum*

Fundamentally, money is a tool. You receive money in exchange for your goods or your time. Then you use it to live. You use it to pay for shelter, buy clothes and food, care for your children, furnish your home.

But of course, money is much more than a tool, because we attach all kinds of meaning to it. The challenge is to use money well and put it in its rightful place as a servant to your greater good and a better world.

Practice:

1. In your journal, explore your feelings about money. Do you feel more important the more money you have? Do you always feel broke? Do you use money to influence or control people? Does your spouse feel different about money? What is your biggest fear about money? Growing up, what did your family feel, say, or argue about money? Did your family donate? How did your family feel and talk about donating? How has that influenced how you feel about donating? How much do you donate now? How often do you donate? What stops you from donating? What do you want to feel about money? What would feel good to believe? Who do you know who can be a role model on a healthy relationship with money?

2. Now that you've completed researching your charities, make a donation to the charity you like the best.

Week 26

Day 182: Breaking Bad (Habits)
Habit: Physical Health

To uproot an old habit is sometimes a more painful thing,
and vastly more difficult, than to wrench out a tooth.
—Samuel Smiles, *Self-Help*

In *The Power of Habit,* Charles Duhigg reveals the psychological framework of a habit. It's quite simple: trigger —> routine —> reward. Something has caused you to act in a certain way so you can get some kind of benefit.[43]

The secret to breaking a bad habit lies in understanding these components of your bad habit so you can reengineer it.

+ *Step 1:* What is the trigger? Where are you? What time is it? Who else is around? What action preceded the urge? What were you thinking or feeling physically and emotionally right before you engaged in the bad habit?
+ *Step 2:* What is the reward? What do you get out of it? Is it an emotional reward like companionship or a feeling of certainty? Does it release stress? Is it a physical reward like a burst of energy, a surge of dopamine, a sensation of movement? What

three words come to mind when you think about why you just did this?

+ *Step 3:* Design a new healthy routine that meets the reward you're getting from this bad habit.

+ *Step 4:* Experiment. It might take a few tries before you correctly identify your trigger (or all your triggers), your reward (or all your rewards), and a new routine that meets those rewards. After you try your new routine, wait fifteen minutes. How did that go? How do you feel? Is the urge still there?

Practice:

1. In your journal, write about a bad habit you want to change. What triggers your habit (i.e., what happens right before you start your bad habit)? What reward do you get from doing your bad habit?

2. Design a new routine that will you give you the same reward but with less harmful consequences.

. . . .
Day 183: Shhhhh
Habit: Mindfulness

*See how nature, the trees, the flowers, and the grass
grow in perfect silence. See how the stars, the moon,
and the sun, how they move in silence. . . .
We need silence to be able to touch souls.*
—Mother Teresa, *Contemplative in the Heart of the World*

Several years ago, I observed Noble Silence during a seven-day meditation retreat. I was dreading it, but I discovered that there is a reason why every religious practice includes silence. Your soul exists before and outside of language. In silence, you can commune with it and hear it in the many different ways it is communicating with you.

Practice:

1. Experiment with a short period of Noble Silence. Choose how long you'll remain silent, and then turn off the radio, the phone, the television. Don't write, don't read, don't surf the Net. Keep still. Listen to the sounds around you. What do you hear? What do you see? Open your eyes, open your ears, open your heart. Perform tasks that don't require you to use words, and observe the details of the act as if it's the first time you've done it. Breathe deeply.

2. Maintain the spirit of silence for the rest of the day. When you speak, do so briefly and quietly, and speak only words that will enhance the silence.

. . . .
Day 184: Judging
Habit: Relationships

You never really understand a person until you consider things from his point of view—until you climb into his skin and walk around in it.
—Atticus Finch in *To Kill a Mockingbird*, Harper Lee

Judging gets a bad rap, but it's actually quite useful. Judging is information gathering. It helps you make sense of the world and clarify how you want to live.

It gets tricky when you've gathered this information about what's right and wrong for you and decided that it's right and wrong for others, too. Now judging becomes controlling. It's used to fix people, to get them to think like you, and to get them to act like you.

When I feel that judging angst rise up in my chest, I tell myself, "Not my circus. Not my monkey." Somehow, it reminds me that my path is not their path, and it gives me permission to respect their journey.

Practice:

1. In your journal, answer these questions: Who are you trying to fix? What do you think they're doing wrong? Why is that wrong for your own life? How could this be useful for them? How can you show respect for their journey, their choices, their life?

2. Perform a random act of kindness today, like giving a compliment, inviting someone to lunch, or spreading the word about someone's fundraising effort, art show, or business.

. . . .
Day 185: Desire
Habit: Connecting with Yourself

It seems to me we can never give up longing and wishing
while we are thoroughly alive. There are certain things we feel
to be beautiful and good, and we must hunger after them.
—Phillip Wakem in *The Mill on the Floss*, George Eliot

It's good to want things. I'm talking about soul wanting. I'm talking about a deep yearning that pulls you toward something beautiful or something more or something better in your life. Whether or not you achieve what you desire is irrelevant right now. Instead, embrace your desire. Imagine it, describe it, bring it alive with luscious details. Let your desire envelop you and get your juices flowing.

Practice:

1. In your journal, write at least five responses to the following sentence-starters.

    I desire to have …

    I desire to achieve …

    I desire to be …

2. Treat yourself to a random act of kindness today, such as starting a new book, taking a yoga class, or going to the movie theater.

Day 186: Gadget Gratitude
Habit: Gratitude

I would maintain that thanks are the highest form of thought;
and that gratitude is happiness doubled by wonder.
—G. K. Chesterton, *A Short History of England*

You can find my favorite gadget in my kitchen. It's an electric teakettle, and it boils water in about thirty seconds. I know it doesn't sound very exciting, but I love this gadget.

I use my electric teakettle no less than three times every single day. I start my morning with a cup of black tea that I sweeten with a little bit of sugar and lighten with a heavy splash of milk. My morning cup of tea is worth getting out of bed for. In the afternoon, I'll have an afternoon pick-me-up of green tea, and at night, I brew a pot of peppermint tea to relax with. Tea is an integral component of my life, and sometimes I think I enjoy everything better with a cup of tea in my hand.

Practice:

What is your favorite gadget? How does it make your life better? Go to this gadget. Examine it. Does it need any care or maintenance? Take a moment to appreciate it and thank it for its service to you.

Day 187: A Pale Blue Dot
Habit: Schedule Simplicity

Astronomy, as nothing else can do, teaches men humility.
—Arthur C. Clarke, "The Star of Bethlehem"

In the *Pale Blue Dot*, Carl Sagan reflects on our place in the universe through a photo of Earth taken millions of miles away. This image of a pale blue dot suspended in a beam of light reminds him of the triviality of human conceits and delusions of grandeur, so he can focus on what's really important.

Practice:

1. In your journal, imagine yourself looking down on your life from space. How do you feel about your life? Are you spending time on what's most important to you? What is one thing you want to spend more time on? What is one thing you want to spend less time on?

2. Spend ten minutes today on an activity you want to spend more time doing and ten minutes less on something you don't.

Day 188: Month 7 Giving Challenge: Social Justice
Habit: Philanthropy

The arc of the moral universe is long
but it bends toward justice.
—Martin Luther King Jr., "Keep Moving from This Mountain"

Martin Luther King Jr. spoke of a dream. It's a dream that many of us share. It's a world where everyone has equal economic, political, and social opportunities regardless of their race, gender, religion, national origin, or sexual orientation.

The world is more just than it used to be, but there is still much injustice to address. In America, racial disparities in law enforcement mean people of color are more likely to be pulled over, arrested, and convicted of crimes. In other countries, dictators oppress entire populations, depriving them of economic and political opportunity. In communities around the world, men and women live in fear for their lives because of their sexuality, their gender, or their religion.

The arc of the moral universe only bends toward justice because people like you take action to make it so.

Practice:

1. What injustice in the world gets you fired up? Slavery, racial or gender inequality, LGBT discrimination, political or religious oppression, treatment of animals?

2. Read an article on the issue.

3. Find a charity working on that cause and sign up for their newsletter.

Week 27

Day 189: Water Is Life
Habit: Physical Health

Water is the only drink for a wise man.
—Henry David Thoreau, *Walden*

Every system in your body depends on water to perform every major function. Water flushes toxins out of your vital organs, through your kidneys, and out of your body. Water dissolves nutrients into small molecules capable of being absorbed by your cells and helps your blood cells deliver those nutrients. Water digests food, lubricates your joints, and regulates your body temperature. Your brain needs even more water because water conducts the electrical signals and chemicals that run your body.

Even mild dehydration causes headaches, drowsiness, and constipation. Severe dehydration can cause palpitations, confusion, seizures, fainting, and eventually death.

How much water you need depends on your level of activity, your age, your percent of body fat, your general health, your diet, and the temperature and humidity of the air around you. Try to drink enough to not feel thirsty and to keep your urine a light yellow.

Practice:

1. How much water do you consume on a daily basis?

2. What health issues do you have that impact how much water you should consume?

3. Do you want to drink more water? What trigger, routine, and reward system will you use (day 44)?

. . . .

Day 190: Physical Body Impermanence Meditation
Habit: Mindfulness

The sun shines not on us but in us.
—John Muir, *John of the Mountains*

Your human body is impermanent and temporary.

Practice:

Close your eyes and take a few centering breaths. As you pay attention to your breath, feel your chest rising and falling. Feel your butt and legs pressing against the ground. Feel your spine holding you upright. Feel the weight of your head as it's balanced on top of your body. Now go deeper. Feel all the bones that make up your body. Feel your heart, stomach, lungs in constant motion that power your body. Go smaller. Feel the blood cells and the white blood cells circulating through your body. Feel the cells that make up your skin, tissue, and organs. Feel that within those cells are organelles that help the cell function, and those organelles are made up of atoms, which are made up of subatomic particles: protons, neutrons, and electrons. At this very moment neutrinos and radio waves are passing through you as if you didn't even exist. Although the surface of your body appears stable and solid, within your body is a constant activity of living, dying, working, and reproducing. Reflect on how this dance in your body began from the moment of your conception, has continued without stopping until this very moment, and will continue until your death. But even though it hasn't stopped, it has changed. As you age, the cells perform different functions, guiding your physical body from fetus to infant to child to teenager to adult to senior. As you age, the cells function less effectively. What does it mean to you that your body changes every single moment? What does the inevitable decline of your physical body mean to you? What are some positive ways you can use this understanding?

· · · · · · · · · · · · · · · · · ·
Day 191: Following Up
Habit: Relationships

In giving, a man receives more than he gives,
and the more is in proportion to the worth of the thing given.
—George MacDonald, *Mary Marston*

Nothing lets people know they are important to you like following up on your past interactions. For example, taking note of a conversation about a favorite author can give you an opportunity to forward an article about the author's next book or local book signing. Or if you know your spouse really enjoys good beer or good chocolate, surprise them with a six pack or a gourmet chocolate bar.

Notice what people around you are doing and enjoying, then look for opportunities to follow up on it.

Practice:

Who do want to make feel special today? What is important to them or what do they enjoy? How can you follow up on it?

. . . .
Day 192: Better Than Perfect
Habit: Connecting with Yourself

Too late, I found you can't wait to become perfect,
you got to go out and fall down and get up with everybody else.
—Charles Halloway in *Something Wicked This Way Comes*,
Ray Bradbury

Did I do it right? Did I live up to other people's standards? Is this what a good (wife, father, husband, employee, student, etc.) would do? Will other people approve? These are the questions that drive perfectionism, hamstring happiness, and stifle your enjoyment of life.

Did I listen to my heart? Did I follow my intuition? Was I kind? Did I speak up? Did I say what was true for me? Did I do the best I could given my circumstances? Did I enjoy it? Was I a good example? These are the questions that wrap your striving for high standards with authenticity and self-compassion, so you can be happier and do more of the things that are right for you.

Practice:

1. Be better than perfect. In your journal, define your new, healthy definition of success: I am successful when…

2. Treat yourself to a random act of kindness, like lying in the grass, listening to your favorite song, or cuddling with a pet.

. . . .

Day 193: Wisdom
Habit: Gratitude

The doorstep to the temple of wisdom
is a knowledge of our own ignorance.
—Charles Spurgeon, "The Anxious Inquirer"

You can find wisdom in religious texts and religious leaders, in movies and TV shows, in books and blogs, in lectures and classes, in other people's conversations, or by watching how a person lives their life. Wisdom is all around you, and it helps you live a better life and be a better person.

Practice:

1. In your journal, consider the following questions: Who and what have been your greatest teachers in the past? What have they taught you? How have their lessons made your life better? Who and what are your current teachers? What are you learning now?

2. Send a thank-you via e-mail, text, or mail to one of your teachers.

Day 194: The Oldest Living Things
Habit: Nature Simplicity

What I see in Nature is a magnificent structure
that we can comprehend only very imperfectly, and that must
fill a thinking person with a feeling of "humility."
—Albert Einstein, draft of a letter from 1954 or 1955

If you live to be ninety, you'll have had a long human life, but you're just a baby compared to other creatures. The pyrogenic geoxylic suffrutex in South Africa's coastal grasslands is an extraordinary tree because it has adapted to live underground. Under the earth, the roots and trunk of the tree are protected from fire, grazing, and drought. What we see of the tree looks like a bush, but it is actually the canopy—the uppermost branches.

This incredible adaptation has been extraordinarily successful, with some of these trees reaching 13,000 years old.[44] Imagine everything it's lived through—starting with our ancestors' domestication of goats to the discovery of the Internet. Today, its biggest threat is habitat loss. A single weekend's work with a Bobcat can destroy 13,000 years of life.

Practice:

1. In your journal, reflect on the difference between the pace of nature and the pace of the modern human world. How does a ninety-year life span affect how you look at the world? What if you lived 13,000 years? How might you look at the

world then? What do we owe living things that can exist for such long periods of time?

2. Perform a generous action for the environment, such as taking shorter showers or reducing food waste by eating your leftovers or starting a compost pile.

. . . .
Day 195: Respecting Their Dignity
Habit: Philanthropy

Give to every human being
every right that you claim for yourself.
—Robert G. Ingersoll, "The Limitations of Toleration"

Help that demeans a person's humanity can damage self-esteem and create a victim mentality that perpetuates a cycle of dependency. Here are three keys for respecting the dignity of the people you are helping.

1. *Use "experiencing" not "is."* Don't limit a person by the problem they have. Adding the word "experiencing" changes it from an identity to a condition. For example, say "This family is experiencing poverty" instead of "This family is poor." Conditions are temporary. Conditions can change. Conditions are learning experiences.

2. *Allow for anonymity and let people ask for help.* Can you imagine people showing up at your house with a holiday dinner because they think you're poor? Maybe you're poor or maybe

you're not, but now you know that everyone thinks you're poor. That can be humiliating. Provide an anonymous way for people to request help.

3. *Allow for choice.* While it might be tempting to think beggars can't be choosers, remember that your intention is to *help*. Unneeded, unwanted, inappropriate help is not helpful. It's a waste. Let people ask for and receive the help they need.

Practice:

Before donating to a charity, ask yourself, "How would I feel if I were in their situation? How would I want to be helped?" Does the charity you support respect the dignity of the people they are helping? If not, choose a new charity to research.

Week 28

Day 196: Liquid Sugar Loop
Habit: Physical Health

If any thing is sacred the human body is sacred.
—Walt Whitman, "I Sing the Body Electric"

Sugar is essential for your body. Your digestive system converts the food you consume into glucose (a type of sugar) and releases it into the blood stream. Once in the blood stream, glucose is trapped. It can only move into the cells if your body has also produced insulin, which tells the cells to let the glucose in. Once in the cells, glucose is converted into energy that is either used right away or stored for later use in the form of fat or protein.

Imbalances in this system impact every part of your body, causing health conditions like excessive urination, mood swings, loss of energy, weight loss or weight gain, injuries that don't heal, diabetes, and vision problems.

One of the easiest ways to reduce excess sugar is to eliminate the kind you drink. Soda has on average 50 grams of sugar per liter and fruit juice delivers nearly the same with 45.5 grams per liter. Diet drinks are just as problematic, with research showing that consumption leads to weight gain and health problems.[45]

Make liquid sugar a special occasion treat that you enjoy only when you are away from home.

Practice:

1. How much liquid sugar do you consume?

2. If you drink more sugar than you want, review "Breaking Bad (Habits)," day 182. What is the trigger for consuming it? What is the reward for consuming it? What routine will you put in its place? A few ideas include coffee or tea (little or no sugar added, decaf if necessary) or water with lemon.

3. Empower your nutritional gatekeeper (day 167) to keep soda and juice out of the home.

. . . .
Day 197: Mini Meditations
Habit: Mindfulness

Nowhere can man find a quieter
or more untroubled retreat than in his own soul.
—Marcus Aurelius, *Meditations*

Standing in line at the grocery store, waiting for someone to answer their phone—any moment is an opportunity to practice meditation.

Practice:

Practice a mini meditation today. Wherever you are, close your eyes and bring your attention to your breath. Count three full inhale-exhale cycles. Slowly open your eyes and resume what you were doing.

Day 198: More Than This
Habit: Relationships

Every man is entitled to be valued by his best moment.
—Ralph Waldo Emerson, "Beauty"

In our polarized world, a different political or religious opinion becomes a case of black and white. But a person's interaction with us based on these issues is only a small piece of who they are. We have so much more in common than we have differences.

Practice:

1. In your journal, write about someone you have strong disagreements with or difficulty appreciating. What else do you know about them? What about them is worthy of appreciation? Do they love animals? Do they coach their kid's soccer team? What is valuable about their perspective or experience? What do they have to teach you? What do you agree on? What do you have in common?

2. Seek out an opinion you disagree with, listen, and make no comment.

. . . .
Day 199: Shame Is a Vampire
Habit: Connecting with Yourself

Maybe ever'body in the whole damn world
is scared of each other.
—Slim in *Of Mice and Men*, John Steinbeck

Shame is a vampire lurking in the dark crevices of your mind, telling you that you're not good enough, that there's something wrong with you, that if people saw certain things about you, they would be horrified and you'd be judged and ostracized from the community.

But it's not true, and shame, like any vampire, is fought with sunlight and a group of vampire-fighting friends. Shame cannot survive in the presence of empathetic friends and courageous self-acceptance.

Practice:

1. In your journal, write about your experiences with shame. Do you have a shameful moment that haunts you? What are the cultural, economic, or political beliefs that define this as a shameful event?

2. Share your experience with a trusted friend who can comfort you.

. . . .
Day 200: Freedom
Habit: Gratitude

*Freedom is indivisible, and when one man is enslaved,
all are not free.*
—John F. Kennedy, *"Ich bin ein Berliner"*

Around the world, an estimated twenty-seven million people are enslaved. Modern-day slaves can be found in brothels, factories, mines, farm fields, restaurants, construction sites, and private homes. They are trapped by phony debts, lured by promises of work or an education, bought and sold, and forced to submit with violence.

Slaves are deprived of their most basic freedoms: the right to life and liberty. But they are also denied freedoms like choosing where to live, what to wear, what to eat, where to go to school, where to work, what to read, what to think, what to say, where to worship or to not worship, and who to vote for.

Practice:

1. In your journal, ask yourself, "What freedoms do you have that other people don't have? What freedoms make the most positive impact in your life?" Choose one freedom. What's important about this freedom? What does this freedom allow you to do? What would someone just getting this freedom be able to think, feel, and do that they can't think, feel, and do now?

2. Take a moment to feel grateful for this freedom.

. . . .
Day 201: Your Kitchen
Habit: Home Simplicity

We owe much to the fruitful meditation of our sages,
but a sane view of life is, after all,
elaborated mainly in the kitchen.
—Joseph Conrad, preface to
A Handbook of Cookery for a Small House

Simplicity in the kitchen is a very personal matter and one that I like to approach from the perspective of usability. Your kitchen has the right amount of stuff when it helps you cook. It has too much stuff when finding something is hard or when putting stuff away is stressful or an exercise in engineering. These are my two favorite kitchen simplicity tips:

1. *Substitute ruthlessly.* While some people can taste the difference between white wine vinegar and regular white distilled vinegar, I can't. And no one I've ever cooked for has said, "This would have been better with white wine vinegar."

2. *Do it the old-fashioned way.* Garlic presses, apple corers, egg-frying rings, citrus juicers, or electric knives have to be washed and put away. It's quicker and easier for me to do it the old-fashioned way.

If organizing your whole kitchen is overwhelming to you, just choose one small part, like the refrigerator or one cabinet.

Practice:

1. *Trash/Donate/Store:* Toss that nonstick frying pan that is no longer nonstick and other kitchen gadgets that are broken or past their prime. Duplicates or special-occasion items you don't use regularly can be donated or stored.

2. *Use Up:* Put all the products that need to be used up in a prominent spot in your kitchen. Make a goal to use up one each week.

3. *Organize:* Replace the remaining items so that you have what you need where you need it.

. . . .

Day 202: Double Your Donation
Habit: Philanthropy

The desire of power in excess caused the angels to fall;
the desire of knowledge in excess caused man to fall;
but in charity there is no excess,
neither can angel or man come in danger by it.
—Francis Bacon, *Of Goodness and Goodness of Nature*

If you could double the amount of food you got at the grocery store without paying more, would you? In a heartbeat! Here are two ways you can double your donation:

1. Many employers offer a matching donation program to encourage you to donate and so they can write off your donation on their taxes. Talk to your human resources department to find out if your employer has one and how it works.

2. Sometimes, a large donor wants to help their favorite charity raise more money, and the charity will tell you something like, "A generous couple is contributing half of the cost to fund three projects in Honduras—$1.5 million—if we can raise the other half from our dedicated, loyal donors." When you donate $50 to this project, this anonymous donor matches $50, so you've effectively donated $100. Watch your favor-

ite charity's website and marketing materials for notifications about matching donation opportunities. When you see one advertised, that's your cue to make your donation now!

Practice:

1. Does your employer match donations?
2. Perform a small philanthropic action like collecting kitchen equipment for a local woman's shelter, collecting school supplies for children, or making a small monetary donation.

Week 29

Day 203: Go Dense
Habit: Physical Health

You would not feed your dog a coffee and doughnut
for breakfast followed by a cigarette. You will kill the damn dog.
—Jack LaLanne, *Live Young Forever*

Making good food choices doesn't have to be that difficult. In fact, it's as simple as avoiding ingredient-dense and energy-dense foods and choosing foods dense in nutrition.

- *Ingredient Dense:* Take a look at the back of that boxed food you're about to eat. How many ingredients does it have? Lots of processed foods have a long ingredients list with a number of ingredients added solely for the purpose of preserving shelf-life and adding back the flavor removed during processing. Avoid highly processed, ingredient-dense food.

- *Energy Dense:* Some foods pack a lot of energy (i.e., calories) into little packages. High in sugar and fat, these foods don't offer a lot of nutrients in return.

- *Nutrient Dense:* These foods are high in nutrients your body needs, such as fiber, potassium, iron, magnesium, antioxidants, flavonoids, etc. Salmon, leafy greens like kale and spinach, nuts, beans, quinoa, blueberries, and eggs are just a few of the simple foods that provide lots of nutrition so your body can thrive.

Make your diet dense in the right foods.

Practice:

1. Evaluate your pantry and refrigerator. Identify your ingredient-dense and energy-dense foods. Choose one to eliminate and empower the nutritional gatekeeper to keep it out of the home.

2. Continue collecting recipes that are easy to make, tasty, and good for you.

3. How many meals are you cooking at home? How many would you like to make? Review day 44 for help on making it happen.

. . . .
Day 204: Material Impermanence Meditation
Habit: Mindfulness

In the presence of eternity, the mountains are as transient as the clouds.
—Robert G. Ingersoll, "The Christian Religion"

Eventually, everything breaks, decays, or dies. With that knowledge comes a reassuring truth: enjoy it while it lasts.

Practice:

Close your eyes and take a few centering breaths. As you pay attention to your breath, reflect on the room around you and some of the material objects in that room. Imagine how this room will look in a month if no human enters it. Has anything begun to rot or smell? How will the room look in ten years? Are the soft surfaces decayed and eaten away by time? Is some of the furniture looking less stable? How will it look in fifty years? Have sunlight and rain begun to penetrate through cracks in the roof? Are the windows cracked and missing? In a hundred years? Have trees begun to sprout in the piles of decayed material? Now bring to mind an object you have a strong emotional attachment to. Is it an heirloom passed down to you from your mother? A special gift? Bring this object to your mind and name all the things you love about it and what it means to you. Feel your love for this object fill you up. Appreciate the gift of enjoying this object. Now imagine some future time when this object is lost or stolen or broken or worn out or passed on to a child who doesn't feel the same way about it as you do. How do you feel? Does it change how you want to treat the object while you have it? What are some positive ways that you can use this experience and this understanding?

. . . .

Day 205: Interview an Elder
Habit: Relationships

*Stories have to be told or they die, and when they die,
we can't remember who we are or why we're here.*
—August in *The Secret Life of Bees,* Sue Monk Kidd

Our elders have so much experience they could share with us, and conversations with them can help us approach life with more wisdom and character. It's also an amazing way of dignifying their life and communicating your love for them. Giving someone the opportunity to be heard and to share their story is a priceless gift.

Practice:

1. In your journal, write about an elder in your life. What have you learned from them? What would you like to tell them about how they've impacted your life?

2. Interview them. Ask questions like "What are the most important lessons you've learned in life?" Check out the StoryCorps website for suggested interview questions. If you use the StoryCorps smartphone app, you can record the interview and archive it at the Library of Congress in one easy step.

. . . .
Day 206: Your Purpose
Habit: Connecting with Yourself

Your task is not to seek for love, but merely to seek and find all the barriers within yourself that you have built against it.
—Helen Schucman, *A Course in Miracles*

What is the purpose of life? It's pretty simple. Your purpose is to love—love yourself, your family, your neighbors, your coworkers, your countrymen, your fellow earthly inhabitants. Your task is to find the barriers that prevent you from loving as much as you are able: fear, apathy, hurt, miscommunication.

How will you do that? There is a different way for each person on the planet. As you consider how you will do it, take into account your occupation; your role as a parent, spouse, neighbor, coworker, and consumer; and your volunteer work and philanthropy.

Practice:

1. In your journal, consider the following questions: In what ways do you express love for yourself, your family, your neighbors, your coworkers, your countrymen, your fellow earthly inhabitants? What keeps you from expressing more love for yourself, your family, your neighbors, your coworkers, your countrymen, your fellow earthly inhabitants? What can you do to better love yourself, your family, your neighbors, your coworkers, your countrymen, your fellow earthly inhabitants?

2. Choose one of the ways you identified to love yourself better and do it.

. . . .
Day 207: Food Gratitude
Habit: Gratitude

And when you crush an apple with your teeth,
say to it in your heart:
"Your seeds shall live in my body,
And the buds of your to-morrow shall blossom in my heart,
And your fragrance shall be my breath,
And together we shall rejoice through all the seasons."
—Kahlil Gibran, *The Prophet*

Food is the gift of life, but it is not guaranteed. In fact, it's a miracle that requires the collaboration of the entire plant. Take a moment today to feel grateful for your food.

Practice:

Choose a meal to feel grateful for. Before beginning the meal, take a moment to think how it came to be on your plate. Thank the farmers, the crop pickers, the delivery drivers, the grocery store, the irrigation systems. Appreciate the warm sunlight, rich earth, and cool rain that nurtured it until it was ready for you. Understand that this food nourishes your mind and body and gives you life. If you will enjoy this meal with others, reflect on the marvelous ability of food to bring people together and that over a meal, we put our differences aside and can appreciate just how much we have in common. The meal that you are about the enjoy is a tangible reminder that your physical well-being depends on the bounty of the earth and the labor of others.

. . . .
Day 208: Needs and Wants
Habit: Mind Simplicity

The art of being wise is the art of knowing what to overlook.
—William James, *The Principles of Psychology*

Fundamentally, you just need the basics of food, shelter, clothing. You don't need filet mignon, because beans and rice will do the job. You may enjoy filet mignon. You may be able to afford filet mignon, but you don't *need* it. You don't need a three-thousand-square-foot house. You may be able to afford a three-thousand-square-foot house. You may love having all that space. But you don't *need* it. Needs make life possible, but wants give life zest. The trick is finding a balance between living like an ascetic monk and a hedonist.

Practice:

1. In your journal, take stock of your current financial situation. Do you spend more than you earn? How much do you have in savings? How much money do you spend on needs? Are any of these needs more expensive than they need to be or you want them to be? How much do you spend on wants? Do those purchases tend to add value to your life, your loved ones, or to the world? Create your rules for purchasing wants.

2. Set an indulgence budget. How much money can you spend a month to treat yourself and your loved ones? Consider transferring this money into a separate account or into cash to reduce the risk of overspending.

· ·

Day 209: Your Bank Account Is a Moral Document
Habit: Philanthropy

In budgets large and small, I'd begun to see the best-kept secret of economists: Economic systems are not value-free columns of numbers based on rules of reason, but ways of expressing what varying societies believe is important.

—Gloria Steinem, *Moving Beyond Words*

Life is made up of time. Life = Time.

Money is received in exchange for time. Time = Money.

Life = Time = Money.

Life = Money.

You spend money to create your life. Money = Life.

Your bank account statement is an impartial record of what you really value. It doesn't care what you say is important. It shows you by your actions what you value and who you are. How you spend your money is how you spend your life.

Practice:

1. Pull up the last few months of your bank statements. In your journal, write about what you spend money on. What do you think you spend money on but don't see? What do you want to spend more money on? What do you want to spend less on? Does what you spend money on reflect your highest values?

2. Today, only spend your money on what makes your life *and* the world better.

. . . .
Day 210: Monthly Check-In

A true commitment is a heartfelt promise to yourself from which you will not back down.
—David McNally, *Even Eagles Need a Push*

Time to check in on your progress. This is not a guilt-inducing exercise designed to shame you for all you haven't accomplished yet.

Instead, it's a gentle reminder about what's important to you and what you want to change.

Enjoy the journey. Be gentle with yourself. Keep growing.

Practice:

+ What did I do last month that I'm proud of?

+ Are my relationships with others improving or deteriorating?

+ What do I need to do less of/quit/get rid of/delegate this month?

+ What experiments did I try? What lessons did I learn? What is going well?

+ What isn't working, and what do I want to change?

+ Habit to focus on next month:

+ Why do I want to establish that habit?

+ What is a first step I can take toward making this a habit?

+ What trigger will I use?

+ How will I reward myself?

+ What obstacles will I face in establishing this habit and how will I overcome them?

+ Notes on successes, long-term goals, and personal changes I'm working toward:

Week 30

Day 211: Your Eyes Are Better Than Your Stomach
Habit: Physical Health

One cannot think well, love well, sleep well,
if one has not dined well.
—Virginia Woolf, *A Room of One's Own*

You might think that you eat when you're hungry and you stop when you're full, but you'd be wrong. Brian Wansink, food researcher at Cornell University, warns you to not rely on your stomach, because your stomach only has three settings: starving, stuffed, and room for more. Your eyeballs are actually a better indicator of how much to eat and can help you feel full. He discovered that people felt more full after eating an extra fluffy milk shake than they did after eating a more compact but otherwise identical shake. Likewise, burgers piled high with lettuce and tomato felt more filling than the same, shorter burger.

He advises serving food on small plates, so they look full and overflowing. Instead of going back for your usual seconds, serve the full amount at the beginning of the meal, so you can see how much you're actually eating. Don't eat from containers, because you can't gauge how much you've eaten. Instead, serve your snack on a cozy-sized dish.[46]

Practice:

1. In your journal, reflect on your eating habits. Do you overeat? What size plates do you use? What strategies can you use to increase how much food it looks like you're eating and only eat as much as you should be eating?

2. Serve dinner on a small plate and don't go back for seconds.

. . . .
Day 212: There's an App for That
Habit: Mindfulness

But they [computers] are useless.
They can only give you answers.
—Pablo Picasso, 1964 interview in the *Paris Review*

And sometimes that's exactly what you need. If you're struggling to be more mindful on a regular basis, technology could be exactly the answer you're looking for. If you need a reminder of just how good mindfulness is for you, review day 2.

Practice:

Continue practicing ten minutes of meditation every day. If you're struggling to create the habit, search for a phone app or other technology that you can use as a tool to gently, consistently prompt you to meditate, breathe, or bring you back to the present.

Day 213: Give It Time
Habit: Relationships

Constant kindness can accomplish much.
As the sun makes ice melt, kindness causes misunderstandings,
mistrust, and hostility to evaporate.
—Albert Schweitzer, *The Teaching of Reverence for Life*

A potter places a piece of clay in the center of the wheel and then propels the kick wheel with her feet. Technologically speaking, the kick wheel is a flywheel. That means that once the kick wheel has amassed enough momentum, it continues spinning with very little effort needed to maintain it. This is great for potters, because they can now focus on molding the clay that continues to spin at a consistent speed.

Relationships are like flywheels. It continues moving in a direction with very little assistance. If you want to change it, it's going to take time and effort.

Practice:

1. In your journal, ask yourself, "What is the momentum in my relationships?" Are they improving or deteriorating? Reflect on a difficult relationship in your life. How long has it been moving in this direction? What actions can you take to change things? Reasonably, how long will you go before expecting to see a change?

2. Perform an action that will improve one of your relationships.

Day 214: Anger
Habit: Connecting with Yourself

When angry, count four; when very angry, swear.
—Mark Twain, *Following the Equator*

There are a lot of rules about when it's okay to be angry, who can be angry, and how to be angry. Express your anger and risk social disapproval, but don't express it or don't even dare to feel it and you risk guilt and depression.

At its core, anger is neither good nor bad. It's an emotion that signals that something is wrong. That's why it's so powerful. Anger gives you the awareness to notice that something is wrong and the energy to do something about it.

Practice:

1. Think about something that makes you angry. In your journal, write about why this makes you angry. Go deeper. What are you really angry about? What is the problem, and whose problem is it? How can you express yourself without attacking, getting defensive, or feeling powerless? If getting angry isn't working, what else can you do?

2. Close your eyes, feel your anger, and appreciate your desire to change something. Embrace the mission to express that desire in a way that is good for you and good for others. Take an action that addresses the area you want to change.

Day 215: Gratitude Trigger
Habit: Gratitude

Give without remembering and take without forgetting.
—Elizabeth Bibesco, *Haven*

Think back for a moment and remember what you've received in your life that has allowed you to become the person you are today. Remember the care you received as an infant that allowed you to survive your helplessness. Think about the nourishment you've received from the planet. Don't forget those kind words and helping hand of a stranger when you stumbled. There's also all that knowledge you've acquired from teachers, leaders, authors. Can you recall the pep talk from a good friend who reminded you to believe in yourself? How many times have people given you a smile, a shoulder to lean on, an ear to talk to, a pat on the back?

Practice:

To help you remember not to forget, find a gratitude charm or trigger, like a bracelet, a stone you carry in your pocket, or the word "gratitude" framed on your wall. When you see this item, it's your reminder to appreciate just one thing. It could be something that happened that day, last week, last year, or this lifetime. It could be something someone has done for you, something you have, something you learned, or a quality about yourself or another person. Anything is a candidate for gratitude!

Day 216: Your Brain Is Limited
Habit: Schedule Simplicity

Your life doesn't get any better than your mind is.
—Sam Harris, "Taming the Mind"

Study after study confirms that humans are terrible at multitasking—even those who believe they're great at it. Multitaskers consistently make more mistakes, are less productive, have difficulty focusing, remember less, and have trouble identifying the information relevant to the task at hand. Recent MRI studies attribute this to the fact that your prefrontal cortex (PFC) has only two hemispheres (you can think of these like potential task slots). The PFC helps you think abstractly, analyze thoughts, regulate your behavior, suppress impulsive behavior, make choices between right and wrong, predict outcomes, focus your attention, coordinate information with other parts of the brain, decide what to do, and create short-term memories, but each activity requires a slot.

Simplicity honors the physical limitations of your brain. Turn off the TV. Choose simple music. Shut down e-mail and social media. Limit your distractions and focus on one thing at a time, so you can get more done, do it better, enjoy it more, and remember more of it.

Practice:

1. Search online for "test your focus" or "test your ability to switch tasks" or "multitasking test." Take the test. How good are you at multitasking?

2. What are your regular distractions? E-mail, social media, TV, family, friends, radio, cell phone?

3. Today, practice limiting your distractions and focusing on one thing at a time.

. . . .

Day 217: Month 8 Giving Challenge: Water and Sanitation
Habit: Philanthropy

> *The true meaning of life is to plant trees,*
> *under whose shade you do not expect to sit.*
> —Nelson Henderson, quoted in *Under Whose Shade*
> by Wesley Henderson

The World Health Organization estimates that 1.7 million people die every year from diarrheal diseases (including cholera), and 600,000 of those are children under five years old. Imagine how awful it would be to watch your child die from diarrhea—something so treatable and easily avoidable. In addition to health costs are the economic costs. Time spent walking to obtain water and time lost due to waterborne illnesses is time that can't be spent on education, building businesses, and other productive efforts. The world loses $260 billion in potential economic activity every year.[47]

Fortunately, this is a problem that can be solved, and it requires economic resources to build wells and toilets in places that don't currently have them.

Practice:

Find a charity working on water and sanitation in the developing world. Use the Charity Evaluation Worksheet in the appendix to evaluate the charity. If you like what you discover, make a donation. Remember, there is no such thing as a small donation. Any donation you make will work to save a life.

Week 31

Day 218: Make It Hard
Habit: Physical Health

I can resist everything except temptation.
—Oscar Wilde, *Lady Windemere's Fan*

Fast food companies invest billions in highly visible, easily accessible locations because they know that if you see it and it's easy, you'll eat there. We can circumvent this human tendency to take the easy route. Brian Wansink studied the workplace candy dish and discovered that secretaries with the dish on their desk consumed 225 calories in candy every day. Moving that candy dish six feet across the room meant the secretaries had to get up and walk to the candy dish, making it harder, and as a result, they ate less than half the amount of candy.[48]

Make it easier for yourself to do the right thing by making it harder to do the wrong thing. Avoid the food commercials, bypass your favorite fast food joint, put the unhealthy treats in an out-of-the-way location, or put your cell phone in the trunk while you're driving.

Practice:

1. In your journal, write about your temptations. What behaviors or foods do you want to avoid? How can you make it more difficult to engage in this behavior?

2. Review day 182, "Breaking Bad (Habits)." How are you doing with breaking that bad habit? Recommit and redesign your environment to make it harder to do your unhealthy routine.

. . . .
Day 219: Body Scan Meditation
Habit: Mindfulness

To become different from what we are,
we must have some awareness of what we are.
—Eric Hoffer, *The Passionate State of Mind, and Other Aphorisms*

The body scan meditation systematically and intentionally examines your body through your mind.

Practice:

Close your eyes and take a few centering breaths. After you get comfortable, bring your attention to the big toe of your left foot. Is it warm or cold? Throbbing? Heavy or light? Itchy? Tingly? Greet each sensation with gentle observation. Now feel each toe, where they touch each other, and if there's clothing touching it or air moving across it. Slowly, systematically, and intentionally examine each part of the rest of foot, up your calf, knee, thigh while noticing the sensations in each part. Repeat for your right leg, and then scan your butt, abdomen, torso, neck, and every nook and cranny of your cranium. Conclude by feeling that your body is whole and complete.

. . . .
Day 220: Life Math
Habit: Relationships

To get the full value of a joy
you must have somebody to divide it with.
—Mark Twain, *Following the Equator*

In math class, you learn that if you have one apple and divide it by two with someone, you only have half an apple left. But in life, division works differently. If you have a candy bar, divide it by two, and give half to your sister, you only have half a candy bar. But if you eat it while lying on your backs, looking up at the stars, and talking about life, you've increased your enjoyment of that candy bar tenfold. In life, division is multiplication because life is better when it's shared with others.

Practice:
Invite someone to share an experience with you.

. . . .
Day 221: The Gift of Sadness
Habit: Connecting with Yourself

Sorrow is one of the vibrations that prove the fact of living.
—Antoine de Saint-Exupéry, *Wind, Sand and Stars*

Feeling sad is as normal and necessary as feeling happy. Sadness often arises when you are dealing with loss. It can be the loss of something tangible like a job or the death of a loved one. But the loss can also be intangible like the death of a dream, the loss of identity, or the end of an experience. Sadness gives you time to heal. It's an opportunity to connect with yourself, to validate your feelings, and to comfort yourself.

Practice:

1. In your journal, write about when you feel sad. How often do you feel sad? What do you feel sad about? Can you identify the loss? Are you afraid of losing something? Is there something missing? Are you struggling with something? What is your sadness trying to tell you? Do you want to talk with a professional?

2. Treat yourself to a random act of kindness, like crawling under a pile of hot laundry, savoring a magazine, or indulging in your favorite TV show.

. . . .
Day 222: If Nothing Else
Habit: Gratitude

If there is a meaning in life at all,
then there must be a meaning in suffering.
—Viktor E. Frankl, *Man's Search for Meaning*

There is at least one thing you can be grateful for in a difficult situation. If nothing else, it gives you the ability to deeply empathize with other people going through the same thing. It's one thing to feel for people who are struggling to find a job. It's quite another to know exactly what it feels like because you looked for a job for two years before getting hired. You know their pain. You can encourage them to persevere, advise them on how to do it better, and even warn them of pitfalls they'll face along the way. This situation can help you help others.

Practice:

1. Are you currently experiencing a difficult situation that you don't feel grateful for? If not, think back to a situation in which you felt hopeless, trapped, and stuck. In your journal, write about what this experience taught you. What would you tell someone going through this same type of difficulty?

2. Take a moment to appreciate your growth and feel compassion for anyone struggling with a similar situation.

· · · · · · · · · · · · ·
Day 223: Layers
Habit: Nature Simplicity

Try and penetrate with our limited means
the secrets of nature and you will find that,
behind all the discernible concatenations,
there remains something subtle, intangible and inexplicable.
—Albert Einstein, quoted in *Diaries of a Cosmopolitan*
by Harry Kessler

Nature reveals itself to you in layers. I have a theory about why that is. Your brain cannot possibly comprehend all the information available at any given time, so it first pays attention to the big, important items on the first layer. Only then can your brain become aware of a smaller layer: "Oh, that tree is flowering, but the flowers are small." Or it notices a quieter layer: "Oh, I hear a bird chirping, and now I see it flitting around in the top of that tree." The more time you spend in one place, the more you'll notice.

Today, be still and discover hundreds of tiny details that remain invisible when you move too fast.

Practice:

1. Find a place near you where you can sit and observe nature. What do you notice first? What is your overall impression of the space? What colors do you see? Do you notice any animals or insects right off the bat? Breathe. Close your eyes. Reopen your eyes slowly without focusing on any one thing while you settle in. Now look down. What else do you see? Are there insects or animals you didn't notice? What materials (leaves, grass, sticks, mulch, sidewalk) do you see? Do all the leaves look the same, or are some different? Is the sidewalk really all the same color, or are there shades? Does something look like it doesn't belong? Why? Look up. Look out. Listen. Just notice everything that could be noticed.

2. Leave the area better than you found it by picking up any garbage you encounter.

Day 224: Accounting
Habit: Philanthropy

People who give will never be poor.
—Anne Frank, "Give!"

In business school, they teach you to keep track of financial categories like assets, liabilities, equity, revenue, and expenses. While these categories are important to your personal financial health, they're not the only items to account for. Here are a few other important categories:

+ *Health:* How well you take care of yourself
+ *Goodwill:* Friendly, helpful, or cooperative feelings or attitude you've engendered in people around you
+ *Love:* Deep feelings of affection you feel for others and others feel for you
+ *Family:* Quality of relationships with those with whom you share a blood (or feels like blood) bond
+ *Friendship:* Quality and number of relationships you hold with others
+ *Peace of Mind:* Absence of mental stress or anxiety
+ *Impact:* The difference you're making in the world

A subtraction in a financial category can increase your goodwill, love, peace of mind, and impact accounts. An increase in revenue due to an increasing number of hours worked can decrease your family and friendship accounts. When your accounting system accounts for all areas of your physical, emotional, and spiritual well-being, it's impossible to become poor from giving.

Practice:

1. In your journal, identify the traditional and nontraditional accounts you think are important. Do you need to make additions or subtractions from some accounts?

2. Perform a philanthropic action like asking for donations instead of birthday presents, redirecting an optional personal expense to a donation, or reading a book on a cause you care about.

Week 32

Day 225: Screw It!
Habit: Physical Health

Every moment is a fresh beginning.
—T. S. Eliot, *The Cocktail Party*

Maybe you overslept and skipped working out. Then for lunch, you caved and ate a bag of potato chips. Now it's dinnertime, and you have a choice. You could have the healthy meal you were planning on, or you could treat yourself to that box of macaroni and cheese. Do you say, "Screw it. It doesn't matter now anyway"?

Scientific studies show that when people believe they've missed their diet goals, they consume way more calories than they normally would, making it even more difficult for them to reach their fitness goals.

Short-circuit the "screw it" response as soon as you notice it happening. Remember, you haven't failed. Each choice is a new opportunity to make a better choice.

Practice:

1. In your journal, reflect on when you have a tendency to say, "Screw it!" When do you intentionally continue unhealthy behavior?

2. Create a trigger or a new empowering phrase so that in the future, you can interrupt your pattern and get back on track with the way you really want to act.

. . . .
Day 226: Mindfulness Trigger
Habit: Mindfulness

Meditation is the tongue of the soul,
and the language of our spirit.
—Jeremy Taylor, "Of Meditation"

It's impossible to be mindful all the time, and for much of your life, you may find yourself on autopilot. A "mindfulness trigger" can be a place, an object, or an event that reminds you to gather your thoughts, collect your emotions, and give your full attention to whatever is going to happen next. For example, a doorknob can be something that causes you say to yourself, "Opening a door, opening my heart." Or a ringing telephone can be an event, and instead of hearing the ring, you hear, "Wake up, wake up!"

Practice:
Choose an object or event that will serve as a mindfulness trigger. How will you remind yourself of the trigger until it becomes a habit? A sticky note on the phone? A ribbon on your front door handle?

· · · · · · · · · · · · · · · · ·
Day 227: Ask for Help
Habit: Relationships

Until we can receive with an open heart,
we are never really giving with an open heart.
—Brené Brown, *The Gifts of Imperfection*

Are you trying to carry it all by yourself? Whether it's something big like coping with the death of a loved one or something little like waking up in a bad mood, burdens are easier when you're not carrying it alone. Just as you want to ease other people's burdens, other people want to ease yours. If they're not helping, maybe they need to know that you need help, maybe they don't know what they could do to help, or maybe you haven't appreciated the help they've given in the past.

Practice:

1. In your journal, ask yourself, "What kind of help do I need? Who can give me that kind of help?"

2. Ask for it. Show your appreciation for their help.

· · · · · · · · · · · · · · · · ·
Day 228: Your Sexuality
Habit: Connecting with Yourself

There is more to sex appeal than just measurements. . . .
I can convey just as much appeal fully clothed,
picking apples off a tree.
—Audrey Hepburn, quoted in *Audrey Hepburn* by Barry Paris

Your sexuality is an important part of your human nature. If you're too busy, too insecure, or too hurt, you may have forgotten what it feels like to be sexy, but sexy feels fabulous. Maybe you don't believe that you could be sexy, but trust me, you're sexy. Maybe you think it's not okay to be sexy, but if you disconnect from your sexuality, you're disconnected from an important part of who you are.

Practice:

1. In your journal, write about what makes you feel sexy. What turns you on? What do you find sexy in others?

2. Lightly run your finger down your arm. Notice the sensations. Admire the contours of your arm. Caress your shoulders and your chest. Lightly travel around your stomach and down your hips. Admire your thighs with your fingertips, cup your calves, and tickle your feet.

. . . .
Day 229: I'm Not Grateful
Habit: Gratitude

[Being grateful] is not only the greatest virtue,
but the parent of all the other virtues.
—Marcus Tullius Cicero, *Pro Plancio*

You aren't always going to feel grateful. Sometimes, your first response is to complain or get angry. I know that I get irritated when I'm waiting on hold only to be hung up on as I'm being transferred to a customer service representative.

A negative thought or two that slips into your mind and then out again is not a big deal. If responding negatively to situations becomes a habit, if you obsess over them, or if the negative thought makes you unhappy, the good news is that you can change it! With just a little bit of effort, you can transform a negative thought into a positive feeling by broadening your perspective and asking a few questions.

Practice:

What was the last ungrateful or negative thought you had? In your journal, consider these questions: What else is true about this situation? Are there compensating factors? Was there a positive intention or benefit you missed? How could the situation have been worse? In the big scheme of things, how important is this? Are you attaching a meaning to this situation that might not be true? What are you grateful for now about this situation?

. . . .
Day 230: Your Home
Habit: Home Simplicity

*Don't own so much clutter that you will be relieved
to see your house catch fire.*
—Wendell Berry, *New Collected Poems*

I have a confession to make. I don't spend a lot of time cleaning my house. I don't especially enjoy cleaning, and I don't have a lot of extra time to do it. Fortunately, maintenance cleaning doesn't take very much time, because there's not much to clean around or put away. And if I don't happen to get around to cleaning, people very often confuse a clutter-free home with a clean home, so I look like a great housekeeper—well, at least not terrible!

Practice:

1. *Take stock.* How cluttered is your home? Are there furniture pieces that are extraneous or too big for their rooms? How much stuff is on display on tables, shelves, walls?

2. *Plan for the furniture.* Can it be removed entirely or does it need to be replaced with something smaller?

3. *Clear the flat surfaces.* Remove all papers, piles of stuff, and knickknacks from shelves, mantels, tabletops, and countertops. Put it all in one place.

4. *Choose the best.* What are your favorite items? Choose the ones that you love and make you smile to display in a place of honor. Treat your home as a museum and curate a careful collection of items for display in the most appropriate and attractive places.

5. *Trash/donate/store/rehome the remaining items.* If in doubt, put it in storage. See if you get used to this new level of decoration. It might feel sparse at first, but does it feel different in a couple weeks? If you absolutely must, in a couple weeks, you can pull out your storage box and carefully choose an item for display in your museum.

Day 231: Start a Giving Circle
Habit: Philanthropy

How wonderful it is that no one has to wait,
but can start right now to gradually change the world!
—Anne Frank, "Give!"

Who said you have to donate alone? Lots of other people care about the same cause you care about, and you can join together in a giving circle or what I like to call your donation team. In a giving circle, you pool your donation with the donations of other people who care about the same cause. Together, you'll make a *bigger* donation than you could alone. Plus, you share the work of finding great charities doing great work, so you're making better donations, too.

You could donate alone, but why?

Practice:

1. Do you want to start a giving circle? Download the Giving Circle Guide at www.givingcircleshelp.com.

2. Check out existing virtual giving circles that you can become a part of right now at www.virtualgivingcircles.com.

Week 33

Day 232: Sleep Epidemic
Habit: Physical Health

A good laugh and a long sleep
are the two best cures for anything.
—Irish proverb

The Centers for Disease Control and Prevention calls insufficient sleep a public health epidemic. If you're not getting at least seven hours of sleep each night, you may be at risk for some of these side effects:

1. Decreased ability to pay attention, be alert, concentrate, reason, and problem solve.

2. Decreased physical safety. The National Highway Traffic Safety Administration estimates 100,000 auto crashes and 1,550 crash-related deaths caused by fatigue. At work, sleepiness leads to significantly more workplace accidents.

3. Depression, heart disease, heart attacks, heart failure, irregular heartbeat, high blood pressure, stroke, diabetes, and lower levels of testosterone.

4. Decreased release of human growth hormones that grow and maintain muscle mass, strong bones, and supple skin.

5. Decreased energy and increased tension, which may lead to decreased interest in sex.

6. Increased weight gain due to decreased levels of leptin and elevated levels of ghrelin leading to stimulated appetites and cravings for high-fat, high-carbohydrate foods.

7. Increased risk of death from all causes.[49]

Practice:

1. Do you have trouble sleeping? Do you feel you're getting enough sleep? Do you feel tired during the day?

2. Keep a sleep journal for the next week and track what time you got into bed, how long it took you to fall sleep, how many times you got up during the night, how many hours you think you slept, and what time you got up. Search the Internet for a printable sleep journal or download a sleep app for your phone. You'll review the journal over the next few weeks.

. . . .

Day 233: "Holding Them in the Light" Meditation
Habit: Mindfulness

From within or from behind,
a light shines through us upon things,
and makes us aware that we are nothing, but the light is all.
—Ralph Waldo Emerson, "The Over-Soul"

Based on a Quaker prayer, "holding someone in the light" is a meditation you can do when someone is going through a difficult time.

Practice:

1. Bring to mind a person you love or are concerned for and visualize them wrapped in warm, soft, healing light. Because it can be hard to know what is best for them, because even they may not be clear about what is best for them, because what we think is best may not happen, simply send out a feeling that they receive whatever may be best for them. Imagine the light lifting them toward peace and healing. Imagine the light giving them strength and love.

2. Send an e-mail or text of love and support to this person.

. . . .
Day 234: A Long, Happy Relationship
Habit: Relationships

"Love" is that condition in which the happiness
of another person is essential to your own.
—Jubal in *Stranger in a Strange Land*, Robert A. Heinlein

Great relationships are the result of love in action. It's not just a feeling. It's the act of giving to each other in countless small and big ways every day. Love is embracing, supporting, surprising, respecting, and listening.

Practice:

1. In your journal, ask yourself how often you act lovingly to your intimate partner. Reflect back on your relationship. What first attracted you to them? What did you get from them in the be-

ginning? What do you get now? What did you give to them in the beginning? What do you give them now? What do they need from you? What keeps you from acting loving? What are you afraid will happen if you give more to your partner? What will you discover if you give more?

2. Take a loving action toward your intimate partner such as greeting them with your full attention when they come home or tucking a love note in their pocket.

· · · · · · · · · · · · · · · · · · ·
Day 235: Your Spirituality
Habit: Connecting with Yourself

All spiritual progress is the growth
of half-knowledge into clear illumination.
—S. Radhakrishnan, *The Principal Upanishads*

Each human harbors a volatile combination of every human emotion. Spirituality is the wrestling we do with our human nature to understand and accept our darkness while learning to live in the light. Spirituality is the expression of love, reverence, harmony, joy, acceptance, and respect. Your spiritual practice is the work you do to express those more often, more fully, and more deeply. And believe me, it takes a lot of work.

Practice:

1. In your journal, consider the following questions: In the past, where have you experienced being connected to something bigger than yourself? Where have you felt peace? What does

a spiritual life mean to you? Where in your life can you express more love, feel more peace, and extend more understanding to yourself and others? What tools will you call on in your spiritual work? Here are a few tools to consider: religions or religious texts; works of art, music, or literature; time with nature, friends, or family; and professional counselors.

2. Use, read, or reach out to one of your spiritual growth tools.

· · · · · · · · · · · · · · · · ·
Day 236: Some People
Habit: Gratitude

When dealing with people, let us remember
we are not dealing with creatures of logic.
We are dealing with creatures of emotion, creatures bristling
with prejudices and motivated by pride and vanity.
—Dale Carnegie, *How to Win Friends and Influence People*

I remember when my mom was dying and a company called because they wanted me to document that I had closed an account *years* ago. After some back and forth, I finally said, "No. This is not my problem. You didn't update your system. You figure it out." And I hung up. Afterward, I felt bad. I know she was just doing her job, and my response was all about my current emotional stress. If I could apologize to her, I would. I hope that as part of their customer service training they gave her some tools for coping with unpleasant customers and that she knows that people who are difficult are often in the most pain. It can be hard to feel grateful for people who are making your life hard, but it's not impossible.

Practice:

1. Who is a difficult person in your life? In your journal, write about what it is about their behavior that bothers you. What gift is this person giving you? Do you need to learn a new skill, like how to set boundaries or say no? Is this an example to learn from? Do you get an opportunity to practice a valuable character trait like patience or understanding?

2. Take a moment to appreciate this person, wish them happiness and peace, and feel grateful for the opportunity to learn an important lesson.

. . . .
Day 237: More Simple Pleasures
Habit: Mind Simplicity

Most men pursue pleasure
with such breathless haste that they hurry past it.
—Søren Kierkegaard, *Either/Or*

The simple pleasures are truly everywhere around you. It's in the first cup of coffee in the morning, the feel of sunshine on your skin, the hot water of a shower, the comfort found in hugging a loved one, or the sound of a child giggling. Some people find simple pleasure in baking cookies, gardening, or reading. An ice cream cone on a hot afternoon, the sound of rain, or warm laundry fresh from the dryer can be opportunities to notice, appreciate, and savor.

Practice:

Choose a simple pleasure to enjoy. Before starting, pause. Feel your body anticipate the pleasure you're about to experience and feel grateful that you get to experience something you love and enjoy. As you begin the experience, notice the sensations. Are you noticing the pleasure on your skin, your tongue? What's happening in your brain as you're soaking up this moment? Do you feel more peaceful, content, happy, grateful? Does closing your eyes help you focus on the feelings of pleasure? Stop thinking about it. Just be right there, in the moment, indulging in it.

. . . .
Day 238: Your Giving Plan
Habit: Philanthropy

What do we live for,
if it is not to make life less difficult to each other?
—Dorothea in *Middlemarch*, George Eliot

Throughout the weeks, you've slowly developed pieces of your donation plan. Now, bring those pieces together into one place. If you're donating as a family, answer these questions together.

Practice:

1. How much money will I/we give? How often?

2. How much time will I/we give? How often?

3. What causes do I/we support?

4. What causes don't I/we support?

5. How will I/we choose where to donate? Here are a few questions to get you started. What, if any, research will we do before we donate? How will we discuss the findings of our research? Do we want to meet to review research, discuss potential charities, or evaluate our giving? If so, how often? Will we choose the same charity every month? How do we find out about new charities to consider? For example, can each family member present a charity? If multiple charities are considered, how will we choose? Will we vote? Will majority vote win? What happens if there's a tie? Will we discuss until we all agree? Will we donate to only one charity at a time or divide our donation among more than one charity?

6. Any other rules? It's okay to break your rules every once in a while. Donating should feel good, and there's room for play and spontaneity in your giving.

Week 34

Day 239: A Good Night's Sleep
Habit: Physical Health

As a well-spent day brings happy sleep,
so life well used brings happy death.
—Leonardo da Vinci, *The Notebooks of Leonardo da Vinci*

A good night's sleep starts with things you do during the day.

1. *Avoid caffeine and alcohol.* Avoid caffeine for four to six hours and alcohol for three hours before bedtime. Sleep studies show that alcohol consumption increases mid-night wakings and decreases the quality of your sleep. Other medications can cause problems with sleep, too, so pay attention to how well you sleep after you take your prescribed and over-the-counter medications.

2. *Eat and drink moderately.* Finish dinner several hours before bed and choose late-night snacks that are easy to digest. Drink enough water so that you won't wake up from thirst but not so much that you wake up to go to the bathroom.

3. *Exercise.* Sleep studies show that regular exercise helps people fall asleep faster and sleep more soundly.

4. *Tap into your circadian rhythms.* Morning sunlight lets your body know it's time to be up, and soft, dim lights at night let your body know it's time to wind down.

5. *Make your bedroom sleep inducing.* Is your bedroom cool, dark, and quiet? Do you feel safe and secure? Is your mattress comfortable?[50]

Practice:

1. Review your sleep journal. Do you notice any patterns? Are there times you have more difficulty sleeping than others? When are you more likely to get a good amount of sleep? What changes do you want to make to improve your sleep? What one change will you make this week?

2. Continue your sleep journal for the next week.

. . . .
Day 240: Monthly Check-In

The wisest man may be wiser to-day,
than he was yesterday, and to-morrow, than he is to-day.
—Charles Caleb Colton, *Lacon*

Time to check in on your progress. This is not a guilt-inducing exercise designed to shame you for all you haven't accomplished yet. Instead, it's a gentle reminder about what's important to you and what you want to change.

Enjoy the journey. Be gentle with yourself. Keep growing.

Practice:

+ What did I do last month that I'm proud of?

+ Are my relationships with others improving or deteriorating?

+ What do I need to do less of/quit/get rid of/delegate this month?

+ What experiments did I try? What lessons did I learn? What is going well?

+ What isn't working, and what do I want to change?

+ Habit to focus on next month:

+ Why do I want to establish that habit?

+ What is a first step I can take toward making this a habit?

+ What trigger will I use?

+ How will I reward myself?

+ What obstacles will I face in establishing this habit and how will I overcome them?

+ Notes on successes, long-term goals, and personal changes I'm working toward:

. . . .
Day 241: In the Moment: Arguments
Habit: Mindfulness

Be calm in arguing: for fiercenesse makes
Errour a fault, and truth discourtesie.
—George Herbert, "The Church-porch"

I'm sure you've never done this, but I have been known to throw my shoe in an argument with my husband. Not at him! Just a general throw to express my extreme frustration at my inability to communicate. Obviously, mindfulness while arguing is an area I need a lot of practice in.

I'm learning to be better by using our wedding photo as a mindfulness trigger to remind me to step back from the heat of the moment. Then, I can ask myself, "Is this true? What else is true? If I wanted to believe that their intentions were good, what would I have to believe about this person? What's more important than being right? How can I communicate this respectfully? What is my goal?"

Practice:

Choose a trigger that will remind you of your love for the person you are arguing with. Share this trigger with them, so they can help you come back to the moment.

• • • • • • • • • • • • • •
Day 242: Go First
Habit: Relationships

Of all forms of caution, caution in love is perhaps the most fatal to true happiness.
—Bertrand Russell, *The Conquest of Happiness*

To get into a relationship, someone has to have the courage to ask someone out first. In an argument, someone has to have the wisdom to stop fighting and apologize first.

Have the courage to give to the other person before they give you what you want. Have the wisdom to do what you know needs to be done.

Practice:

What are you waiting for someone else to do first? Do it.

. . . .
Day 243: You're Going to Be Okay
Habit: Connecting with Yourself

*In the middle of winter I at last discovered that there was in
me an invincible summer.*
—Albert Camus, "Return to Tipasa"

At times in our life, winter hits all of us, and we focus on our own survival. We move inside ourselves and hunker down. But seasons change. Winter makes way for spring when new growth begins, which makes way for summer.

No matter what is going on in your life, you're going to be okay. You've survived everything else in your life so far. You can make it through this, too. Inside you there is an invincible summer.

Practice:

1. In your journal, reflect on a difficult situation you are dealing with. What are the beliefs, relationships, past experiences, and other resources you can call on to create an invincible summer?

2. Treat yourself to a random act of kindness, like taking a nap, coloring in an adult coloring book, or spending time doing your hobby.

. . . .
Day 244: You've Already Won the Lottery
Habit: Gratitude

Your chances of winning the lottery are about the same whether or not you buy a ticket.
—Robert J. Marks II, 2010 interview with Discovery Institute

I used to say, "If I win the lottery, I'll donate a million dollars to charity." I truly wanted to give to charity, but I just didn't feel like there was much I could do—today. Today, I didn't have enough, but someday I would. And if I won the lottery, that someday would arrive much sooner than I thought.

But I'd overlooked that I'd already won the lottery. I already had so much. Reflecting on the lottery I'd already won made me realize that if I didn't already have enough, nothing was going to be enough.

Practice:

1. In your journal, write about your winning lottery. What do you appreciate about your physical body? What can it do? What do you appreciate about your mind? What does it know? What do you appreciate about your emotional life? Who do you love, and who loves you? What do you enjoy? What do you appreciate about your environment? What is great about

your country, your state, your home? What would someone else envy about your life?

2. Take a moment to feel grateful for all these gifts.

. . . .
Day 245: Daily Action Plan
Habit: Schedule Simplicity

More important than how fast you're going,
is where you're headed.
—Stephen Covey, *First Things First*

Simplicity is about doing the things that are most important to you and eliminating all the rest. This daily action plan process can help you get focused.

1. *Remind yourself of your most important priorities.*

2. *Everything in your head must come out.* Write down everything that needs to get done, anything that's worrying you.

3. *Organize.* Go through that list, and organize your to-do list into categories. Star your most important project. Number the one to three most important tasks that will move it forward. Identify one to three other most important tasks/errands you must complete today. If tasks are not consistent with your life priorities, eliminate or delegate. Take a reality check: Is there enough time to get this all done?

4. *Be efficient.* Group items that can be done together. Block out time during your most product time of day so you can focus for maximum effect.

5. *Do.* As you go through your list, ask, "Given the reality of the situation, what is the next most important thing for me to do?" Just keep doing the next most important thing you need to do.

Practice:

1. What are your life priorities?

2. What is your most important project?

3. What are the one to three most important tasks that will move that forward?

4. What are one to three other most important tasks/errands you must complete today?

5. Is today's daily action plan consistent with your life priorities? Do you need to make some changes?

. . . .
Day 246: Month 9 Giving Challenge: Donate Blood
Habit: Philanthropy

*Compassion is probably the only antitoxin of the soul.
Where there is compassion even the most poisonous
impulses remain relatively harmless.*
—Eric Hoffer, "The Human Factor"

It's a dark and stormy night when your mother's car drives off the road and into a tree. She's rushed to the hospital where she receives a blood transfusion that saves her life. That blood transfusion was made possible by people like you. And like me, because I donated blood for the first time today!

I did it because I learned that every two seconds someone needs a blood transfusion, but only 10 percent of the population donates every year. And since donated red blood cells expire after forty-two days, there is a constant demand for blood. I decided that because I *can* give blood, I should give blood.

I didn't really enjoy it, but it wasn't all that bad and didn't take all that long. I do feel great about giving the gift of life, so here begins an annual blood donation from me. Maybe someday, I'll work up to donating more often, but let's just take our small victories where we can get them!

Practice:

Locate your local blood donation center and contact it. Find out if you're an eligible blood donor, and if so, make an appointment to donate blood.

Week 35

Day 247: Create a Consistent Sleep Schedule
Habit: Physical Health

Oh bed! oh bed! delicious bed!
That heaven upon earth to the weary head.
—Thomas Hood, "Miss Kilmansegg and Her Precious Leg"

If you have difficulty falling and staying asleep, the Harvard Medical School suggests going to bed at the same time every night to set your body's internal clock to create a habit of falling asleep at that time. Harder to do but even more important is waking up at the same time each day—even on the weekend. Waking up at the same time not only creates a regular schedule, but waking up even if you're sleepy will make you more tired and more likely to get a good night's sleep the following night.

In the hour or so before it's time to go to bed, slow down by taking a bath, reading a book, or meditating. If you watch TV, avoid intense shows that will trigger your adrenaline. Put away your work and write down any issues that are on your mind so that your mind can relax and know it can pick up tomorrow where you left off.[51] Remember, giving yourself the gift of sleep will improve your mental and physical health.

Practice:

1. Review your sleep journal. Do you notice any patterns? Are there times you have more difficulty sleeping than others? When are you more likely to get a good amount of sleep? What changes do you want to make to improve your sleep? What one change will you make this week?

2. Continue your sleep journal. You'll be reviewing it again next week.

. . . .

Day 248: Forgiveness Meditation
Habit: Mindfulness

*Every time we forgive, we set a prisoner free,
and the prisoner we set free is ourselves.*
—Lewis Smedes, *Keeping Hope Alive*

Adapted from Jack Kornfield's *The Wise Heart*, this forgiveness meditation incorporates Buddhist psychology and other wisdom.

Practice:

Close your eyes and take a few centering breaths. Say to yourself, "There are many ways knowingly and unknowingly that I have hurt others, betrayed them, or abandoned them. I remember now the harm I've caused and feel the sorrows I still carry." After reflecting and feeling those hurts, say, "I have hurt you because of my own suffering, fear, confusion, pain, anger, or misunderstanding. In this moment, I ask for your forgiveness for the many ways I've harmed you. Please forgive me." After reflecting, say, "Just as I have hurt others, so too I have hurt myself. I have betrayed myself, abandoned my own deepest values, I have judged myself. I remember these now and feel what I still carry." After reflecting, say, "I have hurt myself because of my own fear and confusion, my own pain, anger, and misunderstanding. I offer myself forgiveness." After reflecting, say, "There are many ways that others have hurt and harmed me. We have all been betrayed. We've all had harm inflicted upon us. I feel these now, too, the way I've been hurt by others and I feel the sorrow I still carry." After reflecting, say, "To the extent I'm ready, I turn my heart in the direction of forgiveness. To the extent I am ready, I offer you forgiveness. I release you. I will not carry the pain of hating you in my heart."[52]

- - - - - - - - - - - - - - - - - - - -
Day 249: Family Is a Verb
Habit: Relationships

We must take care of our families, wherever we find them.
—Elizabeth Gilbert, *Eat, Pray, Love*

Family isn't just a noun that describes a genetic relationship. At its best, family is a verb. Family is something you do. Family loves, supports, answers the phone, teaches, listens, remembers, inspires, laughs, cooks, cleans, nurtures, heals, cares, supports, cheers. Family is there for each other.

Family is as family does.

Practice:

1. In your journal, consider these questions: What does your family do well? What do you enjoy about your family? What have you learned from your family? What can you do to bring your family closer?

2. Reach out to a family member today.

. . . .
Day 250: Alter Egos
Habit: Connecting with Yourself

Why be you when you can be moi?
—Miss Piggy

Inside you is every conceivable human emotion and personality. If you're like most people, a few of those are your go-to favorites. I know I like being the happy and positive person that everyone can count on. However, different situations require different strengths, and an alter ego can inspire you to ignite the parts of yourself you need to be successful in different scenarios. For example, at the end of the day, you can call on the powerfully sexy alter ego Scarlett to help you let the stress of the day go and be physically intimate with your partner.

Practice:

1. In your journal, list the personality traits you want to call on in the following situations and give a name to your alter ego that will inspire you to bring those traits out of yourself.

The Board Room—a.k.a., when you want to be powerful

The Bedroom—a.k.a., when you want to be sexy

The Ballroom—a.k.a., when you want to be elegant and sophisticated

The Hospital Room—a.k.a., when you need to be nurturing and supportive

Other:

2. Choose an altar ego to play with today. Treat your altar ego to a random act of kindness he or she would enjoy.

. . . .
Day 251: Friends
Habit: Gratitude

Friendship is unnecessary, like philosophy, like art.…
It has no survival value; rather it is one of those things
which give value to survival.
—C. S. Lewis, "Friendship"

I used to not have friends. I was busy working, and I was terrible at keeping in touch with people. In an attempt to socialize more, I started volunteering and met this lively, fun, powerful woman named Christine. She said, "You have to meet Heidi. She would love you!"

I don't know how it happened, but this friendless person made two amazing friends. It's not just that we have a ball hanging out together, although we do. It's that I'm proud of them. I believe in them. I think they're fabulous, and everyone should know them. I like to think they feel the same way about me—not because they have to because they are related to me but because they choose to. And that is a fabulous feeling.

Sending a big thank-you to my friends.

Practice:

1. Take out your journal and list your friends. What do you like about them? What does their friendship mean to you?
2. Send a thank-you e-mail or text to a friend or call them.

. . . .
Day 252: Birding
Habit: Nature Simplicity

The beautiful vagabonds, endowed with every grace,
masters of all climes, and knowing no bounds—
how many human aspirations are realized in their free,
holiday lives, and how many suggestions to the poet
in their flight and song!
—John Burroughs, "Straight Seeing and Thinking"

Birds aren't just important indicators of the environment's health, they are also beautiful. Their blues, reds, and yellows are nature's jewelry. Birds mark the passing of time and let you know when spring is budding or winter descending. They remind us that we, too, used to be free and that we still yearn to take flight.

Birding is a doorway to a deeper relationship with nature and is an activity available to anyone (there are even groups of blind people who bird by ear) at almost any time (birds are everywhere in every season). At any moment, a little piece of the wild can visit you to remind you of your connection with nature and inspire you with the mystery of life. Birds are fascinating, and their behaviors and songs are a constant source of discovery rewarded to the close observer.

Practice:

1. Find a place near you where you can observe some birds. What kind of birds do you notice? Describe them. What kind of shape do they have? What colors are their legs, their eyes, their bills? What patterns do their feathers create? Is the bird by itself or with others of its kind? What is it doing?

2. Connect with your local Audubon club to learn more about the birds in your area.

3. Add bird habitat such as brush piles, a birdbath, or a birdhouse to your yard.

. . . .
Day 253: Ignore the Founder's Story
Habit: Philanthropy

We are not here to curse the darkness,
but to light the candle that can guide us through
that darkness to a safe and sane future.
—John F. Kennedy, 1960 presidential nomination
acceptance speech

Some charities tug on your heartstrings by telling you who started this charity and why. The stories often involve personal difficulty and a search for meaning that results in personal transformation.

You know what I do with these stories? I ignore them. The founder's story doesn't tell me if their work is effective. It doesn't tell me if they're efficient with their money. It doesn't tell me if the founder does a good job of leading their charity. It doesn't tell me if their costs are too high.

Their story tells me that they care. I'm glad they care. But caring isn't enough.

Practice:

1. Take stock of your philanthropic efforts. Are the charities you're supporting working on your favorite causes? If no, should you stop donating to them? Which of your favorite causes do you want to do more for?

2. Perform a philanthropic action like volunteering to help a charity with an upcoming event, signing an online petition, or making a monetary donation.

Week 36

Day 254: Sleep Rules
Habit: Physical Health

There is a time for many words,
and there is also a time for sleep.
—Odysseus in *The Odyssey*, Homer

If you have difficulty falling and staying asleep, these two rules may help:

1. *No naps.* A high level of tiredness encourages you to sleep when you're supposed to be sleeping.

2. *The bed is for sleeping.* Lying in bed and looking at the clock will just stress you out. If you're in bed and struggling to fall sleep or if you wake up in the middle of night and can't get back to sleep, get out of bed, go to another room, and do something relaxing, like reading or listening to music, until you are tired enough to sleep. Keep the lights dim and avoid physical, mental, and emotional stimulation.[53]

Practice:

1. Review your sleep journal. Do you notice any patterns? Are there times you have more difficulty sleeping than others?

When are you more likely to get a good amount of sleep? What changes do you want to make to improve your sleep? What one change will you make this week? Continue with your sleep journal for one more week.

2. In your personal journal, ask yourself, "What would being fully rested allow me to do better? What will my sleep routine be? What are my sleep rules?"

· ·
Day 255: Moving Meditation
Habit: Mindfulness

In the marriage of flesh and spirit, divorce is impossible.
—Gabrielle Roth, *Maps to Ecstasy*

Any form of conscious movement can become a moving meditation and is often an intentional part of many practices such as martial arts, sacred dancing, tai chi, qigong, and vinyasa and other types of yoga. These moving meditations can foster a truly generous understanding and acceptance of one's own body. They are often best experienced with instruction, so consider watching YouTube videos or signing up for tai chi, qigong, or yoga classes.

Practice:

Close your eyes and take a few centering breaths. Bring your attention to your hands. Wiggle your fingers, and when your hands feel energized, place them palm up on your thighs. Can you feel the pulse in your fingertips, the air touching your palms, and the space between your fingers? Gently lift your hands, moving slowly, almost imperceptibly. Feel the air parting and the energy in your hands. Slowly, bring your palms close to each other. Imagine a ball of pulsing energy between your hands. Explore this feeling and energy, and when you're ready, rest your hands in your lap and sit for a few more minutes in silence.

· ·
Day 256: Be a Good Neighbor
Habit: Relationships

Neighbors bring food with death and flowers with sickness and little things in between.
—Harper Lee, *To Kill a Mockingbird*

Neighbors aren't always easy to live with, so they give us the perfect opportunity for practicing our relationship building and conflict resolution skills. The skills we develop with our neighbors help us build better relationships out in the rest of the world, too. The world is really just one big neighborhood made up of lots of tiny neighborhoods. If we can turn our neighborhoods into vibrant and supportive communities, imagine how the world's neighborhoods could change, too.

Practice:

Treat your neighbor to a random act of kindness, such as a yummy treat or fresh flowers (not picked from your neighbor's yard!). You could mow the lawn or run a few errands for an elderly or ill neighbor. If you're thinking big, you could host a neighborhood block party or begin a neighborhood babysitting swap where parents take turns babysitting the neighborhood kids.

. . . .

Day 257: Regret
Habit: Connecting with Yourself

Of all the words of mice and men,
the saddest are "It might have been."
—Kurt Vonnegut, *Cat's Cradle*

I regret that my mom passed away before we got to be good friends. Regret is a powerful emotion, and what I wouldn't do to avoid feeling that. What I wouldn't give to go back and just enjoy my mom.

But I can't change the past, so I have to use that regret. I can use it to make sense of the world. I can use it change my behavior. In the future, I won't miss an opportunity to enjoy someone I love. That's the real power of regret. It's the power to change your life and the world for the better. So use your regret. Use the fear of having regret.

Practice:

1. In your journal, write about a moment in your past you regret. How will you use it to avoid future mistakes? What would you regret having left undone or unsaid if you died tomorrow?

2. If your regret involves another person, write them a note. Otherwise, write a promise to yourself expressing your regret and how you will rectify it.

. . . .
Day 258: The Magic of Music
Habit: Gratitude

Music expresses that which cannot be said
and on which it is impossible to be silent.
—Victor Hugo, *William Shakespeare*

After my mom passed away, I noticed that nothing could bring her to mind more quickly than the right song. My mother loved music in a way I haven't experienced. For her, music was deep and personal, and it's one of her legacies to me.

She grew up in a large Italian, Catholic family. At one point, she and her seven siblings squeezed into a small apartment over a bar in the Italian part of town. At night, the bar would turn up the music, and the old Italian crooners like Jerry Vale and Jimmy Durante would serenade the neighborhood. She never tired of listening to those standards.

But my mom was born in 1954, and Motown changed everything. When Martha Reeves sang "Nowhere to Run," Mom sat in her bedroom and listened to this song over and over. It's the first song she remembered obsessing over.

More than anything though, my mom loved women with strong voices. You know, the ones who can just belt it out. Barbra Streisand's album *Guilty* was one of mom's favorites. It turns out that she wasn't the only one in the house who loved that album. When I was a freshman in college, I called home. My dad answered. We talked for a few minutes, and I asked to speak to Mom. But he told me Mom wasn't home. And I was confused.

"Yes, she is."

"No, she isn't."

"But I hear Barbra in the background. Dad, are you listening to Barbra?"

Practice:

1. In your journal, list your favorite song, a song that makes you feel young at heart, a song that makes you want to dance, and a song you would want played at your memorial service. Write down songs that bring back special memories of people or places.

2. Take a moment to appreciate the artists who create the soundtrack for your life.

3. Listen to one of these songs.

. . . .
Day 259: Your Desk
Habit: Home Simplicity

If a cluttered desk is a sign of a cluttered mind,
of what, then, is an empty desk a sign?
—Laurence J. Peter, *Peter's Quotations*

Some people like a meticulously organized desk, and some like their desk to reflect the creativity of their process. In any case, the trick is finding a system in which you can be confident that you can find whatever you need and that nothing important is going to get overlooked, so you can focus on giving more to yourself and to others.

Practice:

1. *Keep an Inbox:* See day 71, "Your Brain Is for Processing." If you don't already have an inbox, create one now.

2. *Collect:* Clear the top of your desk and any drawers that need to be organized. Place all paper into the inbox to be processed.

3. *Discard Trash:* Toss the old receipts, gum wrappers, and old sticky notes.

4. *Prioritize:* Place the items you use most frequently in or on your desk. Items you don't use regularly can be stored in a filing cabinet, on a shelf, or even in a closet.

5. *Sort and Organize:* Group like things together. Use bags or trays to keep similar items contained.

6. *Make an Active Project Strategy:* What is your strategy for staying on top of ongoing projects? I like to keep mine in separate stacks on a bookshelf left open for this purpose. Hanging baskets, to-do lists, and calendar appointments could also work. Check out the Internet for lots of great suggestions on how to keep track of your ongoing paperwork and projects.

7. *Process Your Inbox.* See day 143, "Papers."

8. *Review Regularly:* Schedule an hour each week to organize your desk, review paperwork, and check on ongoing projects.

Day 260: Charity Races
Habit: Philanthropy

Many persons have a wrong idea of what constitutes
true happiness. It is not attained through self-gratification
but through fidelity to a worthy purpose.
—Helen Keller, *The Open Door*

Every year tens of millions of Americans ask friends to sponsor them in events ranging from three-mile "fun runs" to hundred-mile bike treks, so it's very likely that a well-meaning family member, friend, coworker, or boss will ask you to support them in a charity race.

There are two reasons to say yes to these requests.

1. To support them. This reason can trump all others. Do you want to support your friend or family member in this effort? Then donate.

2. You believe the cost is worth the publicity. Taking into consideration costs like toilets, signage, fences, barricades, permits, security, water, entertainment, and online fundraising commissions, a charity will only keep about 48 percent of all the money raised.[54] But an event can raise public awareness. Is it worth it?

If you disagree with these reasons, if you don't support the cause, or if you already support the cause through more cost-effective methods, it's okay to say no.

Practice:

1. If you are asked to donate to a friend or family member's walk or run, when will you say yes? When will you say no? How will you say no?
2. Set a budget for supporting your friends' and family's charity requests.

Week 37
· · · · · · · · · ·

Day 261: Sleeping and Happiness
Habit: Physical Health

Laugh and the world laughs with you,
snore and you sleep alone.
—Beatrice Stella Tanner Campbell,
1912 letter to George Bernard Shaw

When you sleep, your body produces hypocretin. Hypocretin is a hormone that promotes wakefulness. The more sleep you get, the more hypocretin you'll accumulate and the more awake you'll feel.

But hypocretin isn't just about wakefulness. There's another time your body produces hypocretin—when you're happy! When you're experiencing joy and pleasure, your body is producing hypocretin. Get enough sleep, and you'll wake up with more hypocretin in your system, giving you a good foundation from which to experience more joy and pleasure during your day.

If you are still struggling to fall asleep quickly and sleep through the night, you may have a sleep disorder or an underlying health problem and should consult with a physician or a sleep specialist. Beware of relying on over-the-counter medications for a long period of time, which could mask your underlying health problem, make your sleeping problems more difficult to solve, or cause their own side effects.[55]

Practice:

Are you getting at least seven hours of sleep a night? Do you need to consult with a physician or sleep specialist? If so, what is the first step you need to take to make that happen?

. . . .
Day 262: Breathing Regulation
Habit: Mindfulness

If you want to conquer the anxiety of life, live in the moment,
live in the breath.
—Amit Ray, *Om Chanting and Medition*

If you don't think about breathing, your brainstem—the ancient brain you've inherited from your lizard ancestors—makes sure it happens for you. But when you take control of your breathing, you engage your cerebral cortex—the most sophisticated and newly evolved section of your brain that you use for thinking, perceiving, and producing and understanding language. For this reason, the conscious manipulation of breath can calm and focus your mind. *Pranayama* is just one style of breathing-regulation meditation, and the four-four-four-four pattern that follows is just one suggested breathing pattern.

Practice:

Close your eyes and take a few centering breaths. Take a breath in through your nose, if possible, for a count of four. Hold it in for a count of four. Exhale for a count of four, and finally, hold empty for a count of four. Repeat for as short or as long as you'd like.

. . . .
Day 263: Stewardship
Habit: Relationships

Real generosity toward the future
lies in giving all to the present.
—Albert Camus, *The Rebel*

What does it mean to own something when you can't take it with you when you go? Nothing really belongs to you. You are the steward, and your job is not just to enjoy it while you have it but to care for it, nurture it, and safeguard it. When you pass it on to others, it should provide them with the same joy, beauty, and benefit it gave you.

Practice:

1. Imagine the ideal world you'd like your children to grow up in. When your children have children and you are a proud grandparent or great-grandparent, what kind of world do you want those children to have? How would that world be better than it is today? How would the world be the same? What needs to be preserved?

2. Take a generous action toward the environment, such as switching to nontoxic cleaners, performing car maintenance to reduce your pollution and increase your gas mileage, or not letting the water run while you brush your teeth or wash dishes.

. . . .
Day 264: Be Honest
Habit: Connecting with Yourself

If you look for truth, you may find comfort in the end; if you look for comfort you will not get either comfort or truth—only soft soap and wishful thinking to begin with and, in the end, despair.

—C. S. Lewis, *Mere Christianity*

When I moved to a new city, I expected to make new friends and have a busy social calendar. It didn't happen, and that was probably because I rarely left my house. I had to be honest that what I said I wanted wasn't lining up with my actions. So I joined a couple Toastmasters Clubs and my local Audubon group to go birdwatching. Slowly but surely, I grew a network of friends where I lived.

Practice:

1. In your journal, write about what you want in your life that you don't have. Where are your actions not lining up with what you want? What behaviors do you have to start doing? What behaviors do you have to stop engaging in? How are you sabotaging your own success and happiness?

2. From your list, do something you know you should be doing, or don't do something you know you shouldn't be doing.

· ·
Day 265: Expressing Gratitude
Habit: Gratitude

In the end, though, maybe we must all give up trying to pay back the people in this world who sustain our lives. In the end, maybe it's wiser to surrender before the miraculous scope of human generosity and to just keep saying thank you, forever and sincerely, for as long as we have voices.
—Elizabeth Gilbert, *Eat, Pray, Love*

Gratitude at its most powerful is a force for deepening our relationship with other people. Gratitude that is expressed multiplies, brings people closer together, and creates a positive cycle where more gratitude is felt, expressed, and shared.

Practice:

1. In your journal, identify someone you're grateful for. List five reasons why you are grateful for them. You can include personality traits and specific actions they've taken or experiences you've shared together. Be specific and detailed.

2. Express your gratitude to this person either face to face or via text, phone, or letter. If you want to get creative, feel free to do so, but not at the expense of actually doing it. The most important thing is to let them know. The more specific you

are with them about why you're grateful for them, the more they will feel understood, seen, accepted, and loved.

. . . .
Day 266: In Case You Missed It
Habit: Mind Simplicity

The real trick to life is not to be in the know,
but to be in the mystery.
—Fred Alan Wolf, *Dr. Quantum's Little Book of Big Ideas*

In his day, Thomas Jefferson was one of the most learned men on the planet and knew something about nearly everything. He was an accomplished gardener who could speak knowledgeably and authoritatively on topics ranging from Greek mythology to economic theory to philosophy. He was the architect of his Virginian home, Monticello.

He collected nearly all the significant authors and thinkers of the world in the library in his home. In fact, in 1815 the Library of Congress purchased Thomas Jefferson's personal library of 6,487 books to start their collection.

Today, the Library of Congress is adding 12,000 publications every single day. At your fingertips, you have access to more information than Thomas Jefferson could have possibly imagined.

Have you felt overwhelmed by the sheer number of e-mails to open, articles to read, and videos to watch? If so, you're not alone, and the cure is to embrace the fact that you will miss out. Don't try to consume as much information as possible from as many sources as possible. Instead cultivate knowledge and entertainment from the sources that add value to your life.

Practice:

1. In your journal, reflect on the limits of time and space in your life. How much time do you have for cultivating information? How much time do you have for cultivating entertainment? What sources provide you with the best knowledge? What entertainment do you enjoy the most? How will you prioritize that knowledge and entertainment? For example, live performances are experiences that are enjoyed as they are happening and can't be saved for later, so these may be more important than other entertainment. How will you limit the information you consume? Do you want to put an expiration date on new material? If you didn't get to it that week, can you just delete it? What sources provide thorough and thoughtful information?

2. Today, miss out on something like a TV show, a social media meme, or water cooler gossip.

. . . .
Day 267: Disaster Donations, Part 1
Habit: Philanthropy

Being myself no stranger to suffering,
I have learned to relieve the sufferings of others.
—Virgil, *The Aeneid*

On the evening news, you see demolished homes and children crying. A disaster struck, and you want to help. This is the most important time to donate because there is a need right now that needs to be addressed, and without help, people will die. But it's also the time when it can be the most difficult to make good donations.

Additional tips will follow on day 282. In the meantime, follow these three principles when donating during a disaster:

1. *Do not donate goods.* Collecting goods after a disaster is a common practice, but donated goods take time and labor to receive, assess for safety, sort, clean, and transport. About 60 percent of donated clothes, food, medicines, and toys will be trashed and can wreak havoc on emergency efforts. Rest assured that disaster relief agencies and first responder units are usually well stocked with provisions or can get them directly from companies at discounted prices.[56]

2. *Do not go to the scene.* In a disaster, food and lodging resources are decimated. If you show up, where will you sleep, and what will you eat? Are you using resources that could go to survivors? Are you taking away work from local survivors who could use that income to get back on their feet sooner rather than later?

3. *Give money.* The most effective thing you can give during a disaster is money.

Practice:

Create an emergency donation budget. If a disaster strikes and you want to help, how much will you donate?

Week 38
· · · · · · · · · · ·

Day 268: Snacking
Habit: Physical Health

My weaknesses have always been food and men—
in that order.
—Dolly Parton

There's nothing wrong with snacking as part of a healthy diet. An apple, carrot slices with peanut butter, or yogurt sprinkled with walnuts and drizzled with honey can be a great source of fiber, vitamins, and antioxidants.

But if you're snacking because you're bored or in the habit of eating certain foods or at certain times, then pause. If you're snacking when really you're thirsty or tired, then pause. If you're feeling lonely or disconnected from yourself, then pause. Notice the urge to snack, identify your trigger, and choose a new routine. Alternatives to snacking could include sucking on a breath mint, chewing gum, or brushing your teeth. Maybe you want to take a walk, read a book, play with your kid, or chat with your coworker. Maybe it's time to go to bed.

Practice:

1. In your journal, reflect on your snacking. How often do you snack? Are there times when you snack when you're not hungry? What is your trigger for snacking? What reward do you get for snacking?

2. What new routine will you create to replace unhealthy snacking? See day 182 for "Breaking Bad (Habits)." Set yourself up for success by having healthy snacking options where you need when you need to snack.

3. Before snacking, try just feeling hungry for a little while. What does that feel like? Does it pass? How do you respond emotionally when you feel hungry?

. . . .
Day 269: How to End a Meditation Session
Habit: Mindfulness

The secret of change is to focus all of your energy,
not on fighting the old, but on building the new.
—Dan Millman, *Way of the Peaceful Warrior*

Use the end of your meditation session to set yourself up for a day where you're focused and motivated to do and give for yourself and others.

Practice:

When you are ready to stop meditating, spend two minutes on the loving kindness meditation (day 38). If you feel moved, offer a prayer or other guiding words of wisdom. Then, before you open your eyes, feel the intention to open your eyes. Experience your eyes opening and each sensation that occurs as they open. Feel the intention to stand up or resume your activities, and feel yourself taking those actions and reorienting to the world around you.

. . . .
Day 270: Monthly Check-In

*As human beings, our greatness lies not so much in being able
to remake the world … as in being able to remake ourselves.*
—Michael N. Nagler, foreword to *Gandhi: The Man*
by Eknath Easwaran

Time to check in on your progress. This is not a guilt-inducing exercise designed to shame you for all you haven't accomplished yet. Instead, it's a gentle reminder about what's important to you and what you want to change.

Enjoy the journey. Be gentle with yourself. Keep growing.

Practice:

+ What did I do last month that I'm proud of?

+ Are my relationships with others improving or deteriorating?

+ What do I need to do less of/quit/get rid of/delegate this month?

+ What experiments did I try? What lessons did I learn? What is going well?

+ What isn't working, and what do I want to change?

- Habit to focus on next month:
- Why do I want to establish that habit?
- What is a first step I can take toward making this a habit?
- What trigger will I use?
- How will I reward myself?
- What obstacles will I face in establishing this habit and how will I overcome them?
- Notes on successes, long-term goals, and personal changes I'm working toward:

. . . .

Day 271: Spread Light
Habit: Relationships

There are two ways of spreading light: to be
The candle or the mirror that reflects it.
—Edith Wharton, "Vesalius in Zante"

I'm not the only person who's had those dark moments of the soul, right? At those times when we feel most hopeless, worthless, or tired, an act of kindness from another human being can remind us of our good qualities, reignite a passion for life, or restore our faith in the human race. You may not realize just how dark someone's world is, and your time and attention might light it up.

Practice:

Who do you know who is going through a difficult time, like fighting an illness or going through a divorce? Treat them to a random act of kindness, like taking them out for coffee, sending them flowers, or leaving a thoughtful voicemail.

. . . .
Day 272: Invest in Yourself
Habit: Connecting with Yourself

The heights by great men reached and kept
Were not attained by sudden flight,
But they, while their companions slept,
Were toiling upward in the night.
—Henry Wadsworth Longfellow, "The Ladder of St. Augustine"

You invest in stocks and bonds because they are valuable. You are also valuable, so invest time and money in yourself. Books, trainings, formal education, spiritual advisors, and coaches are just a few resources that can help you close the gap between where you are and where you want to be.

Practice:

1. In your journal, consider investing in your mind. What do you need to know, do, or change to grow your skills and education? Where can you get this? What about your body? What do you need to know, do, or change to improve your health? Where can you get this? And what about your spirit? What do you need to know, do, or change to have more connection with something bigger than yourself, more peace of mind, and less stress? Where can you get this?

2. Invest in yourself today. For example, buy an educational book, listen to an informational podcast, or consult with an expert.

. . . .

Day 273: What Can You Do with What You Have?
Habit: Gratitude

You are braver than you believe,
and stronger than you seem, and smarter than you think.
—Christopher Robin in *Pooh's Grand Adventure*

What Don't I Have?

That's a crappy question, and when you ask a crappy question, you'll get a crappy answer that makes you feel crappy. I don't have the right pair of shoes to go with that outfit or a big enough house or a new enough car. I don't have enough time or energy or money or someone to hang out with this weekend. I don't have a perfect body.

What Do I Have?

Now that's a better question. I have two arms, legs, eyes, and ears that all work. I have a sharp mind and a big heart, a great family and lovely friends, a roof over my head, a bed to sleep on, and food in my refrigerator.

What Can I Do with What I Have?

This is an even better question that puts you in problem-solving mode and reminds you that you can do something! I can use the

Internet, which puts me in contact with millions of people and a gazillion pieces of information. I can use my past experience to offer advice, experience, and support to someone who needs it.

Practice:

1. Think about a situation in which you feel incomplete, less than, or unsatisfied or one with which you are unhappy. In your journal, identify what you don't have in that situation that is causing your struggle. Then, create a list of assets that could help you in this situation. Be sure to include people, knowledge, skills, and resources.

2. Reflect on how lucky you are to have so many resources to call on.

. . . .
Day 274: It's Not a Priority
Habit: Schedule Simplicity

The purpose of life, after all, is to live it,
to taste experience to the utmost, to reach out eagerly
and without fear for newer and richer experience.
—Eleanor Roosevelt, *You Learn by Living*

Often people say that they don't have time or they're too busy as a reason for not doing something. While that may be true, it may be something you should make time for. Saying "It's not a priority" may help you become more aware of these times. For example, does saying "My health is not a priority" instead of "I don't have time to exercise" change how you feel about exercising?

Not everything is a priority. Remove yourself from activities and commitments that don't serve your highest purpose so that you have time and energy for what does.

Practice:

1. In your journal, list your commitments—work, side work (freelancing, odd jobs, home business, etc.), family, your children's commitments that you help make happen, civic commitments (volunteer work, board membership, and other civic or political engagement), religious commitments, hobbies, home, health, online activities, and any other commitments.

2. Now take a close look at each item on the list and consider these questions: How does this give my life value? How important is it to me? Is it in line with my life priorities and values? How would it affect my life if I dropped out? Does this further my life goals? What does this commitment cost me in terms of time, energy, and other opportunities?

3. Which commitment or commitments are not a priority for you? What are your concerns about quitting that commitment?

4. Quit at least one commitment.

Day 275: Month 10 Giving Challenge: Health
Habit: Philanthropy

Here let me say that there is no finer investment
for any community than putting milk into babies.
Healthy citizens are the greatest asset any country can have.
—Winston Churchill, "Four Year Plan"

In 2012, the Integrated Benefits Institute estimated that poor health costs the US economy $576 billion a year[57]—which includes disability, worker's comp, sick days, and days when people are at work but can't perform at their best because of illness. The personal costs are much harder to quantify but are no less dramatic. Illness and poor health drain financial resources, strain marriages, limit a parent's ability to participate in their child's activities, and reduce a person's ability to excel and get promoted at work.

Practice:

1. Do you have a personal connection to a health condition and does it interest you to support awareness or funding research for this disease? Or are you more interested in supporting initiatives that promote a healthy lifestyle, such as encouraging youth exercise or making fresh fruits and vegetables available and affordable to inner-city communities?

2. Sign up for a newsletter from a charity working on a health cause that interests you.

Week 39

Day 276: Give Your Heart Legs
Habit: Physical Health

He who has a Why? in life can tolerate almost any How?
—Friedrich Nietzsche, *Twilight of the Idols*

Change is difficult, but if your reason for changing connects with your heart, you may discover a lot more commitment to your goal. Take, for example, the bad habit of interrupting people while they're talking.

A regular reason might look like this: I will stop interrupting people because it's rude.

But a reason with heart might look like this: I want to stop interrupting people because when I interrupt them, I don't get to hear what they were going to say. It might have been fun or interesting, and now I'm missing out. Plus, I've communicated to them that I don't care what they have to say, and that's hurtful. I wouldn't want someone to think that what they have to say is unimportant. So even though I'm burning with desire to jump in, I will respect them and wait for them to finish.

Practice:

In your journal, choose a habit to break. Why is it so important to make this change? What will it mean for your life? What will it let you accomplish or feel? What will it cost you if you don't make this change? Refer to day 182, "Breaking Bad (Habits)," and make a plan. Consider all your resources, including day 227, "Ask for Help," and day 97, "Enlist Support."

. . . .
Day 277: In the Moment: Implicit Bias
Habit: Mindfulness

The eye sees only what the mind is prepared to comprehend.
—Robertson Davies, *Tempest-Tost*

Research reveals that despite our best intentions and best effort, every person has an unconscious implicit bias. This means that you respond differently to different people—even though you truly believe that you treat everyone equally. Although you can't and probably shouldn't eliminate bias entirely, mindfulness has been shown to alleviate the negative impacts of implicit bias, and you can't be fully generous if you're not seeing people clearly.[58]

Practice:

Today while engaging with a person who looks different from you in race, gender, age, or ability, notice what thoughts and emotions you are feeling. Try this exercise suggested by Rhonda Magee, professor of law at the University of San Francisco. Silently say, "This person is just like me. They love and have been loved. They have been hurt. They have known loss. This person is just like me."[59]

. . . .
Day 278: Surprise!
Habit: Relationships

Our brightest blazes of gladness are commonly kindled by unexpected sparks.
—Samuel Johnson, *The Idler*, No. 58

Surprises are fun to give and to receive. Big events like birthdays or graduations can be occasions for a surprise, but truly no occasion is needed. In fact, there is no better way to let someone know they are special and loved than the unsuspected, undeserving surprise.

Practice:

1. In your journal, choose someone to surprise. Brainstorm ideas for a surprise. What do they need help with? What would make their life better? What do they enjoy? What can you make a big deal about? What makes them feel loved?

2. Surprise them!

. . . .
Day 279: I Might Be Wrong
Habit: Connecting with Yourself

I wish to say what I think & feel today, with the proviso that
tomorrow perhaps I shall contradict it all.
—Ralph Waldo Emerson, 1939 journal entry

I joke that I want to start an "I might be wrong" support group because everyone wants to be right all the time. Somehow being wrong is a cardinal sin, and people would rather stop talking to friends and family than change their mind. But an open, curious mind reflects the reality that the world changes. Our knowledge about the world changes. We change. What used to be true for us changes.

Practice:

1. In your journal, consider a scenario in which you know others disagree. Why are you so sure of your opinion? Is there information you haven't considered? Has something new developed since you last made up your mind? By what standards are you judging right? Is that fair to you? Is it fair to others? Could more than one position be true? What's more important than being right?

2. Ask someone who has a different opinion why they believe that way without offering your opinion in return.

······················
Day 280: Deep Gratitude
Habit: Gratitude

*In ordinary life, we hardly realize that we receive
a great deal more than we give, and that it is only
with gratitude that life becomes rich.*
—Dietrich Bonhoeffer, *Letters and Papers from Prison*

Researchers at the University of Southern California wanted to know if *how* people practiced gratitude impacted how much benefit they got from it. In their study, some people wrote one thing they were grateful for, some wrote five things they were grateful, and some wrote five reasons they were grateful for one thing. They concluded that being more grateful about one thing leads to greater emotional well-being, unless that gratitude was directed at a person.[60]

For example, I am grateful for my home because it's my sanctuary where I always feel safe, comfortable, and loved. I love its built-in bookshelves that display my favorite books and the dining room that is bathed in warm afternoon sunlight and is the perfect size for sharing meals with friends and family. I adore my front porch, which is perfect for enjoying the spring and fall weather.

Practice:
Choose one object or event you are grateful for. In your journal, write for two minutes every possible reason that you are grateful for it. Be specific, detailed, and creative.

Day 281: Life and Death in Nature
Habit: Nature Simplicity

One's life has value so long as one attributes value
to the life of others, by means of love, friendship,
indignation and compassion.
—Simone de Beauvoir, *The Coming of Age*

For ancient humans, survival was uncertain and unpredictable, and from this fact of life, ancient humans came to understand that their life was not entirely in their own hands. They were just a single thread in an intricate web of creation and destruction. They saw that the animals, trees—all life—always chose life over destruction, and for this reason, all life deserves respect. It has value without regard to its usefulness to man. There was no escaping the knowledge that life was made possible by death, and death for all was inevitable.

Practice:

1. If possible, sit outside in nature. Close your eyes. Feel your life as a single thread in the web of the entire world. How does your thread impact other threads? How do they affect you? Consider the food you eat, the way you travel, the way you entertain yourself, and where you live. Reflect on the ways your life causes death and destruction in nature. Where can you treat the life you are taking with greater respect? Reflect on your inevitable death; does it change how you want to interact with the natural world? Does it change the things

you want to do or say on a daily basis? To close, thank the natural world around you that makes your life possible and promise to honor both nature's life and its death.

2. Be generous to the environment by making food choices that respect life. This can include purchasing sustainably harvested seafood, purchasing animal welfare–ensured meats, and avoiding products like palm oil that are causing environmental damage.

. . . .
Day 282: Disaster Donations, Part 2
Habit: Philanthropy

Do good with what thou hast, or it will do thee no good.
—William Penn, *Some Fruits of Solitude in Reflections and Maxims*

On day 267, you learned three principles to follow when donating during a disaster. Here are two more tips to consider:

1. *Choose experienced charities.* Emotions are high after a disaster, and scammers take advantage of that. Is that new charity a fraud? Maybe they're not scammers, but have they dealt with emergencies before and do they have relationships with other disaster relief charities? During a disaster, coordination is critical. Infrastructure is damaged, so getting in and getting out can be a logistical nightmare. Charities that are not familiar with and involved in that coordination can cause havoc in ports and on roads. In addition, if they are delivering supplies but are not

part of the official reporting chain, no one knows who has received what. As a result, some areas get more assistance than they need while other areas get less than they need. Because aid that is incorrectly disbursed can destabilize the local labor market and economies, emergency aid is best left to those with experience.

2. *Choose charities already in the community.* They already know the needs of the communities and have the experience and resources to get the assistance to those who need it. Outside charities can waste precious time and resources before learning what is really needed, where it's really needed, and how to best deliver it. Get your donation to the people with boots already on the ground.

Practice:

You've already set your disaster donation budget; now get clear on the kind of disasters you will support. Consider size, severity, and a country's relative wealth and access to resources.

Week 40

Day 283: Love Your Body
Habit: Physical Health

*People are crying up the rich and variegated plumage of the
peacock, and he is himself blushing at the sight of his ugly feet.*
—Sa'di, *The Gulistan*

A *Glamour* survey of more than three hundred women of all sizes
found that women have on average thirteen negative body thoughts
a day with 97 percent having at least one "I hate my body" thought
each day. So if you're like most women, you're not happy with your
body. But the truth is that it's not really about your body. That survey discovered that women who were unsatisfied with their career
or relationship reported more negative body thoughts and started
berating their looks when they were feeling uncomfortable emotions like stress, loneliness, and even boredom.[61] These negative
thoughts take a psychological and physical toll, and it is a deeply
ungenerous way to treat yourself.

Practice:

1. In your journal, make a list of all the wonderful things your
   body does for you (for example, your eyebrows keep sweat
   from stinging your eyes, your ears treat you to the sound of

children laughing). What do you like about your body? Is it the smoothness of your skin, the gentleness of your hands, the strength in your legs, the roundness of your shoulders? How often do you feel bad about your body? When do those thoughts arise (i.e., what triggers your self-abuse)? What reward do you get for engaging in those thoughts?

2. Stand in front of a full-length mirror and thank your body for what is does for you. Admire the parts of your body that you like and say, "This is my body. It's not perfect, but it belongs to me. I accept it and value it. I am grateful for it."

. . . .
Day 284: Exercise Mindfulness
Habit: Mindfulness

To connect with our bodies is to learn to trust ourselves, and from that comes power.
—Mirka Knaster, *Discovering the Body's Wisdom*

Practicing mindfulness while exercising is a wonderful opportunity to connect with, to listen to, and learn from your body. A deep connection and trust with your body creates a foundation that will allow you to accomplish more in the world.

Practice:

Be mindful while exercising today. No music or TV. Just you and whatever physical activity you've chosen. Before beginning, notice how your body feels. Is anything tense or sore? Warm up with some slow arm swings or lunges and notice how your body is moving and responding to this movement. As you begin your exercise, notice how quickly your breathing changes. Do you feel your heart rate accelerating? Do you feel air moving or clothing brushing up against your skin? Feel your muscles expanding and contracting while you're exercising. Which ones are working harder? Anything feel strained, in a bad way? What thoughts pop up in your head? How are you responding emotionally to exercising?

. . . .
Day 285: Tell Me More
Habit: Relationships

A good listener helps us overhear ourselves.
—Yahia Lababidi, *Signposts to Elsewhere*

I love giving advice, but there's a dark side to giving advice. Sometimes I jump in to solve a problem or give a new perspective before I truly understand someone's problem. Sometimes they don't want a solution; they just need to talk. Sometimes it's not my problem to solve, and if I just listened more, they'd figure it out on their own. There is no better way to short-circuit giving advice too soon than to be a good listener. There is no better way to discover more from a person than to say to them, "Tell me more."

Practice:
In a conversation today, invite a person to tell you more about their idea, situation, passion, or problem.

Day 286: Comparing
Habit: Connecting with Yourself

*How much time he gains who does not look to see what his
neighbor says or does or thinks, but only at what he does himself, to make it just and holy.*
—Marcus Aurelius, *Meditations*

Comparing yourself to others is unfair to yourself. In some cases,
you're comparing your insides to other people's outsides. Sure,
they look like they have it all together, but their lives are messy and
complicated, too. Or you're comparing the game you're playing to
theirs. But you're in the first inning, and they're in the fourth. Or
you're playing football, and they're playing soccer. Instead of comparing yourself to others, create the standards by which you judge
yourself to yourself.

Practice:

1. In your journal, ask yourself, "Am I proud of the choices I'm
   making at home? Am I proud of the choices I'm making at
   work? What would make me more proud?"
2. Today, do something you'd feel proud of, like cleaning up
   your front yard, cleaning out your car, or answering that difficult e-mail.

Day 287: Getting Older
Habit: Gratitude

*We delight in the beauty of the butterfly, but rarely admit
the changes it has gone through to achieve that beauty.*
—Maya Angelou, *Rainbow in the Cloud*

In our youth-obsessed culture, getting older may feel like a series of losses. Skin loses its firm elasticity. Bodies lose their resilience and strength. Hair loses its pigmentation and turns gray. Children move out. Careers end.

But if you consider that the human being is the only species to live well beyond their prime years for reproduction, you may very well ask what is so important and valuable about our elders that evolution made sure we had them around for fifty more years. I'm glad you asked!

Practice:

1. In your journal, consider the benefits of aging. What do you know about yourself, others, and the world now that you didn't know at twenty? What resources do you have now? In what way can you help others that you couldn't have done when you were twenty? What have the older people in your life taught you? What will you teach others? Who do you know who didn't get the opportunity to live to old age?

2. Take a moment to appreciate the gifts of getting older and the opportunity to help others for as long as possible.

Day 288: A Little Mess Is Okay
Habit: Home Simplicity

Give me the discipline to get rid of the stuff that's not im-
portant, the freedom to savor the stuff that gives me joy, and
the patience not to worry about the stuff that's messy but not
hurting anybody.
—Vinita Hampton Wright, *Simple Acts of Moving Forward*

A mess may mean you've been playing with your kids. It may mean that a nutritious meal was prepared and enjoyed by loved ones. Sometimes, a mess means you've been loving and living well, and generosity means being tolerant of messes and those who make them. If keeping a clean house is stressing you out, today's practice might help.

Practice:

1. In your journal, take a reality check. Are you keeping your home clean because you feel judged by the cleanliness standards of others? Is that a reasonable standard? Are you respecting other family members' different standards of cleanliness or methods of cleaning? How important is it that this be clean right now? Can some places in the home be allowed to be messy? Are you trying to do it all on your own? Can chores become a family activity that is fun or happens before fun? Do you have clutter that is adding to the feeling of messiness?

2. Review "Your Home" on day 230 and declutter a room in your home.

· ·
Day 289: Giving with Teens
Habit: Philanthropy

Kindness can become its own motive.
We are made kind by being kind.

—Eric Hoffer, *The Passionate State of Mind: And Other Aphorisms*

Surviving the tumultuous teenage years can be challenging. Would you love to help your children navigate the hazards and become healthy, happy adults? Fortunately, there's something you can do!

Stephen Post, PhD, a bioethics professor at Case Western Reserve University School of Medicine and author of *Why Good Things Happen to Good People* summarizes the research on teens and volunteering: "Teens who actively volunteer do better in life: they have higher grades in school, use less drugs and alcohol, have lower pregnancy rates, and are likely to continue volunteering for the rest of their lives."[62]

Giving as a teenager creates lifelong benefits.

Practice:

1. If you have teenagers, what is their past experience with giving time or money? How would you like it to change? Does your teen obviously lean toward giving in certain ways (in person, skills from home, money, etc.) or for certain causes (animals, environment, seniors, etc.)? What opportunities can you structure to introduce your teen to more giving while not making it feel like another chore?

2. Either by yourself or with your teenager, perform a small philanthropic action like writing a testimonial for your favorite charity, contributing an item for a fundraising raffle, or making a monetary donation.

Week 41
· · · · · · · · ·

Day 290: You Are Beautiful
Habit: Physical Health

Though we travel the world over to find the beautiful,
we must carry it with us, or we find it not.
—Ralph Waldo Emerson, "Art"

Become more generous in your appreciation of beauty. There are beautiful people of all different sizes, colors, shapes, and styles. Notice when someone's internal beauty is expressed physically—in a smile or in the light of their eyes. Every person's beauty is different and unique, and so is yours.

Practice:

1. In your journal, consider how often you judge someone else's looks. When do you tend to do that? What reward do you get for engaging in those thoughts? Create a list of admirable people and reflect on all the different ways they are beautiful.

2. If you have nothing nice to say, don't say anything at all. Today, make no disparaging judgments about your looks or anyone else's.

. . . .

Day 291: Soft Front, Strong Back
Habit: Mindfulness

The place in your body where these two meet—
strong back and soft front—is the brave, tender ground in
which to root our caring deeply.
—Joan Halifax, *Being with Dying*

In *Being with Dying*, Joan Halifax writes that the ideal posture for meditation is a strong spine that holds the body upright while keeping a soft front to facilitate breathing. But, as she points out, it's really a metaphor for life. When our stomach, diaphragm, and chest are soft and open we can give more love to the world. But connecting with others can be risky, so it requires strength. A strong spine provides the confidence and grounding needed to see others and to be seen by others. Often people get the two confused and approach life hard in the front: defensive and angry. This facade makes it appear as though they are strong, but in truth they are protecting a weak spine that's afraid to be hurt.[63]

Practice:

1. Feel the strength in your spine, your values and your beliefs that hold you upright in this world. Feel the softness, the vulnerability, and the tenderness in your belly. Know that together this means you will meet life's challenges with strength, love, and compassion. Know that you have the courage and con-

fidence to go out in the world with a soft front and a strong spine. You will be okay.

2. Are you practicing ten minutes of meditation every day? If not, get back on the wagon. Review day 44 and come up with a plan for making this a regular part of your day.

. . . .
Day 292: Ask for Advice
Habit: Relationships

Old men are fond of giving good advice, to console themselves
for being no longer in a position to give bad examples.
—François de La Rochefoucauld, *Reflections*

People love to give advice. They'll give advice on something even if they don't know anything about it! Asking for advice is a great way to connect with people—just make sure to ask the right people. Ask people who have been where you are but are now where you want to be.

Practice:

What situation are you dealing with and could get a second opinion on? Whose opinion do you trust? Do you know someone who's gone through it? Ask, "Have you dealt with a situation like this before? How did you handle it?" Thank them for sharing their experience with you. You are not obligated to implement their advice. Just take it into consideration.

· · · · · · · · · · · · · · · · ·

Day 293: Used To…
Habit: Connecting with Yourself

I am always at a loss to know how much
to believe of my own stories.
—Washington Irving, *Tales of a Traveler*

Everybody has stories about what happened to them and why they are the way they are. When these stories undermine your self-esteem, limit your expectations, or hamper your ability to get what you want, it's time to tell a better story.

Practice:

1. In your journal, reflect on a disempowering story in your past. How is this story hurting you? How is it hurting others? Is it true? Really, really, really true? What else is true about it? Who would you be without this story?

2. Rewrite it.

   I used to … but now I …

   I thought I learned … but the real lesson was …

· · · · · · · · · · · · · · · · · · ·
Day 294: Your Ancestors
Habit: Gratitude

We all grow up with the weight of history on us. Our ancestors dwell in the attics of our brains as they do in the spiraling chains of knowledge hidden in every cell of our bodies.
—Shirley Abbott, *Womenfolks*

Traditional Mexican culture recognizes that life and death exist because of each other, so death is not something that should be feared. Día de los Muertos is a holiday that celebrates the cyclical nature of life and death and is a time for the living to remember and honor the dead.

Some of the Día de los Muertos traditions include decorating and placing offerings on an altar. I have personally adopted the practice of displaying an elaborately decorated skull made from sugar. Death, of course, is painful, but the sugar skulls act as a reminder that death can be sweet, too.

If you listen closely and look carefully, you might just see and hear your departed loved ones all around you.

Practice:

1. Bring to mind a departed family member. In your journal, consider the following questions: How well did you know this person? What influence did they have on you? How were you impacted by their death? What would you tell them if you had the opportunity to talk to them again?

2. Dedicate a random act of kindness to the memory of this loved one.

. . . .
Day 295: Finding Quiet
Habit: Mind Simplicity

True silence is the rest of the mind, and is to the spirit what sleep is to the body, nourishment and refreshment.
—William Penn, *The Advice of William Penn to His Children*

Downtime is hard to come by these days. If it's not work, appointments, and other obligations, then it's movies, television, and music. As a result, your brain is a noisy place, and it needs quiet to unwind. It needs space to follow its own meandering thoughts. It needs permission to create, explore, and be bored. Give your brain and yourself the gift of quiet.

Practice:

1. In your journal, consider the following questions: How much quiet do you have in your life right now? If you have children, how much quiet do they have in their lives? Is there a time of day when there is more quiet than others? How can you set aside some time to enjoy quiet by yourself? What is something you can do or not do that will quiet your brain? How can the family enjoy quiet time together?

2. Lie in bed and spend a few minutes enjoying some peace and quiet. What would it feel like to have nowhere to go and nothing to do? Maybe, just maybe, you can take a nap.

. . . .
Day 296: A Successful Donation
Habit: Philanthropy

The spirit in which a thing is given determines that in which the gift is acknowledged; it is the intention, not the face-value of the gift, that is weighed.
—Seneca the Younger, *Moral Letters to Lucilius*

After September 11, my dad donated a thousand dollars to one of those big charities. You know, one of those charities constantly on TV asking for money. Now, my dad never made more than fifteen dollars an hour, so a thousand-dollar donation was a big deal for him. *Huge*, even. Guess what he got in return? A form thank-you letter. He was hurt and disappointed that this charity didn't appreciate what this thousand dollars meant to him.

I've donated to hundreds of charities, and across the board, big or small, charities are terrible at thanking their donors. I know it's shocking, and I'm not sure how to explain it. Unless you are writing *very large* checks, it is rare to receive any personal attention or thanks from a charity.

Practice:

1. In your journal, write about why you donate. Donating for thanks and recognition will be unfulfilling. Instead, define what makes a donation successful according to your own internal criteria. Write five responses to the following sentence starters:

   I am happy with my donation if…

   My donation was successful if…

2. Make an anonymous donation to a charity of your choice.

Week 42
· · · · · · · · · ·

Day 297: How to Visualize Success, Part 1
Habit: Physical Health

So many of our dreams at first seem impossible,
then they seem improbable, and then,
when we summon the will, they soon become inevitable.
—Christopher Reeve, 1996 speech
at the Democratic National Convention

Visualization can be a powerful tool to help you achieve your goals—if you do it correctly. Researchers from the University of California, Los Angeles, have been doing their best to discover if it makes a difference if you (1) visualize just the outcome, (2) visualize just the process, (3) visualize the process and the outcome, or (4) don't visualize at all.

After reviewing the results of multiple visualization studies, they concluded, "Mental simulations in which people focus exclusively on the outcomes they want to achieve may succeed in making them feel good, but these emotional regulation benefits may be achieved at the expense of effective planning and problem solving." They describe it as "a form of wishful thinking that not only fails to help in the achievement of goals but at least in some cases may actively interfere with it."[64]

The magic of visualization comes from visualizing the *process* of achieving your *outcome*. On day 305, you'll work on the process, but first, we'll start with the outcome.

Practice:

1. In your journal, create a vision of your physical fitness outcome. Using all of your senses, vividly imagine your physical health results. Close your eyes. What does it look like (how do you look, what are you wearing, where are you, who's around you)? How are you feeling? What do you hear? What do you smell? Do you taste anything? If it helps, you could make a vision board or place inspiring photos on your bathroom mirror.

2. Stand up, close your eyes, and imagine this outcome. Feel it. Taste it. Hear it. Today, walk around as if you've already achieved that outcome.

. . . .
Day 298: Saying Grace
Habit: Mindfulness

Would that you could live on the fragrance of the earth, and like an air plant be sustained by the light. But since you must kill to eat, and rob the young of its mother's milk to quench your thirst, let it then be an act of worship.
—Kahlil Gibran, *The Prophet*

Saying grace is an opportunity to be mindful about your food and is a generous outpouring of respect.

Practice:

Before a meal today, reflect on the place you occupy in the natural world and feel the weight of the knowledge that your life comes at the expense of the living creatures in the world around you who also want to live. Admire the bounty of the earth and recognize that such bounty is not guaranteed and others did not receive a bounty. If you are so moved, you may choose words from your religious tradition or create your own language to express, out loud or silently, your gratitude for your food and for the opportunity to live another day.

. . . .
Day 299: What You've Meant to Me
Habit: Relationships

The bitterest tears shed over graves are for words left unsaid and deeds left undone.
—Harriet Beecher Stowe, *Little Foxes*

Delivering my mother's eulogy was the greatest privilege of my life. I loved standing up there and telling the world about what she meant to me and the wonderful things she accomplished. I only wish I'd told her while she was still alive.

Practice:

1. Who has made an impact on your life? Who will you miss dearly when they go? In your journal, write about what you admire about them, what you're grateful to them for, and how they've made a difference in your life.

2. Share this with them.

Day 300: Monthly Check-In

*There's only one corner of the universe you can be certain
of improving, and that's your own self.*
—Carlo in *Time Must Have a Stop*, Aldous Huxley

Time to check in on your progress. This is not a guilt-inducing exercise designed to shame you for all you haven't accomplished yet. Instead, it's a gentle reminder about what's important to you and what you want to change.

Enjoy the journey. Be gentle with yourself. Keep growing.

Practice:

+ What did I do last month that I'm proud of?
+ Are my relationships with others improving or deteriorating?
+ What do I need to do less of/quit/get rid of/delegate this month?
+ What experiments did I try? What lessons did I learn? What is going well?
+ What isn't working, and what do I want to change?
+ Habit to focus on next month:
+ Why do I want to establish that habit?
+ What is a first step I can take toward making this a habit?
+ What trigger will I use?
+ How will I reward myself?
+ What obstacles will I face in establishing this habit and how will I overcome them?

+ Notes on successes, long-term goals, and personal changes I'm working toward:

. . . .
Day 301: Have Some Fun
Habit: Connecting with Yourself

When I'm caught between two evils,
I generally like to take the one I never tried.
—Mae West as The Frisco Doll, *Klondike Annie*

Having fun isn't just for kids. Even as an adult, having fun is essential for your mental and emotional well-being. It lowers stress, increases creativity, and improves relationships with friends and family. In short, having fun makes you happier. Give yourself permission to do something that has nothing to do with work or family responsibilities. Enjoy yourself.

Practice:

1. In your journal, list ten activities you enjoy. List three activities that you haven't done before but sound like fun.

2. Do something fun either by yourself or with someone else.

Day 302: Work Gratitude
Habit: Gratitude

To set out boldy in our work, is to make a pilgrimage of our labors, to understand that the consummation of work lies not only in what we have done, but who we have become while accomplishing the task.
—David Whyte, *Crossing the Unknown Sea*

You might have a job, a calling, a career, or a purpose. Wherever you do it and whatever form it takes, you work. Whether your work is a joy or feels like a burden, there is a beauty in it, a purpose to it, and an opportunity to express yourself through it.

Practice:

1. In your journal, write about your work. How does your work impact people inside your company, outside your company, and in your family? What does the income from your work allow you to do? Who at your work do you look forward to seeing? What are you good at at work? What do you enjoy doing at work? What are you learning at work?

2. Invest in your work by enrolling in a class, reading a book in your field, or putting together a new résumé to find work that is more enjoyable to you.

. . . .
Day 303: Busyness
Habit: Schedule Simplicity

It is not enough to be industrious; so are the ants.
What are you industrious about?
—Henry David Thoreau, 1857 letter to Harrison Blake

When people ask "How are you?", do you respond with "Busy!"? If so, you may be suffering from chronic busyness.

Busyness proves to other people that you are important and productive. You are a good employee, parent, friend, business owner, etc. Busyness assuages your guilt, reassures you that you are doing enough, and confirms that you belong to your tribe of fellow busy friends. Busyness prevents you from feeling your feelings, because if you are busy, then you don't have to time to feel bored, dissatisfied with your life, alone, or sad. Busyness hides the changes you need and want to make in your life under the fluster and bluster of getting things done.

The question is not "Are you getting things done?" The question is "*What* are you getting done?"

Practice:

1. In your journal, answer these questions: How busy are you? What does being busy keep you from doing, noticing, feeling? What is the most important thing you should be working on right now? What are the less important activities that keep you too busy to work on it?

2. Eliminate one task, activity, or commitment that keeps you busy but isn't a priority (day 274).

. . . .

Day 304: Should I Start My Own Charity?
Habit: Philanthropy

Nothing happens unless first a dream.
—Carl Sandburg, "Washington Monument by Night"

Have you thought about starting your own charity? Here are a few questions to consider first:

1. *Are you able to invest the money necessary?* You'll have to pay several hundred dollars to the IRS to get your 501(c)(3) status. Each year, you'll have to renew your charity with the Secretary of State. You'll have to maintain a checking account and pay any fees associated with that account. Each year, you'll have to file a tax return for the charity.

2. *Are you willing to spend the time it takes to run a charity?* Creating financial reports, holding board meetings, raising money, and doing the actual charitable work takes a lot of time.

3. *Are you duplicating efforts?* If there are other charities already supporting the cause you care about, what are you doing differently that will justify starting your own charity instead of just supporting theirs?

4. *Do you have the skills?* What skills are required to run a successful charity? What skills do you have, and which are missing? Can you learn or hire those skills?

Practice:

1. In your journal, ask yourself, "If I were going to start a charity, what would it be and do? Do I want to pursue my own charity or support the work of others?"

2. Identify three charities that are working on your favorite cause and are new to you. Sign up for their newsletters.

Week 43

● ● ● ● ● ● ● ● ● ●

Day 305: How to Visualize Success, Part 2
Habit: Physical Health

All our dreams can come true—
if we have the courage to pursue them.
—Walt Disney, quoted in *How to Be Like Walt* by Pat Williams

Last week, on day 297, you discovered that the magic of visualization comes from visualizing the *process* of achieving your *outcome*. The process helps you understand how to accomplish what you want, and when you understand how to accomplish what you want, you have less anxiety about failing, less confusion about what to do and when to do it, and more inspiration to actually perform those actions. That means you're better able to live the generous life you imagine.

Practice:

1. Review your physical fitness outcome from last week. Now visualize the process of achieving that goal. In your journal, list the actions that need to happen and the steps you need to take. What challenges will you face and how will you deal with them? Imagine yourself putting your tennis shoes on in the morning, running around the block, and working up a

sweat and loving it. Imagine your kids getting up earlier than you expected and now your morning physical fitness routine turns into a dance party.

2. Take one action right now that will move you toward your desired outcome.

. . . .
Day 306: Wait Patiently
Habit: Mindfulness

*[Christopher Robin] thought that if he stood on the bottom rail
of the bridge, and leant over, and watched the river slipping
slowly away beneath him, then he would suddenly know
everything that there was to be known.*
—A. A. Milne, *The House at Pooh Corner*

In line, on hold, at the light. Waiting is a part of life and creates an opportunity to practice mindfulness, so you can bring a more generous energy to the world than irritated impatience.

Practice:
While waiting, take a few centering breaths. Notice your surrounding. Notice when you become irritated or impatient. How long do you feel that way before it changes into something else. Notice the impulse to check your phone. How long does the urge last before it changes into something else? Notice when your mind jumps for-

ward to anticipate something in the future or jumps back to think on a past event. Bring your attention back to your breath and wait, patiently.

. . . .
Day 307: Reconnect with an Old Friend
Habit: Relationships

Sweet, O Asem! is the memory of distant friends! Like the mellow ray of a departing sun, it falls tenderly yet sadly on the heart.

—Washington Irving, *Salmagundi*, No. IX

People come into and out of your life all the time. You move, get busy, change schools or employers, and you lose track of people you used to consider friends. Reconnecting with an old friend can remind you of where you used to be, who you used to be, and what you used to do. It can illuminate you how you've changed and how far you've come.

Practice:

1. Who from your younger days do you miss?
2. Reach out by phone, e-mail, or social media to say you are thinking of them and ask how they're doing.

. . . .
Day 308: Your Escapes
Habit: Connecting with Yourself

The best way out is always through.
—Robert Frost, "A Servant to Servants"

Too much. Too bored. Too scared. Too lazy. Too tired. Too stressed. Any number of emotional reactions can trigger a desire to escape. The TV, drugs or alcohol, Facebook, video games, reading. Any vehicle can be used to let off steam, to lessen internal pressure, to distract, to soothe. Sometimes it can be healthy to get away from your problems for a little while, and sometimes it keeps you stuck. Sometimes you just need to feel, so you can spend less time escaping and more time giving to yourself and others.

Practice:

1. What vehicles do you use to escape? When do you feel the need to escape? What are you trying to escape? What are you afraid will happen if you feel your fear?

2. Practice the emotional pain meditation from day 146.

. . . .
Day 309: Facing It as a Family
Habit: Gratitude

Whether it's the best of times or the worst of times,
it's the only time we've got.
—Art Buchwald, quoted in 2006 CNN Newsroom profile

After my mom's diagnosis, she lived ten months. Each day robbed her of more functionality, and it was brutal to watch. It was a challenge we went through as a family, and together we learned a few things.

1. *Accept the brutal facts and maintain faith.* Very likely, her brain cancer was going to kill her very quickly. But at the same time, some people beat the odds—it could be Mom. So we did our part, but whether or not she beat the disease was out of our hands and no one's fault.

2. *Know you're doing the best you can.* Are you doing enough? Is there a treatment you should have done? Shouldn't have done? There is so much second-guessing. Trust yourself that you are making the best decisions you can at the time.

3. *Apologize often.* Emotions and tensions are high, and as a result, we often misunderstood each other or jumped to conclusions. Believe that everyone is doing their best and that their hearts are in the right place, apologize, and move on.

4. *Hospice is a gift.* The six weeks my mom was in hospice were the best and worst days of my life. It was a relief to be with her without treating her. The family came together, we reconciled ourselves to the inevitable, and we held her in a sacred space as she transitioned out of this world.

Practice:

1. In your journal, write about a challenge you've gone through as a family. How has it made your relationships stronger or

brought you closer? What did you learn about your family and about yourself? How have you changed? In the next family challenge, how will you behave?

2. Take a moment to appreciate your family and then reach out to a family member to let them know what you appreciate about them.

. . . .
Day 310: The Great Outdoors
Habit: Nature Simplicity

There is a love of wild Nature in everybody,
an ancient mother-love ever showing itself whether recognized
or no, and however covered by cares and duties.
—John Muir, *John of the Mountains*

Wilderness is the place you meet the ancient part of yourself that grew up in the wild, whose bare feet padded the forest floors, and whose life depended on noticing the sights, sounds, and smells of the wild. Gazing out at the ocean or over a meadow, your ancient self is calmed by nature's music and yearns to return home.

Although our wild and ancient spirit craves wilderness, we also need it for our physical well-being. A healthy wilderness provides critical habitat for plant and wildlife that can only thrive far from human development and creates healthy ecosystems that protect our watersheds and filter our air. A healthy wilderness means we have cleaner water to drink and fresher air to breathe.

Allow your ancient mother-love of the wild to awaken, so it can nurture and protect the wilderness. The value it brings to our spiritual and physical lives is irreplaceable.

Practice:

1. Contact your congressional leader, and let them know you want to protect our wild places.

2. Search online for local outdoors groups to meet up with others for hiking and other adventures.

3. Find the principles of Leave No Trace online and learn how to enjoy the wild while maintaining its integrity and character for all living things for generations to come.

. . . .
Day 311: Month 11 Giving Challenge: Veterans
Habit: Philanthropy

Patriotism ... is not short, frenzied outbursts of emotion, but the tranquil and steady dedication of a lifetime.

—Adlai Stevenson, 1953 speech at American Legion convention

Twenty-two veterans commit suicide every day, their unemployment rate is higher than the national average, and even though they are only 1 percent of the population, they make up 12 percent of the homeless.

This happens in part because we avoid honest conversations about war. We pretend there is a morality on the battlefield separate from the rest of our everyday morality. We pretend the actions of the men and women in uniform belong only to the men and women in uniform, so we fail to own that they are only an extension of the morality of our society. As a result, we can't help the men and women who are burdened with guilt, anger, fear, and possibly missing the thrill of battle. To truly help veterans, we have to ask about and listen to their experiences. We have to have honest conversations about what it means to kill a person, to cause suffering, and when is it necessary to do those things anyway.

Practice:

1. Call your congressional leader to advocate for responsible military action. Remind them that our commitment to a veteran is a lifetime commitment and that they must fund veteran services.

2. Like anyone else facing difficult financial circumstances, veterans need jobs and housing. In addition, they have mental health challenges. Sometimes providing mental health services and reestablishing a sense of community and camaraderie can be enough to get the veteran moving in the right direction. Sometimes there needs to be a comprehensive solution, such as partnering emergency housing with counseling. Find a charity helping veterans. Use the Charity Evaluation Worksheet, located in the appendix, to evaluate the charity. If you like what you discover, sign up for their newsletter or make a donation.

Week 44
· · · · · · · · · ·

Day 312: Sonic Impact
Habit: Physical Health

The words peace and quiet are all but synonymous,
and are often spoken in the same breath.
A quiet place is the think tank of the soul,
the spawning ground of truth and beauty.
—Gordon Hempton, *One Square Inch of Silence*

We live in a noisy world. While that may seem harmless, the World Health Organization considers noise pollution a serious health risk and identifies seven ways people are damaged by too much noise.

First, even moderate levels of noise, like heavy truck traffic or factory machinery, can damage hearing. Second, noise interferes with spoken communication, causing uncertainty, lack of self-confidence, irritation, misunderstandings, stress, and accidents, while decreasing working capacity and disturbing interpersonal relationships. Third, noise leads to difficulty falling asleep, frequent awakenings, waking too early, and disturbances in sleep stages and depth. Fourth, noise damages cardiovascular health, causing (even while sleeping) increased blood pressure, heart rate, vasoconstriction, levels of epinephrine, norepinephrine, and cortisol. Fifth, noise causes or aggravates anxiety, stress, nervousness, nausea, headache, emotional instability, argumentativeness, sexual impotence, changes in mood, increase in social conflicts, neurosis, hysteria, and psychosis. Sixth, noise impairs task performance, making reading, problem-solving, and memory creation more difficult, especially among children. Finally, if you've ever spent a night listening to your neighbor's dog bark, you know that noise can cause antisocial behavior, anger, disappointment, dissatisfaction, withdrawal, helplessness, depression, anxiety, distraction, agitation, or exhaustion. All these impacts add up to millions of productive hours lost and increased medical costs for those affected by noise pollution.[65]

Practice:

1. In your journal, list all the sources of noise in your life. What machines inside your home make noise? What machines do you use outside your home that create noise? What noise do you have control over and what noise don't you? How does the noise impact your life?

2. Today, avoid intruding on the silence by choosing the manual over motorized option, observing quiet time between 8 p.m. and 8 a.m., or turning off a noisy appliance.

. . . .
Day 313: In the Moment: Safety
Habit: Mindfulness

Let's not look back in anger or forward in fear,
but around in awareness.
—James Thurber, *Lanterns & Lances*

Mindfulness can be an important tool for ensuring your personal safety. Put your phone away and walk confidently through the street. Notice your surroundings. Who is around you? What are they doing? Trust your feelings. If something feels out of place or an interaction with a person doesn't feel right, trust that feeling. Be confident enough to protect your personal space or safety by not engaging, by saying no loudly, or by calling the police, if necessary. You can't be generous if you don't feel safe and if you aren't aware of your environment.

Practice:

1. In your journal, write about when you feel physically safe and when you don't. How do you respond to that fear? Are those fears real? What would a healthy response to fear look like?
2. Today, walk mindfully from your car into a building.

· ·
Day 314: The Fear We Share
Habit: Relationships

I learned that courage was not the absence of fear, but the triumph over it. The brave man is not he who does not feel afraid, but he who conquers that fear.
—Nelson Mandela, *Long Walk to Freedom*

It doesn't matter if you're the richest person in the world or the poorest. It doesn't matter if you've devoted your life to serving the poor or if you're in prison at San Quentin for murder. We all have the same fear: you are afraid that you aren't worthy of love. The fear of being judged, looking stupid, failing, being unimportant, and being alone all spring from that root fear.

You're afraid that you're not worthy of love.

Just as important as understanding that this is your deepest fear is understanding that it's true for everyone else, too. Anger, defensiveness, disconnectedness, apathy, materialism, violence, manipulation, facades, substance abuse: these are the emotional handicaps people have developed to help them cope with this fear.

Practice:

1. In your journal, consider these questions: How do you protect yourself from feeling you're not worthy of love? How is that preventing you from connecting with other people? How do you know you are worthy of love? What are the emotional handicaps of the people around you? What are yours?

2. Perform a random act of kindness, like calling your parents to say you love them, sending a photo you have to the person in the image, or dropping off dinner for your busy friend.

. . . .
Day 315: I Am…
Habit: Connecting with Yourself

Today you are you! That is truer than true!
There is no one alive who is you-er than you!
—Dr. Seuss, *Happy Birthday to You!*

Who you are is unique, interesting, and valuable. But I can only know you and experience you if you give yourself permission to let me see you. I'd really like to meet you.

Practice:

1. Write five to ten responses to the following sentence starters:
   I am ...
   I wish people knew about me that I ...
   I will express more of who I am by ...

2. Do something that expresses your you-ness, like sharing these answers with a trusted friend, creating an art project, or speaking your mind (respectfully, of course).

. . . .
Day 316: What Do You Have to Give?
Habit: Gratitude

What we have done for ourselves alone dies with us; what we have done for others and the world remains and is immortal.
—Albert Pike, *Ex Corde Locutiones*

You started your journey in life with empty hands, and you will leave it empty handed. In between, you travel from place to place, from relationship to relationship, from year to year, acquiring material objects and experiences. But these are just borrowed. You cannot hold on to them, and when you leave this world, it is only what you've given to others that remains.

Nothing is yours to keep, but everything is yours to give.

Practice:

1. What do you have to give? In your journal, list all your assets: time, money, passion, expertise, and presence. Note that just because you have it to give does not mean you must give it. Just brainstorm all your assets. What passions do you have that you can share? What do you know how to do that you could teach someone? What insight do you have that others can benefit from? How can you serve others by listening? How can you use your money to make the world a better place? Can your body serve others such as through a donation of blood or hair?

2. Take a moment to appreciate how much you have to give and then give something from one of the assets you just listed.

. . . .
Day 317: Stuff
Habit: Home Simplicity

Every increased possession loads us with new weariness.
—John Ruskin, "Contentment in Science and Art"

Making careful purchases that add value to your life is an act of generosity to the planet, your wallet, and your peace of mind. Before you buy, here are a few questions that may help you maintain simplicity of mind, home, and schedule.

1. Where did the impulse to buy it come from?

2. What need will this purchase meet? What problem does this solve?

3. Is my purchase based on a genuine need or a cultural pressure?

4. What are the additional expenses associated with this purchase?

5. Is it worth the money, space, and emotional energy?

6. Can I afford it?

7. Am I choosing quality over quantity?

8. Who am I supporting with this purchase?

9. Does the price reflect the true cost of producing this item, or are there hidden costs paid by other people in the form of exploited resources, pollution, low wages, or toxic chemicals? Are you okay with knowing how your purchase supports the system that produced it?

Practice:

1. In your journal, create a few rules for bringing new stuff into your home. When is it okay for you to buy something? What role do you want stuff to play in your life?

2. Replace a common purchase with a better option, like rain forest–certified coffee, recycled paper, or sweatshop-free clothing.

. . . .
Day 318: Give Monthly
Habit: Philanthropy

The most dangerous risk of all—
the risk of spending your life not doing what you want
on the bet you can buy yourself the freedom to do it later.
—Randy Komisar, *The Monk and the Riddle*

I know the siren song of someday. Someday when I have more time
and money, then I'll give. I know how the best of intentions can go
astray and that extra money I thought I'd have at the end of the
month is gone.

The best way to make sure you donate is also the best way to
make sure you save: do it first! Most people discover that once the
money is out of their checking account, they don't miss it.

Practice:

Choose an amount that is affordable for your budget (day 79) and
set up a recurring monthly donation to your favorite, researched
charity.

Week 45

Day 319: The Mental Game of Physical Activity
Habit: Physical Health

Strength does not come from physical capacity.
It comes from an indomitable will.
—Mahatma Gandhi, "The Doctrine of the Sword"

I hate running. I really do. But I run once a week—not far and not fast, but I run. And I have to coach myself all the way through it. I say, "Sharon, you can do this. Your job is to put one foot in front of the other. That's all. You can put one foot in front of the other, right? Yes, you can. Just keep moving. You're not a quitter."

For me, running is more about exercising my mind than it is about exercising my body. It builds my mental muscles of determination and perseverance. It gives me more practice at accomplishing something I say I'm going to accomplish, which gives me more confidence in every other area of my life.

Practice:

1. In your journal, write about your current level of physical activity. Do you feel healthier? happier? Does thinking about exercising your body as exercising your mind make it easier for you to exercise?

2. Perform an exercise that you don't enjoy but would improve your physical and mental health.

· ·
Day 320: Being with Dying
Habit: Mindfulness

The sooner we can embrace death, the more time we have to live completely, and to live in reality. Our acceptance of our death influences not only the experience of dying but also the experience of living.
—Joan Halifax, *Being with Dying*

In the world, at every moment, countless people and animals are dying.

In our bodies, at every moment, cells are dying.

In our hearts, at every moment, we walk hand in hand with the possibility of death—our own and our loved ones'.

Death is our companion, and even though it will come for us all, few people have spent much time preparing for it.

Practice:

1. While meditating, contemplate how deeply you've accepted your mortality. How do you feel and what thoughts do you have when you imagine your heart ceasing to beat and your body decomposing? How would you live differently if you accepted this more? What do you need to do to prepare yourself for your own death? What do you need to do to prepare yourself for being there for others who are dying?

2. Do you have a will and medical directives? You never know when you'll need them, and it's a gift to your loved ones who will want to honor your wishes but can't if you haven't prepared these documents. If not, make an appointment with an attorney.

. . . .

Day 321: Compassionate Empathy
Habit: Relationships

Pain and suffering are always inevitable for a large intelligence
and a deep heart. The really great men must,
I think, have great sadness on Earth.
—Fyodor Dostoyevsky, *Crime and Punishment*

By itself, compassion can be apathetic. By itself, empathy can be overwhelming.

Compassionate empathy partners the ability to understand the feelings of another person with the desire to help. It channels anger and indignation toward solving a problem. Compassionate empathy has an element of disconnection, which allows you to assess a situation and act. Compassionate empathy calls on you to be brave, to understand what other people are going through, to experience your own emotions, and to discover solutions together.

Practice:

1. In your journal, reflect on when you are most likely to help someone else. Do you try to solve problems that aren't yours

to solve? Where have you avoided helping because you feel overwhelmed, lost, or insignificant?

2. Perform a random act of kindness, like being someone's cheerleader, stopping to offer directions to someone who's lost, or babysitting so that a couple of busy parents can have a date night.

. . . .
Day 322: Dance with Fear
Habit: Connecting with Yourself

We look at the dance to impart the sensation of living
in an affirmation of life, to energize the spectator into keener
awareness of the vigor, the mystery, the humor, the variety,
and the wonder of life.
—Martha Graham, "The American Dance"

On day 314, you discovered that we all share the same fear. This fear will never go away. It is part of your human nature, and it can have a paralyzing effect. Since fear will not be ignored, it is better to dance with it. In dancing with your fear, you breathe life back into it. Don't freeze. Move. Dance.

Practice:
Thank your fear for alerting you that something is about to happen that you want to pay attention to. In your journal, ask yourself, "What is my fear trying to tell me?" Specifically, what is the fear? Reflect on what avoiding this situation will cost you. Imagine what a successful

outcome would do for you. Extend your hand to your fear and ask it to come along with you. Invite it to dance with your courage.

. . . .
Day 323: Group Gratitude
Habit: Gratitude

As we express our gratitude, we must never forget that the highest appreciation is not to utter words but to live by them.
—John F. Kennedy, 1963 Thanksgiving Day proclamation

Gratitude is often a private act, but it's also wonderful done as a group. Here are a couple group gratitude activities that are perfect for holiday dinners and birthday parties:

1. *Thankful Tree:* Cut out paper leaves from construction paper. Create a tree to hang the leaves from—maybe real branches strategically arranged in a vase or a tree drawn on poster board. Place the leaves and some magic markers near the tree and invite your guests to write something they're grateful for and hang it from the tree.

2. *Appreciation Cards:* Place a card and a pen at each person's place setting. After everyone sits down, ask them to write the name of the person to their left at the top of the card followed by something they appreciate about that person. Then, passing the card to the right, the next person adds an item to the list. Keep passing the card to the right until everyone has written something on everyone's card and they get the card with their

own name on it. Each person can then read aloud what other people appreciate about them.

Practice:

Today, express gratitude publicly. Share a positive acknowledgment with your friends, family, or coworkers. You could even ask for the manager at an establishment you patronize to compliment the staff.

. . . .
Day 324: Take a Break
Habit: Mind Simplicity

Besides the noble art of getting things done,
there is the noble art of leaving things undone.
—Lin Yutang, *The Importance of Living*

Breaks restore your sense of calm. They help you be more productive, refocus your attention on what's really important, and improve your problem-solving, so you can actually get more done in less time.

You can find breaks in small places throughout the day, like when you are standing in line, sitting at the doctor's office, waiting for a bus, or waiting for a plane. When you find these moments, instead of reading the news, making a phone call, checking Facebook, replying to e-mail, or writing out your to-do list, just take a break. Under serious stress and chaos, you may need to make an extra effort to take a break.

Be generous to yourself, close the door to your office, sit in a bathroom stall, go for a walk, and take a break.

Practice:

Today, take an intentional break. For five to ten minutes, concentrate on your breathing, observe the people around you, notice your environment, or use another relaxation method that works for you.

. . . .
Day 325: Build the Giving Muscle
Habit: Philanthropy

To accomplish great things we must not only act,
but also dream; not only plan, but also believe.
—Anatole France, 1896 speech to the French Academy

Giving on a regular basis isn't easy, but it's just like any muscle. Start small, increase the weight, and over time, it just gets easier. If you're not quite sure how to reach your monthly donation goal (day 318), I suggest a plan to gradually increase your giving.

For example, if your goal is to give twenty-five dollars every month, in the first month you can donate one dollar. The next month you donate five dollars. The next month you give ten dollars, then fifteen, then twenty, and then, finally it's twenty-five. So in six months you work up to twenty-five dollars per month.

If at any point in time you begin to feel financially strained, pause your increase. Give at the same level for a month or two. Go back and look at your account statements and look for places you are spending more than you thought or more than you want. It's okay to wait until you get a raise before increasing your monthly donation.

Practice:

Are you meeting your monthly donation goal? If no, what is your plan for increasing your monthly giving to reach that goal? If yes, can you do more?

Week 46

Day 326: Put Your Scale in Its Place
Habit: Physical Health

Not to have confidence in one's body
is to lose confidence in oneself.
—Simone de Beauvoir, *The Second Sex*

You are not your weight. How much you weigh measures one thing: the amount of gravity exerted on your body. That's it. It doesn't tell if you're healthy. It doesn't tell if you are a good person or a bad person. It doesn't tell you how much willpower you have.

If losing weight is part of your vision for a healthy body and you want to measure your weight, then weigh yourself once a week around the same time of the day and on the same day of the week while wearing similar clothing and on the same scale. Be reasonable about sustainable weight loss and look for half a pound to two pounds each week.

Remember, your weight fluctuates constantly, so no single weight number should cause alarm. Use your scale as a long-term indicator of the direction you are heading. It's feedback. That's it.

Practice:

1. In your journal, write about your feelings about your weight. Do you think you're too heavy? Too thin? Just right? What is your ideal weight? What do you feel your weight says about you? Is that true? Who are you besides your weight?

2. Stand in front of a full-length mirror and thank your body for what it does for you. Admire the parts of your body that you like and say, "This is my body. It's not perfect, but it belongs to me. I accept it and value it. I am grateful for it."

· · · · · · · · · · · · · · · · · · · ·
Day 327: Being with Living
Habit: Mindfulness

The question is not whether we will die, but how we will live.
—Joan Borysenko, *Guilt Is the Teacher, Love Is the Lesson*

I learned how to live by watching my mom. I learned that life was about caring for others, working hard, facing my fears, and being honest. But she didn't just teach me how to live. At the end of her life, she taught me how to die. Every morning through her illness, she'd wake up and say, "Another beautiful day in Colorado," and she'd go to bed saying, "Thanks for giving me another good day." And that was in essence who my mother was. She was full of gratitude for what she had and was appreciative of those around her. And she didn't just do it when times were easy. She did it when it was the hardest experience she would go through. She died with the same grace and dignity with which she lived.

Practice:

1. During your meditation today, contemplate that with every moment, your life span is decreasing. How does this thought make you feel? What are you doing now to live a good life? What does it mean to you to have a good death?

2. In your journal, create a bucket list for things you want to do, say, feel, or be before you die.

. . . .
Day 328: Intimacy
Habit: Relationships

It is not time or opportunity that is to determine intimacy;—it is disposition alone. Seven years would be insufficient to make some people acquainted with each other, and seven days are more than enough for others.
—Marianne in *Sense and Sensibility*, Jane Austen

Intimacy happens between people when they can reveal their true feelings, thoughts, fears, and desires. Intimacy flourishes when giving time, emotional support, and physical affection creates an environment of unconditional trust. Here are some ideas to create intimacy in your relationships:

• *Gifts of Time:* Going out on date nights, on picnics, to dance lessons, or to the theater; serving breakfast in bed; opening the door.

- *Gifts of Emotional Support:* Praising publicly, reminiscing about romantic memories, talking about your goals and dreams, supporting their goals and dreams, sharing your fears, alleviating their fears, sharing your needs, asking about and meeting their needs, writing a love letter.

- *Gifts of Physical Affection:* Hugging, snuggling, making eye contact, holding hands, squeezing their hand, gently kissing their neck, brushing their hair away from their face.

Practice:

1. In your journal, consider the following questions: How intimate you are with your partner? Do you need more time, emotional support, or physical affection? What do they need?

2. Give your intimate partner a gift of time, emotional support, or physical affection.

- - - - - - - - - - -

Day 329: No
Habit: Connecting with Yourself

This is the hardest of all: to close the open hand out of love, and keep modest as a giver.
—Friedrich Nietzsche, *Thus Spoke Zarathustra*

Stop. Before you say yes, remember you have a choice. You always have a choice. You can say yes or no. Both are perfectly valid answers. Breathe and say to yourself, "My needs and feelings are as important as your needs and feelings." If you weren't feeling guilty or responsible for their happiness, what would your first response be? Do you have the time, energy, and desire? If the answer is no, then say no with confidence, and know that you are saying yes to yourself.

Practice:

1. In your journal, ask yourself, "In the past, where have I said yes when I wanted to say no?" Why? Who in your life doesn't listen to your no? In the future, if your personal integrity or safety is compromised by someone not taking no for an answer, what will you do?

2. What are you currently doing that you wish you would have said no to? Extract yourself from this obligation.

. . . .
Day 330: Monthly Check-In

The condition of all progress is experience. We go wrong a thousand times before we find the right path. We struggle, and grope, and hurt ourselves until we learn the use of things, and this is true of things spiritual as well as of material things.
—Felix Adler, *Life and Destiny*

Time to check in on your progress. This is not a guilt-inducing exercise designed to shame you for all you haven't accomplished yet. Instead, it's a gentle reminder about what's important to you and what you want to change.

Enjoy the journey. Be gentle with yourself. Keep growing.

Practice:

+ What did I do last month that I'm proud of?

+ Are my relationships with others improving or deteriorating?

+ What do I need to do less of/quit/get rid of/delegate this month?

+ What experiments did I try? What lessons did I learn? What is going well?

+ What isn't working, and what do I want to change?

+ Habit to focus on next month:

+ Why do I want to establish that habit?

+ What is a first step I can take toward making this a habit?

+ What trigger will I use?

+ How will I reward myself?

+ What obstacles will I face in establishing this habit and how will I overcome them?

+ Notes on successes, long-term goals, and personal changes I'm working toward:

. . . .
Day 331: Teacher Gratitude
Habit: Gratitude

A teacher affects eternity;
he can never tell where his influence stops.
—Henry Adams, *The Education of Henry Adams*

Education means that you can read legal and health documents and make better choices regarding important issues like business contracts, insurance benefits, and health needs. Math education means you can evaluate income, assets, and expenses and make more profitable decisions running your business and home. Critical thinking skills means you can listen to people in power while asking questions, evaluating arguments, and electing better leaders. Education gives you the ability to imagine future scenarios, compare alternatives, and plan accordingly.

Education doesn't just give you information and facts. It transforms the way you think, expands the capacity of your brain, and helps you reach your full potential.

Practice:

1. Take out your journal. Who was your most important teacher? Why?

2. Write a thank-you note to this teacher. If you know how to reach them, send it.

. . . .
Day 332: Acts of Love
Habit: Schedule Simplicity

The often heard lament, "I have so little time," gives the lie to the delusion that the daily is of little significance.
—Kathleen Norris, *The Quotidian Mysteries*

Dishes must be cleaned, groceries purchased, gardens tended, laundry cleaned, toilets scrubbed, and bank accounts balanced. Calling these activities "errands" or "chores" fails to appreciate the value they bring to your life. Truly, they are acts of love. When you love something or someone, you take care of it.

It's not always easy to find time and energy to do these activities, but having a routine in your schedule can help. Today, organize and simplify your weekly and monthly acts of love into a manageable routine.

Practice:

1. List tasks that need to be done daily, weekly, and monthly.
2. Group tasks that can be done together.
3. Eliminate unnecessary tasks, delegate, and enlist help to keep your list manageable and focused.
4. Make room for these activities on your schedule.

. . . .
Day 333: Volunteering
Habit: Philanthropy

I believe that the experience of love is the most human and humanizing act that it is given to man to enjoy and that it, like reason, makes no sense if conceived in a partial way.
—Erich Fromm, *On Being Human*

There are 63.4 million Americans who volunteer on an annual basis. As you consider volunteering, note that skills such as listening, teaching English, tech skills, graphic design, repair and handyman skills, and financial and bookkeeping skills are valuable to charities.

Also think about activities that you do on a regular basis that you could do with or for another person without a big time burden, like grocery shopping for an elderly person while doing your own grocery shopping.

Practice:

1. Review your answers for day 28. Have your feelings about giving time changed? What keeps you from volunteering? What are you afraid might happen if you volunteer? Growing up, did your family volunteer? How did your family feel and talk about volunteering? How has that influenced how you feel about volunteering?

2. Contact your favorite charity and commit to volunteering at least one hour per month.

Week 47

· · · · · · · · · · ·

Day 334: Be Strong
Habit: Physical Health

To resist with success the frigidity of old age,
one must combine the body, the mind and the heart; to keep
these in parallel vigor, one must exercise, study and love.
—Bonstettin in *Madame de Staël*, Abel Stevens

Strength training exercises are terrific for your health—especially as you age. Studies show that strength training reduces the severity of arthritis, osteoporosis, diabetes, back pain, obesity, and depression. Strength training improves balance, which means fewer injury-inducing falls. A twelve-month study on strength training in postmenopausal women at Tufts University resulted in 1 percent gains in hip and spine bone density, 75 percent increases in strength, and 13 percent increases in dynamic balance with just two days per week of progressive strength training. Additionally, muscle mass helps manage your body's insulin and metabolism levels, leading to overall better health and weight management.[66]

While some women are afraid of looking masculine, don't worry. Women weight lifters work incredibly hard and sometimes take anabolic steroids to achieve their bulky and chiseled look. For the rest of us, we don't have enough testosterone for that to happen.

Practice:

1. In your journal, consider these questions. How strong are you? Given your current physical condition, what strength training exercises can you do? Do you need to enlist some professional support?

2. Incorporate strength training into your physical fitness. You could go to the gym and lift weights, or you can do squats, push-ups, planks, and dips wherever you are.

. . . .

Day 335: Sound Meditation
Habit: Mindfulness

*Music, verily, is the mediator between the life
of the mind and the senses.*
—Attributed to Ludwig van Beethoven,
1810 letter from Bettina von Arnim to Goethe

Whether it's nature sounds, guided meditations, gongs, chanting mantras, or producing the om sound, some people find meditating with sound useful for changing the body's state and giving the wandering mind something to focus on.

Practice:

Search online for "chanting meditation," "guided meditation," or "music for meditation" and choose one for your meditation today. Meditating with sound is best experienced with instruction, so consider signing up for classes.

Day 336: Be Contagious
Habit: Relationships

I will not follow where the path may lead;
instead I will go where there is no path and leave a trail.
—Muriel Strode, *My Little Book of Prayer*

James Fowler of the University of California, San Diego, and medical sociologist Nicholas Christakis of Harvard University designed an experiment where everyone would benefit the most by being selfish. Participants were organized into groups of four to play a game where the rational decision was to keep as much of your own money as possible. They discovered that some people didn't play the game rationally. Instead of keeping all their money, one person, whom we'll call the "giver," would give it all away to the other members of the group; we'll call them the "receivers."

When the participants changed groups, the receivers were more generous in their next group—even though they no longer had the giver in their group. The members of this new group, whom we'll call the the "next generation," didn't know it, but they benefited from the giver's generosity.

Here's where it gets even more interesting. Participants would change groups again. The next generation went on to be more generous in their next groups, even though neither the giver nor the receivers were in their new groups. The researchers concluded that "each person in a network can influence dozens or even hundreds of people, some of whom he or she does not know and has not met."[67]

Well, that's a hell of a lot better than passing around the flu bug. Your behavior inspires others. Make it worth catching.

Practice:

Perform at least one random act of kindness today, like putting in a good word for a coworker, leaving five dollars in the Redbox movie case for the next person to buy snacks with, or surprising your office with a bouquet of flowers.

. . . .
Day 337: Problem-Solving, Step 1
Habit: Connecting with Yourself

A problem well put is half-solved.
—John Dewey, *Logic: The Theory of Inquiry*

When you're struggling with a problem, sometimes you might feel like the problem is too big to be solved. You've been struggling with it for too long. You've tried too many times. It's overwhelming and unchangeable, so you stop trying to change it. On the other hand, you might say the problem isn't such a big deal. After all, you've lived with it for this long. So you resign yourself to accepting it. Unfortunately, neither of these approaches helps you solve your problem. But being generous means giving intentionally to improve your own life.

The first step is to see the problem as it is. Don't sugarcoat it to make yourself feel better. But don't make it worse than it is, either, by burying yourself in guilt and feeling overwhelmed.

Practice:

1. In your journal, identify a situation or problem in your life that you want to change. See it as it is. What is it costing you now? What will it cost you in the future? What has it cost you already? How is it hurting you or those you love?

2. Stand in front of a mirror in your power pose (day 54) and tell yourself that you are committed to solving this problem.

. . . .
Day 338: What You Gain
Habit: Gratitude

Gratitude is a currency that we can mint for ourselves,
and spend without fear of bankruptcy.
—Fred De Witt Van Amburgh, *The Mental Spark Plug*

Giving can feel like losing. Writing a check to a charity means less money for you. Spending two hours on the weekend volunteering means less time for you. As a result, many of us give less and volunteer less than we think we should. If that's true for you, perhaps it's because you are not fully appreciating what you gain in return. You might gain stronger relationships, knowledge, laughter, the satisfaction of unleashing someone's potential, or any number of other benefits.

Practice:

1. In your journal, consider these questions. What do you gain when you donate? What do you gain when you volunteer?

What you do you gain when you give to your children, intimate partner, yourself, or your work?

2. Take a moment to appreciate how remarkable it is that when you give, you receive. Feel grateful for the gifts you've gotten from those around you. Choose someone and thank them.

. . . .
Day 339: Nature at Home
Habit: Nature Simplicity

Nature is not a place to visit, it is home.
—Gary Snyder, *The Practice of the Wild*

Sometimes, people think that nature is out there. Somewhere else. But nature is all around, even in the midst of the busiest city. Beautifying your surroundings is an opportunity for you to slow down, look around you, believe in something bigger than yourself, and hope for a better world.

Practice:

Choose an activity to beautify your neighborhood. It can be done by yourself, with friends or neighbors, or with the backing of your local government. It can be a one-time effort or something you do regularly.

1. Pick up trash by yourself or organize a neighborhood cleanup.
2. Plant a tree, a bush, or a flowerpot with a native plant that is good for birds or bees.
3. Replace part of your front yard with a garden.

4. Install a "pick up after your dog" or community library stand.

5. Provide food or shelter for local wildlife. Contact your local experts on native plants that provide food and shelter for wildlife.

6. Install a bird feeder, a birdbath, a birdhouse, or even a bee house.

· ·
Day 340: Month 12 Giving Challenge: Arts
Habit: Philanthropy

All creative art is magic, is evocation of the unseen
in forms persuasive, enlightening, familiar and surprising,
for the edification of mankind, pinned down by the
conditions of its existence to the earnest consideration
of the most insignificant tides of reality.
—Joseph Conrad, "Henry James: An Appreciation"

A community rich in the arts is rich in a number of other ways. Economically, art generates $135 billion of economic activity, supports 4.1 million full-time jobs for $86.68 billion in resident household income. Socially, communities with a strong presence of the arts have a higher level of civic engagement, more social cohesion, and lower poverty rates. Academically, students perform better when also involved in art classes.[68] Spiritually, although these benefits are less tangible, art is healing, inspiring, and enjoyable.

Practice:

Support your local art community. For example, you can visit a museum, pop into an art gallery, or donate an instrument to a school band.

Week 48

· · · · · · · · · ·

Day 341: Plowing through Plateaus: Intensity
Habit: Physical Health

There are no limits. There are plateaus,
but you must not stay there, you must go beyond them.
—Bruce Lee, *The Art of Expressing the Human Body*

The human body is amazing at adapting. The first time you run a mile, your heart is pumping and you can hardly catch your breath. Run that mile every couple of days and in no time you're running it faster and easier. Now, you're not improving your health, you're maintaining it. In order to get healthier, you need to step up the difficulty by increasing the distance or speed with which you run.

To increase the difficulty of your workout, you can increase the speed, weight, or number of reps. For example, you can transition from pushups on your knees to pushups on your toes.

Practice:

1. In your journal, reflect on your physical health. What exercises have you been doing? Has your body adapted to any of these exercises? Are you enjoying your physical activity?

2. Increase the intensity of one of your physical fitness activities.

··

Day 342: The Wandering Mind
Habit: Mindfulness

Don't seek, don't search, don't ask, don't knock,
don't demand—relax.
—Osho, *Zen: The Path of Paradox*

The mind will always wander. Emotions will always surface. Thoughts will always visit you. Meditation is just the practicing of noticing when it happens, how you respond when it happens, and bringing your attention back to a point of focus. In this way, you build your mental strength. More generosity to yourself and others blossoms naturally from your increased calm, focus, and peacefulness.

Each meditation will be different. Not good or bad. Just different. Not right or wrong. Just different. Not easy or hard. Just different.

Relax. Just notice.

Practice:

If you're struggling to maintain the meditation habit, brainstorm in your journal possible solutions, including exploring some different types of meditation that you may enjoy more (days 125, 219, 255, 262, and 335). Just do one or two minutes on the days you don't want to meditate (day 96).

Day 343: Support a Friend
Habit: Relationships

*If you could only sense how important you are to the lives of
those you meet; how important you can be to the people you
may never even dream of. There is something of yourself that
you leave at every meeting with another person.*
—Fred Rogers, *You Are Special*

All around you people are starting something: a new club, a new
business, a new habit. They're doing cool things: volunteering, organizing events, running for charity. Getting support from other
people inspires them to continue, gives them the resources to do it
better, and makes them feel that what they are doing is worthwhile.

Practice:
Look through your friends, family, coworkers for people doing cool
things. Support someone's project by giving either moral or financial support.

• •
Day 344: Problem-Solving, Step 2
Habit: Connecting with Yourself

*Optimism is the faith that leads to achievement;
nothing can be done without hope.*
—Helen Keller, "Optimism"

On day 337, you saw the problem as it is. Now imagine this problem is solved. Create an inspirational vision for your life when you've overcome this situation. What's waiting for you on the other side?

Practice:

Look back in your journal to the problem you wrote about on day 337. Now consider the following: What will solving this problem do for you? How will your life improve? What will it mean for you or your family? How will you feel? What will that let you achieve? How will you be better able to help others? Stand in front of the mirror in your power pose, envisioning your future without this problem. Stay tuned for one more step next week.

. . . .
Day 345: Community
Habit: Gratitude

No man is an island, entire of itself; every man is a piece of the continent, a part of the main.
—John Donne, "Meditation XVII"

Rural or urban, town or city, small or large—whatever shape and form your community takes, it exists because it is easier to survive and thrive together than it is alone. Who makes your community possible?

Practice:

1. Think about the people who make your community function: the garbage collectors, the mail carriers, the supermarket

stockers, the produce pickers, the school teachers, the restaurant cook, the waitstaff, the small business owners, the nurses. Pause to appreciate the innumerable people who make your community function and thrive.

2. Reach out to your local city government to thank them for their work.

. . . .
Day 346: What's Left?
Habit: Home Simplicity

Have nothing in your houses that you do not know to be useful, or believe to be beautiful.
—William Morris, "The Beauty of Life"

Of the areas of your home we didn't have a chance to organize yet, choose one. Below is the basic process to organize and simplify any area of your life, but remember to learn from others. Ask friends and family and check the Internet for more tips and advice.

Practice:

1. *Empty and Collect:* Put whatever needs to be organized all together in one place where you can go through it.

2. *First Pass:* Organize into three piles: (1) trash/recycle, for what is no longer good or useful; (2) donate, for things that others can use; and (3) store, for what may be of use in the future or you're not ready to let go of.

3. *Simplify:* Choose the best and identify what you really need. What really serves you? What do you really love?

4. *Second Pass:* Of the remaining items, what's left? Now, what can be trashed, donated, or stored?

5. *Organize:* Group and put away items. Store similar items together and put things back so that they are easy to see, take out, and replace.

. . . .

Day 347: Spread the Word
Habit: Philanthropy

To have a respect for ourselves, guides our morals;
and to have a deference for others, governs our manners.
—Laurence Sterne, *The Koran: Or, Essays, Sentiments,*
Characters, and Callimachies

Generosity is contagious, so do share with others where and why you give. When you talk about your giving, do so in a respectful and easygoing manner without guilting or pressuring those around you. A statement like "I'm so excited—I just discovered this great charity that is doing this amazing work" or "I love donating to this charity because they make such a difference in their community" raises awareness of your favorite charities and causes.

Just as the where and why you give are deeply personal issues, the reasons and places other people give are deeply personal matters. It's important to treat everyone's donation choices with respect.

Sometimes other people will not treat your giving with respect. They may call you naive. They may dismiss your ability to make the world a better place. They may think your cause pales in comparison to the "real" issue you should care about. That's okay. Thank them for their input and stand your ground. You know what you're doing.

Practice:

At home, at work, or on social media, respectfully but enthusiastically share with friends, family, or coworkers a little about the last charity you donated to and why.

Week 49

Day 348: Plowing through Plateaus: Variety
Habit: Physical Health

The joy of life is variety; the tenderest love requires
to be rekindled by intervals of absence.
—Samuel Johnson, *The Idler,* No. 39

Have you lost weight at the start of a diet, but then it just stopped? That's because your body adjusts. It becomes more efficient and burns fewer calories. To continue losing weight, you can decrease your caloric intake even further (e.g., increase the intensity, as on day 341). But consume too few calories, and your body thinks it's starving and burns even fewer calories.

Increasing the intensity isn't the only way to break through a plateau, and a little variety in your diet can do wonders. So take a day here and there when you treat yourself to comfort food and extra calories and reset the hormones in your brain that are telling your body to burn less fuel.

Incorporate some variety in your exercise, too. You can try out the treadmill, elliptical, squats, yoga, Crossfit, spinning, Zumba, TRX, or P90X. Choose a combination of cardio and strength training to do on a regular basis, and mix it up every now and then by adding something new.

Remember, you are the expert on your own body, so pay attention to how your body is responding to diet and exercise. Call on the expertise of nutritionists or fitness trainers, or consult a doctor who might identify underlying health issues causing your plateaus.

Practice:

1. In your journal, reflect on your eating habits. What changes have you made in the food you eat? How has your body responded to those changes? Are you enjoying your new food lifestyle, and can you maintain it for the long haul?

2. Add something new to your diet or physical fitness activities.

. . . .
Day 349: The Zone
Habit: Mindfulness

May what I do flow from me like a river,
no forcing and no holding back,
the way it is with children.
—Rainer Maria Rilke, *The Book of Hours*

Athletes covet getting into "the zone." It's a state of mind where they are fully immersed, totally focused, and completely enjoying their sport. Time ceases to pass normally. They're not thinking about themselves or how to shoot or the score. It's just them in this moment doing this activity that they love doing. The zone is a unique state of mindfulness and may be a difficult state to create intentionally. You'll give yourself the best shot by eliminating all distractions while doing an activity you know well and enjoy doing.

Practice:

Eliminate all distractions and spend ten minutes doing an activity you love.

· · · · · · · · · · · · · · · · · ·
Day 350: Vulnerability
Habit: Relationships

Vulnerability sounds like truth and feels like courage.
Truth and courage aren't always comfortable,
but they're never weakness.
—Brené Brown, *Daring Greatly*

Vulnerability is risky. Being vulnerable means sharing what you're really feeling and what you really want out of life. And yes, that means you could get hurt. But it doesn't hurt as bad as the alternative. If you're not vulnerable, no one can know who you really are, so they can't love you for who you really are.

I'm sorry. I'm lonely. I'm afraid. I made a mistake. I'm hurting. I'm overwhelmed. I'm lost. I'm disappointed.

When you have the courage to share your truth and be more of who you are, you inspire other people to share their truth and be more of who they are. Together, you'll form more meaningful relationships.

Practice:

1. In your journal, write five to ten responses to the following sentence starters:

    If people really saw me …

If I fully accepted myself…
I wish I…

2. Share your responses with a trusted, supportive friend.

. . . .
Day 351: Problem-Solving, Step 3
Habit: Connecting with Yourself

I suppose it is tempting, if the only tool you have is a hammer,
to treat everything as if it were a nail.
—Abraham Maslow, *Psychology of Science*

Once you've seen your problem as it is and imagined a better future, do something to make your vision a reality. As you outline the steps toward your better future, consider all your tools and resources such as those in the "Ask For Advice" (day 292), "Enlist Support" (day 97), and "Role Models" (day 148) entries.

Practice:

1. Look back to the problem you've been working on in "Problem-Solving, Step 1" (day 337) and "Problem-Solving, Step 2" (day 344). In your journal, consider the following questions: What do you need to believe about yourself to solve this problem? What alternative solutions are there to your problem? What resources will help you solve this problem? List actions that would resolve this situation.

2. What one action step will you take today?

• • • • • • • • • • • • • •
Day 352: Bravery
Habit: Gratitude

When the will defies fear, when the heart applauds the brain,
when duty throws the gauntlet down to fate, when honor
scorns to compromise with death—this is heroism.
—Robert G. Ingersoll, 1882 Decoration Day speech

Bravery is a unique type of courage. Bravery happens in the presence of physical danger when a person reaches inside themselves to risk their own well-being to help others and save lives. Some people do it for a living, and those people deserve our thanks.

Practice:

1. Think about the soldiers, the police officers, the firefighters, the paramedics, and the everyday heroes who run toward danger to help and to do what's right. Reflect on the sacrifices they make and the risks they take in service to something bigger than themselves.

2. Take a moment to feel grateful to those men and women, and then reach out with a call or a social media post or drop by with a box of donuts.

· · · · · · · · · · · · · · · · · · ·
Day 353: Drive Slowly
Habit: Mind Simplicity

The most important reason for going from one place to another
is to see what's in between.
—Alec in *The Phantom Tollbooth*, Norton Juster

For years, I had a dog with serious separation anxiety, and it was easier to take him with me everywhere than to leave him at home. Together, we drove through twenty-eight states and over a hundred thousand miles. His favorite part was when I would roll down the window. Then he would rest his chin on the edge of the window, close his eyes, and lose himself in the smells. For him, it was all about the journey, and he helped me learn to love driving.

Practice:

Leave earlier than you normally would, so you can go slower than you normally go. Allow others to pass you by. If you're listening to something, choose music or trainings that you enjoy. Or even turn it off and just be in quiet.

Day 354: The Practice of Philanthropy
Habit: Philanthropy

To the wrongs that need resistance,
To the right that needs assistance,
To the future in the distance,
Give yourselves.

—Carrie Chapman Catt, "The World Progress of Women"

After all these weeks of philanthropic training, you are an agent for powerful philanthropy. Here are some of the best practices you've discovered this year.

1. Research charities before you give (days 123, 137, 144, 152, and 166 and the Charity Evaluation Worksheet in the appendix).

2. Stick to your giving plan (days 86, 94, 238, and 296).

3. Give money instead of goods (days 267 and 282).

4. Give what you can. No amount is too small (days 50, 79, 318, and 325).

5. Support only your favorite causes (days 57 and 65).

Practice:

In what area do you have room for improvement? Choose an entry from that category, reread it, and do the practice for that entry.

Week 50
· · · · · · · · · ·

Day 355: Define Your Healthy Body Rules
Habit: Physical Health

*Order and simplification are the first steps
toward the mastery of a subject.*
—Thomas Mann, *The Magic Mountain*

Very likely, you have a set of unconscious rules that make it easy for you to feel bad about your health and body but very difficult to feel good. Some of these rules may even contradict each other, so you can never feel good!

Rules are important because they guide your behavior and give you a yardstick with which to judge yourself, so take control of your rules and craft a set that empowers you.

Here are the rules for making rules:

1. Only make rules about things you can control. You can't control other people, and you can't always control the results. You *can* control your own behavior and your own choices.
2. Your rules should be simple.
3. You should have as few of them as possible.

For example, here are my healthy body rules: I am healthy when I eat food, mostly plants, and not too much (day 87). I am healthy when I am physically active every single day. I am healthy when I drink soda and alcohol no more than twice a week.

Practice:

1. In your journal, craft your healthy body rules: I am healthy when _____. Are your rules, clear, consistent, and within your control?

2. Print these rules so that you can remind yourself of what you need to do.

. . . .

Day 356: The Practice of Having Strong Relationships
Habit: Relationships

Souls are like athletes, that need opponents worthy of them,
if they are to be tried and extended and pushed
to the full use of their powers.
—Thomas Merton, *The Seven Storey Mountain*

Congratulations on coming so far! Over the course of the book, you've done a lot to develop and maintain strong relationships. Here are the three main ways you connect with others and the entries that can help you practice that skill:

1. *Be Interested:* Pay Attention (day 89), Get Curious (day 155), Ask for Advice (day 292), Interview an Elder (day 205), Tell Me More (day 285)

2. *Engage:* Five-Minute Favor (day 147), Appreciate (day 133), Send a Card (day 169), Cluster Giving (day 176), Be a Good Neighbor (day 256), Celebrate Their Success (day 104), Checking In (day 126), Following Up (day 191), Enlist Support (day 97), Life Math (day 220), Ask for Help (day 227), A Long, Happy Relationship (day 234), Spread Light (day 271), Surprise! (day 278), What You've Meant to Me (day 299), Reconnect with an Old Friend (day 307), Support a Friend (day 343), Intimacy (day 328)

3. *Be You:* Boundaries (day 3), Powerful Body Language (day 140), Judging (day 184), More Than This (day 198), Give It Time (day 213), Go First (day 242), Vulnerability (day 350), The Fear We Share (day 314), Compassionate Empathy (day 321)

Practice:

Which area do you need more practice with? Choose an entry from that category, reread it, and redo the practice it suggests.

. . . .

Day 357: The Practice of Connecting with Yourself
Habit: Connecting with Yourself

*What lies behind us and what lies before us
are but tiny matters compared to what lies within us.*
—Henry Haskins, *Meditations in Wall Street*

Connecting with yourself is a lifelong practice. Here are the three main ways you can connect with yourself and the entries that can help you practice that skill:

1. *Allowing Your Emotions:* Anger (day 214), Shame Is a Vampire (day 199), Your Sexuality (day 228), Desire (day 185), Fake It Until You Become It (day 54), Regret (day 257), Comparing (day 286), Have Some Fun (day 301)

2. *Valuing Yourself:* Self-Confidence (day 25), Be Proud (day 177), Negative Self-Talk (day 62), I Love You! (day 69), Feeling Important (day 98), Repetition (day 127), Problem-Solving (days 337, 344, and 351), Something New (day 156), Better Than Perfect (day 192), Be Honest (day 264), Your Escapes (day 308), Feedback Loops (day 141)

3. *Acting Intentionally:* Your Eulogy (day 40), Prepared for Anything (day 163), Three Words (day 170), Be Honest (day 264), Alter Egos (day 250), I Might Be Wrong (day 279), Used To ... (day 293)

Practice:

Which area do you need more practice with? Choose an entry from that category, reread it, and do the practice for that entry.

. . . .
Day 358: The Practice of Simplicity
Habit: Schedule Simplicity

The sculptor produces the beautiful statue by chipping away
such parts of the marble block as are not needed—
it is a process of elimination.
—Elbert Hubbard, *The Philistine*, vol. 25

A simple life is built around the big rocks (so that you can spend your precious time on what's most important to you), is organized (so that you have what you need where you need it), is productive (because you have lots to do), and is focused (so that you can get it done in less time).

1. *The Big Rocks:* Short Life in an Old World (day 13), Curate Your Time (day 42), Pale Blue Dot (day 187), It's Not a Priority (day 274), and Busyness (day 303)

2. *Organize:* The Linen Closet (day 56), Clothes Closet (day 85), Your Purse (day 114), Papers (day 143), Your Kitchen (day 201), Your Desk (day 259)—and in your day: Your Brain Is for Processing (day 71), Daily Routine (day 129), Acts of Love (day 332)

3. *Do:* Get Things Done (day 158), Daily Action Plan (day 245)

4. *Focus:* No Dinging (day 100), Your Brain Is Limited (day 216)

5. *Review:* The check-ins appear every thirty days, so you can check your progress and make any course corrections.

Practice:

In what area do you have room for improvement? Choose an entry from that category, reread it, and do the practice for that entry.

Week 51: Year in Review

Day 359: Year in Review: Physical Health
Habit: Physical Health

There will stretch out before you an ever-lengthening,
ever-ascending, ever-improving path.
You know you will never get to the end of the journey.
But this, so far from discouraging,
only adds to the joy and the glory of the climb.
—Winston Churchill, "Painting as a Pastime"

Congratulations on completing this book. You are remarkable. So few finish a book, a goal, a week-long training program. You are amazing.

I don't expect you are perfect. Not now. Not ever. There is no perfection. Only progress. And only your progress. Not compared to anyone else's progress.

This is the final week of the book, so look back, reflect on your changes, celebrate your progress, and look forward to the growth still awaiting you.

I am proud to call you a friend and compatriot on our journey to being our best selves. Thank you for spending this year with me.

Practice:

1. In your journal, consider the following questions: How did you feel about your physical health when you started the year? What were your biggest health challenges? What are your current health challenges now? What healthy habits did you adopt this year that you're proud of? What healthy habits do you want to continue or make more challenging? What did you learn about your health and your body this year? Looking forward to next year, what habits do you want improve? Why?

2. Use the monthly review format to develop your game plan for adopting this new healthy habit.

. . . .
Day 360: Year in Review: Mindfulness
Habit: Mindfulness

Today is only one day in all the days that will ever be.
But what will happen in all the other days
that ever come can depend on what you do today.
—Ernest Hemingway, *For Whom the Bell Tolls*

The Romans named the first month of the year after their god Janus, the god of transitions. Life is full of transitions. From birth to infancy to childhood to adolescence to adulthood to old age to death. From periods of conflict to times of calm. From a vision of yourself as one thing to a rebirth of who you are now. From one city to another, one job to another, one step of personal development to another. Each moment is a transition from the last moment to the newest moment.

All periods of transitions are fraught with challenges and emotions, and so Janus has two faces. One face looks back at the past and one looks forward to the future. With the wisdom gained from the past and with eyes directed toward the new goal, times of transition can be more easily navigated.

Practice:

This morning in your meditation, look back at the year and honor your journey. Appreciate the person you were at the start of the year, the person who cares so much about himself or herself and the world in which they embarked upon this journey of self-improvement and self-care. Feel yourself understanding the lessons you encountered through the year. Feel the wisdom sinking into your body, becoming part of who are now. Now look forward to the future. Wherever you've been and whatever you've done will help you on your future journey. Feel yourself navigating the future with grace and ease. Feel grateful for the new experiences and wisdom you will acquire next year. At this time, you can either imagine specifically what you'd like to accomplish next year or just feel the potential of the future awaiting you. Leave the future, and come back to who are now, where you are sitting, and feel grateful that that future is possible because of the potential within you right now. The seeds for accomplishing your future are already planted in your heart, but the fully grown plant is no more valuable than the seeds in their infancy. Now is where the future is born. Imagine yourself caring for the seedlings that live in your heart now and each day and nurturing them as they grow.

. . . .

Day 361: Year in Review: Relationships
Habit: Relationships

Love one another and you will be happy.
It's as simple and difficult as that.
—Michael Leunig, *When I Talk to You*

It is often the case that the times we need people the most are the times we are most likely to withdraw. And yes, by withdrawing you can avoid the pain of being judged or rejected, but you also miss out on the joy of connecting with someone else—experiencing their joy vicariously, surprising them, helping them with something they need, and receiving their insight and support.

Throughout the year, you've had over one hundred opportunities to connect with family, friends, and strangers through meaningful conversations, philanthropy, random acts of kindness, and other interactions. As these opportunities came up each week, I hope you discovered that, indeed, making other people feel better can make you feel better.

I honor you for your efforts and for your courage, and I'm awfully glad to be living in the better world you are creating.

Practice:

1. In your journal, consider the following questions: What kind of impact were you making on other people at the beginning

of the year? How has that impact changed over the year? How have you changed because of your interaction with others? Looking forward, what kind of impact would you like to make on others? What would you like to do more of or less of?

2. Invite someone to celebrate your year of connection with you!

• •

Day 362: Year in Review: Connecting with Yourself
Habit: Connecting with Yourself

If you asked me for my New Year resolution,
it would be to find out who I am.
—Cyril Cusack, quoted the *Irish Times* in 1975

On the calendar, the end of the year happens in the middle of winter. In the old days, life slowed down in the winter. There was less work to do because the harvest had been reaped. There was less light to do things by because the shorter days couldn't be augmented by artificial light sources.

As we turned our attention from our outside activities, I suspect that we sat down around the fire and looked inward. Aside from doing more sleeping, I imagine that we used to do lot of sitting around in the winter. When people gather together and sit, we also talk, sing, laugh, eat, tell stories, and imagine. When I say "imagine," I don't mean fanciful constructions. I mean forming new images and sensations that are not perceived through sight, hearing, or our other senses.

When we imagine, we ask questions and then open our hearts and minds to possible answers. We imagine why we're here. We imagine where we came from. And through our imaginings, we find meaning and purpose.

As in the dead of winter, when there is the least reason to be outside, the end of this book provides the perfect opportunity to go inside ourselves and find our meaning and our purpose.

Practice:

1. In your journal, consider the following questions: How was your self-esteem at the beginning of the year? How well did you know yourself and what you needed and wanted? What were your biggest challenges to knowing and liking all parts of yourself last year? What changes did you make in your life that you're proud of? What did you learn about yourself this year? What do you like about yourself? What are you still challenged to love about yourself? My purpose is to live fully, love unconditionally, and to inspire others to do the same. What is your purpose?

2. Treat yourself to an extra-special act of kindness today to celebrate coming so far.

. . . .
Day 363: Year in Review: Gratitude
Habit: Gratitude

Write it on your heart
that every day is the best day in the year.
—Ralph Waldo Emerson, *Society and Solitude*

What a year! Each week, you discovered more and more things to be grateful for in your life and in the world. People, places, experiences, objects, stories, lessons, tools. Nothing was too big or small to escape the reach of your appreciation.

You discovered that life is not nearly as much about what you have as how you feel about what you have. There will always be good days and bad days, but every day you're alive is a day you can feel grateful.

I am grateful to have spent this year with you. Thank you for believing in yourself and trying your best. Thank you for sharing your path with me.

Practice:

1. In your journal, consider the following questions: How often did you feel grateful at the beginning of the year? What benefits have you noticed from feeling more gratitude? What are you most grateful for this past year?

2. Take a moment to appreciate the remarkable accomplishment of completing this book!

. . . .

Day 364: Year in Review: Simplicity
Habit: Simplicity

Music is an outburst of the soul.
—Frederick Delius, quoted in *Delius as I Knew Him*
by Eric Fenby

Simplicity. Ah. Just hearing the word, I breathe a little easier. It reminds me that life is very simple. There are only a few things that are really important. The rest is noise, and the sweet, clear sound of the word "simplicity" gives me permission to let the noise go and instead create my own song composed of the notes that I choose, creating a melody that makes my heart sing, and a rhythm that makes my body move.

This year, your music found more room for expression in the space and silence you created in your schedule, your home, and your mind. You helped your soul be heard over other people's music, creating a symphony that is distinctly your own. You chose your own notes, your own rhythm, your own pace, and your own instruments and allowed the rest to be played by someone else.

Next year, continue to intentionally create your own music.

Practice:

1. In your journal, consider the following questions: At the beginning of the year, how stressed were you? How cluttered was your schedule, your house, and your mind? How stressed are you now? What do you wish you had done more of last year? What do you wish you had done less of? What emotional baggage will you let go of next year?

2. Use the monthly review to continue your mission to eliminate the unnecessary and focus on the necessary.

Day 365: Year in Review: Philanthropy
Habit: Philanthropy

If Nature has made you for a giver, your hands are born open,
and so is your heart; and though there may be times when
your hands are empty, your heart is always full, and you
can give things out of that—warm things, kind things, sweet
things—help and comfort and laughter—and sometimes gay,
kind laughter is the best help of all.
—Frances Hodgson Burnett, *A Little Princess*

It's no coincidence that holidays of giving happen in the middle of winter. Before grocery stores and shopping malls, the dead of winter meant there would be no replenishing. We must make do with what we have managed to put away in good times.

And yet, when we should feel the most scarcity, the most fear about having enough to survive, we are called upon to be generous. We are called to give, because giving connects our spirit with our fellow humans to create love and abundance. And there is no better time to create love and abundance than in the middle of winter. Whether that winter is real or metaphorical, giving brings life back into the hibernating landscape of our hearts.

Giving is living. May your generous spirit create a life filled with love and joy for you, your family, and the world today and every day.

Practice:

1. In your journal, consider the following questions: How much were you giving to charity at the beginning of the year in terms of money and time? What were your biggest challenges in giving? What are you currently giving to charity? Where did you give this year? Which ones did you enjoy the most? What ones are you most proud of? What did you learn about philanthropy this year? What do you want or need to learn next year? Do you want to increase the time and money you give next year? Why or why not?

2. Use the monthly review to create a game plan for donating more money or time.

3. Congratulate yourself for being an amazing, well-rounded, powerful giver who is a force for good in this world!

Table of Contents by Habit

Physical Health

Mindfulness

Relationships

Connecting with Yourself

Gratitude

Simplicity

Schedule Simplicity

Nature Simplicity

Home Simplicity

Mind Simplicity

Philanthropy

Charity Evaluation Worksheet

Level 1: Orientation

What does the charity do?

How do they do it?

How do they know they are making a difference?

Is it something you want to support? Why?

Level 2: Reputation Research

Check online sources: Philanthropedia, Give Well, Charity Navigator, Better Business Bureau, Guidestar, or Charity Rater. What do you find?

Google the charity's name with the word "problem," "concern," "controversy," or "criticism." What do you find?

Google the charity's work (examples: orphanage, food aid, microfinance, etc.) with the word "problem," "concern," "controversy," or "criticism." What do you find?

Level 3: Impact Evaluation

On what research or evidence did the charity design its programs?

What information does the charity collect about the results of its programs?

How does the charity systematically analyze the information it collects?

How has the charity adjusted its activities in response to new information?

Does the charity have an absolute focus on producing results?

Level 4: Financial Review

Does this charity file a 990 (check the Guidestar website)?

If the charity does not, ask, "Where does your income come from? How do you spend it? How has your financial situation changed over the past few years? How do you feel about the financial future of your charity?"

If the charity files a 990, review the last three years. Over the last three years, what patterns do you notice? Is revenue going up or down (line 12)? Do they typically run a deficit (line 19)? Do they have assets to withstand tough times (line 22)? Are they heavy on a primary funding source that could leave them vulnerable if that source dried up (Section VIII, and for large donors or private foundations check Schedule B, Part 1) Are there at least five board members, most of whom are not paid (Section VII)?

Notes
· · · · · · ·

1 H. Roger Segelken, "'Holier Than Thou' Morality Study by Cornell Psychologists Shows Why Americans Aren't as Smart as They Think They Are," *Cornell Chronicle*, accessed January 15, 2016, http://www.news.cornell.edu/stories /2001/03/americans-are-not-nice-they -think-they-are.

2 "What Is Mindfulness?," Greater Good Science Center at Berkeley University of California, Berkley, accessed October 8, 2015, http://greatergood.berkeley.edu/topic/mindfulness/definition.

3 "What Is Mindfulness?," Greater Good Science Center at Berkeley University of California, Berkley, accessed October 8, 2015, http://greatergood.berkeley.edu/topic/mindfulness/definition.

4 Robert Emmons, "Why Gratitude Is Good," Greater Good Science Center at Berkeley, University of California, November 16, 2010, http://greatergood.berkeley.edu/article/item/why_gratitude_is _good.

5 *Cosmos: A Spacetime Odyssey*, episode no. 1, "Standing Up in the Milky Way," first broadcast by Fox, March 9, 2014, directed by Brannon Braga and written by Ann Druyan and Steven Soter.

6 "Cost Savings with Permanent Supportive Housing," National Alliance to End Homelessness, March 1, 2010, http://www.endhomelessness .org/library/entry/cost-savings-with-permanent-supportive-housing.

7 Mark Williams, John Teasdale, Zindel Segal, and Jon Kabat-Zinn, *The Mindful Way through Depression: Freeing Yourself from Chronic Unhappiness* (New York: Guilford Press, 2007).

8 John de Graaf, David Wann, and Thomas H. Naylor, *Affluenza: The All-Consuming Epidemic* (Oakland, CA: Berrett-Koehler Publishers, 2001).

9 Kristin Harmel, "Adding Variety To An Exercise Routine Helps Increase Adherence," University of Florida News, October 24, 2000, http://news.ufl.edu/archive/2000/10/adding-variety-to-an-exercise-routine-helps-increase-adherence.html.

10 "What Is Mindfulness?," Greater Good Science Center at Berkeley University of California, Berkley, accessed October 8, 2015, http://greatergood.berkeley.edu/topic/mindfulness/definition.

11 Wendy Smith, *Give a Little: How Your Small Donations Can Transform Our World* (New York: Hyperion, 2009), xiv-xv.

12 Phillippa Lally, Cornelia H. M. van Jaarsveld, Henry W. W. Potts, and Jane Wardle, "How are habits formed: Modelling habit formation in the real world," *European Journal of Social Psychology* 40 (July 16, 2009): 998–1009, doi:10.1002/ejsp.674.

13 Richard M. Lee, Matthew Draper, and Sujin Lee, "Social Connectedness, Dysfunctional Interpersonal Behaviors, and Psychological Distress: Testing a Mediator Model," *Journal of Counseling and Psychology* 48, no. 3 (2001): 310–18, doi:10.1037/0022-0167.48.3.310.

14 Julianne Holt-Lunstad, Timothy B. Smith, J. Bradley Layton, "Social Relationships and Mortality Risk: A Meta-Analytic Review," *PLOS Medicine* 7, no. 7 (July 7, 2010), doi:10.1371/journal.pmed.1000316.

15 Amy Cuddy, "Your Body Language Shapes Who You Are," filmed June 2012, TED Talks video, 21:02, http://www.ted.com/talks/amy_cuddy_your_body_language_shapes_who_you_are.

16 Richard M. Lee, Matthew Draper, and Sujin Lee, "Social Connectedness, Dysfunctional Interpersonal Behaviors, and Psychological Distress: Testing a Mediator Model," *Journal of Counseling and Psychology* 48, no. 3 (2001): 310–18, doi:10.1037/0022-0167.48.3.310.

17 James S. House, Karl R. Landis, and Debra Umberson, "Social Relationships and Health," *Science*, n.s., 241, no. 4865 (July 29, 1988): 540–45, doi: 10.1126/science.3399889.

18 Elizabeth W. Dunn, Lara B. Aknin, and Michael I. Norton, "Spending Money on Others Promotes Happiness," *Science* 319, no. 5870 (2008): 1687–88, doi:10.1126/science.1150952.

19 United Nations, *The Millennium Development Goals Report 2015*, ed. Catharine Way, United Nations, http://www.un.org/millennium goals/2015_MDG_Report/pdf/MDG%202015%20rev%20 %28July%201%29.pdf.

20 Bill Bryson, *A Short History of Nearly Everything* (New York: Broadway Books, 2003), 9–18.

21 Bill Bryson, *A Short History of Nearly Everything* (New York: Broadway Books, 2003), 246–50.

22 Kaiser Permanente, "Kaiser Permanente Study Finds Keeping a Food Diary Doubles Diet Weight Loss," press release, July 8, 2008, http:// share.kaiserpermanente.org/article/kaiser-permanente-study-finds -keeping-a-food-diary-doubles-diet-weight-loss/#sthash.UrfUZgpY .dpuf.

23 Adam Grant, *Give and Take* (New York: Viking, 2013), 7.

24 Michael Pollan, *In Defense of Food* (New York: Penguin, 2009).

25 Christof Koch, "Neuroscientists and the Dalai Lama Swap Insights on Meditation," *Scientific American*, July 1, 2013, http://www.scien-tificamerican.com/article/neuroscientists-dalai-lama-swap -insights-meditation.

26 CMO Council, "Facts and Stats: Marketing Spend," CMO Council, accessed March 20, 2016, https://www.cmocouncil.org /facts-stats-categories.php?view=all&category=marketing-spend.

27 Statistic Brain Research Institute, "Television Watching Statistics," Statistic Brain Research Institute, accessed March 20, 2016, http://www.statisticbrain.com/television-watching-statistics/.

28 Krista Casazza et al., "Myths, Presumptions, and Facts about Obesity," *New England Journal of Medicine* 385, no. 5 (January 31, 2013): 446–54. doi:10.1056/NEJMsa1208051.

29 Thomas William Jackson, Ray Dawson, and Darren Wilson, "Case study: evaluating the effect of email interruptions within the workplace," Conference on Empirical Assessment in Software Engineering, Keele University, EASE Conference 2002, April 2002, https://dspace.lboro.ac.uk/2134/489.

30 Christof Koch, "Neuroscientists and the Dalai Lama Swap Insights on Meditation," *Scientific American*, July 1, 2013, http://www.scientific american.com/article/neuroscientists-dalai-lama-swap-insights -meditation.

31 Elizabeth Bernstein, "To Build Intimacy, Trust, Satisfaction, Celebrate the Good Times," *Wall Street Journal*, April 7, 2014, http://www.wsj.com/articles/SB1000142405270230464010457948745213 9791452.

32 Shakar Vedantam, "How Scarcity Trap Affects Our Thinking, Behavior," NPR, January 2, 2014, http://www.npr.org/2014/01/02 /259082836/how-scarcity-mentaly-affects-our-thinking-behavior.

33 Koji Miyamoto, "What Are the Social Benefits of Education?" Education Indicators In Focus, Organization for Economic Co-operation and Development, January 2013, http://www.oecd.org/edu/skills -beyond-school/EDIF%202013--N%C2%B010%20%28eng%29--v9 %20FINAL%20bis.pdf.

34 Roy F. Baumeister and John Tierney, *Willpower: Rediscovering the Greatest Human Strength* (New York: Penguin, 2012).

35 Mona Chalabi, "What Are the Demographics of Heaven?," Dear Mona, FiveThiryEight, October 4, 2015, http://fivethirtyeight.com /features/what-are-the-demographics-of-heaven/.

36 Amy J. C. Cuddy, Caroline A. Wilmuth, and Dana R. Carney, "The Benefit of Power Posing Before a High-Stakes Social Evaluation," (working paper no. 13-027, Harvard Business School, September 2012), https://dash.harvard.edu/handle/1/9547823.

37 Sean Stannard-Stockton, "Probing Questions All Donors Should Ask Before Making a Significant Gift," Opinion, *The Chronicle of Philanthropy*, October 3, 2010, https://philanthropy.com/article/Opinion -5-Questions-to-Ask/159851.

38 Adam Rifkin, "Five Minute Favor!," PandaWhale, June 19, 2012, http://pandawhale.com/post/2500/five-minute-favor.

39 Debbie Hadley, "10 Fascinating Facts About Ants," About.com, updated June 20, 2016, http://insects.about.com/od/antsbeeswasps /a/10-cool-facts-about-ants.htm.

40 Brian Wansink, *Mindless Eating: Why We Eat More Than We Think* (New York: Bantam, 2007), 165.

41 Brendon Burchard, *The Charge: Activating the 10 Human Drives That Make You Feel Alive*, (New York: Simon & Schuster, 2012), 83–84.

42 Sonia Lyubomirsky, Kennon M. Sheldon, and David Schkade, "Pursuing Happiness: The Architecture of Sustainable Change," *Review of General Psychology* 9, no. 2 (June 1, 2005): 111–31, http:// escholarship.org/uc/item/4v03h9gv.

43 Charles Duhigg, *The Power of Habit: Why We Do What We Do In Life and Business* (Random House: New York, 2012).

44 Rachel Sussman, "The 13,000-Year-Old Underground Forest of South Africa," The Long Now Foundation, filmed November 15, 2010, 2:13, FORA.tv video, http://library.fora.tv/2010/11/15

/Rachel_Sussman_The_Worlds_Oldest_Living_Organisms/The
_13000-Year-Old_Underground_Forest_of_South_Africa.

45 Maria Godoy, "Diet Soda: Fewer Calories in the Glass May Mean
More on the Plate," NPR, January 17, 2014, http://www.npr.org/blogs
/thesalt/2014/01/17/263141134/diet-soda-drinkers-calories-you
-don-t-guzzle-end-up-in-your-belly-anyway.

46 Brian Wansink, *Mindless Eating: Why We Eat More Than We Think*
(New York: Bantam, 2007).

47 Guy Hutton, "Global Costs and Benefits of Drinking-Water Supply
and Sanitation Interventions to Reach the MDG Target and Universal Coverage," World Health Organization, 2012, http://www.who
.int/water_sanitation_health/publications/2012/globalcosts.pdf.

48 Brian Wansink, *Mindless Eating: Why We Eat More Than We Think*
(New York: Bantam, 2007), 78–81.

49 Camille Peri, "10 Things to Hate about Sleep Loss", WebMd, updated
February 13, 2014, http://www.webmd.com/sleep-disorders/features
/10-results-sleep-loss.

50 "Twelve Simple Tips to Improve Your Sleep," Healthy Sleep, Division
of Sleep Medicine at Harvard Medical School, updated December 18,
2007, http://healthysleep.med.harvard.edu/healthy/getting
/overcoming/tips.

51 "Twelve Simple Tips to Improve Your Sleep," Healthy Sleep, Division
of Sleep Medicine at Harvard Medical School, updated December 18,
2007, http://healthysleep.med.harvard.edu/healthy/getting
/overcoming/tips.

52 Jack Kornfield, *The Wise Heart: A Guide to the Universal Teachings of
the Buddhist Psychology* (New York: Bantam Dell, 2008), 349–51.

53 "Twelve Simple Tips to Improve Your Sleep," Healthy Sleep, Division
of Sleep Medicine at Harvard Medical School, updated December 18,

2007, http://healthysleep.med.harvard.edu/healthy/getting
/overcoming/tips.

54 Anne Kadet, "Are Charity Walks and Raves Worth the Effort?," Mar-
ketWatch, updated June 21, 2011, http://www.marketwatch.com
/story/are-charity-walks-and-races-worth-the-effort-1306536923690.

55 Ashley M. Blouin, Itzhak Fried, Charles L. Wilson, et al., "Human
hypocretin and melanin-concentrating hormone levels are linked to
emotion and social interaction," *Nature Communications* 4 (March 5,
2013): 1547, doi:10.1038/ncomms2461.

56 Pierre Boulet-Desbareau, "Unsolicited In-Kind Donations & Other
Inappropriate Humanitarian Goods," Office for the Coordination of
Humanitarian Affairs, May 2013, http://emergency-log.weebly.com
/uploads/2/5/2/4/25246358/ubd_report_eng_-_final_for_printing
_2.pdf.

57 Bruce Japsen, "U.S. Workforce Illness Costs $576B Annually From
Sick Days to Workers Compensation," Forbes.com, September 12,
2012, http://www.forbes.com/sites/brucejapsen/2012/09/12/u-s
-workforce-illness-costs-576b-annually-from-sick-days-to-workers
-compensation/#36fcb2c47256.

58 Adam Lueke and Bryan Gibson, "Mindfulness Meditation Reduces
Implicit Age and Race Bias: The Role of Reduced Automaticity of
Responding," *Social Psychological and Personality Science* 6, no. 3 (April
2015): 284–91, doi:10.1177/1948550614559651.

59 Rhonda V. Magee, "The Way of ColorInsight: Understanding Race
and Law Effectively Through Mindfulness-Based ColorInsight Practices," *Georgetown Law Journal of Modern Critical Race Perspectives*
(University of San Francisco Law research paper no. 2015-19), Social
Science Research Network, http://ssrn.com/abstract=2638511.

60 Ravi Iyer, "Adding Complexity to the Grattitude-Affect Relationship"
(master's thesis, University of Southern California, 2010), http://digital
library.usc.edu/cdm/ref/collection/p15799coll127/id/287343.

61 Shaun Dreisbach, "Shocking Body-Image News: 97% of Women Will Be Cruel to Their Bodies Today," *Glamour*, Feb 2, 2011, http://www.glamour.com/health-fitness/2011/02/shocking-body-image-news-97-percent-of-women-will-be-cruel-to-their-bodies-today.

62 Stephen Post and Jill Neimark, *Why Good Things Happen to Good People: How to Live a Longer, Healthier, Happier Life by the Simple Act of Giving*, (New York: Broadway Books, 2007): 63.

63 Joan Halifax, *Being with Dying: Cultivating Compassion and Fearlessness in the Presence of Death* (Boston: Shambhala, 2009 Boston): 17.

64 Shelly Taylor, Lien B. Pham, Inna D. Rivkin, and David A. Armor, "Harnessing the Imagination Mental Simulation, Self Regulation, and Coping," *American Psychologist* 53, no. 4 (1988): 429–39, http://www.culturedesoi.fr/wp-content/uploads/2012/07/Taylor-et-al-Harnessing-the-imagination-Mental-simulation-self-regulation-and-coping.pdf.

65 World Health Organization, "Guidelines for Community Noise," ed. Birgitta Berglund, Thomas Lindvall, and Dietrich H. Schwela, World Health Organization (1999): 39–52, http://www.who.int/docstore/peh/noise/guidelines2.html.

66 Tufts University and Centers for Disease Control and Prevention, "Strength Training for Older Adults," Growingstronger.com, Tufts University and Centers for Disease Control and Precention, accessed October 8, 2015, http://growingstronger.nutrition.tufts.edu/why_grow_stronger/index.html/.

67 James H. Fowler and Nicholas A. Christakis, "Cooperative behavior cascades in human social networks," *Proceedings of the National Academy of Sciences* 107, no. 12 (March 2010): 5334–38, doi:10.1073/pnas.0913149107.

68 Randy Cohen, "Top 10 Reasons to Support the Arts in 2014," *Americans for the Arts* (blog), March 20, 2014, http://blog.americansforthearts.org/2014/03/20/top-10-reasons-to-support-the-arts-in-2014.

To Write to the Author

If you wish to contact the author or would like more information about this book, please write to the author in care of Llewellyn Worldwide Ltd. and we will forward your request. Both the author and publisher appreciate hearing from you and learning of your enjoyment of this book and how it has helped you. Llewellyn Worldwide Ltd. cannot guarantee that every letter written to the author can be answered, but all will be forwarded. Please write to:

Sharon Lipinski
c/o Llewellyn Worldwide
2143 Wooddale Drive
Woodbury, MN 55125-2989

Please enclose a self-addressed stamped envelope for reply,
or $1.00 to cover costs. If outside the U.S.A., enclose
an international postal reply coupon.

Many of Llewellyn's authors have websites with additional information and resources. For more information, please visit our website at http://www.llewellyn.com.